HARRY POTTS

MARGARET'S STORY

HARRY POTTS

MARGARET'S STORY

Margaret Potts &
Dave Thomas

SPORTS
BOOKS

Published in Great Britain by
SportsBooks Limited
PO Box 422
Cheltenham
GL50 2YN

© Margaret Potts & Dave Thomas 2006
First Published October 2006

Front cover designed by Kath Northam.

A catalogue record for this book is available from
the British Library.

ISBN 1 899807 41 1

Printed and bound in England by
Cromwell Press

DEDICATIONS

To Alan and Muriel Reid who, at all times over the years, have given so much comfort and support.

Margaret Potts. October 2006

Billy Dougal and Ray Bennion were backroom servants of Burnley Football Club for decades, from the 1930s into the '60s. The number of players they nurtured, trained and coached, including Harry Potts, runs into the hundreds. They were two truly inspirational characters and the foundations they laid at the club were immense. Because they were Burnley's backroom team their names rarely come to the fore, but the 'bootroom' they had at Burnley Football Club, where they would meet and talk about football matters for hours with Harry Potts, was there long before Bill Shankly's famous Anfield 'bootroom'. For more than thirty years, everybody in football knew of them. Burnley Football Club owes them a huge debt of gratitude, and the wonderful triumphs of the 1960s, and a procession of great Burnley players, are their legacy.

Dave Thomas. October 2006.

Contents

ACKNOWLEDGEMENTS

Ray Simpson. Before Ray handed me the task of writing this book, he had spent a considerable amount of time talking to Margaret Potts and tape recording his interviews. These were then transcribed and provided many pages of notes. Ray also sifted through the boxes and boxes of cuttings, clippings, newspaper articles, documents and pictures Margaret had saved over the years. He organised them into files and folders in chronological order and in so doing saved me weeks of preparation. His generosity and willingness to hand over the results of his months of work and research cannot be emphasised too much.

Alan Bailey. Before he died at the beginning of 2005 Alan gave me all the scrapbooks he had so lovingly collected between 1961 and 1980. He had read my anthology of writings about Burnley FC, *No Nay Never* and rang me to say he wanted his collection to go where they would be used and appreciated. They filled four huge tote boxes and a suitcase. The reports and articles they contained cover most of the Harry Potts managerial years and saved me from making a dozen visits to Burnley library from Leeds. Alan, if you are watching, from wherever you are, I can't thank you enough.

Players, friends and colleagues of Harry Potts readily gave their time and I thank them for their contributions. I am indebted to all of them. I met some great people, great players and heard many great stories. Arthur Bellamy, Brian and Mary Miller, Willie Irvine, Barbara Lord, Paul Fletcher, Dave Thomas, Reverend Alan Reid, Joe Brown, Ralph Coates, Andy Lochhead, Albert and Muriel Maddox, Les and Pam Latcham, Jimmy McIlroy, Martin Dobson, Steve Kindon, Colin Waldron, Ray Pointer, Des McBain, Cyril Law, Clive Bennett, Peter Pike, Tony Scholes, Rebekah Jackson, Marilyn Jackson.

Burnley Football Club for access to club documents.

Harriet Thomas for, as usual, keeping the computer going.

PROLOGUE

IN HIS final days, as he took imaginary penalty kicks in the hallway of his bungalow, Harry Potts barely knew what day it was or who he was with. Parkinson's Dementia took an ever-increasing hold on his mind and body, playing endless tricks, and disorienting him with incurable, slow relentlessness.

Towards the end, in moments of calm as he sat resting in his chair in Dove Court nursing home in the mid-nineties, or walking in the garden on a summer's evening, looking so slight and frail, he might recognise the loved ones and friends who came to see him. But most of Harry Potts' final days were marked by his uncomprehending confusion. Sometimes at Dove Court, where he spent his last months, he would believe he was in a hotel with his former players. There were days he did not recognise his own wife Margaret. To some who knew him from their playing days, it was more than they could bear to see him like that.

It started, his family now suspect in hindsight, in the late 1970s with the slightest of tremors and shakes they used to notice in his hands on the occasions he took a glass of sherry at a special occasion. Then later, there was the forgetfulness of simple ordinary things.

Parkinson's belongs to a group of conditions called motor system disorders and is the result of the loss of dopamine-producing brain cells. Loss of dopamine causes the nerve cells to fire out of control, leaving sufferers unable to direct or control their movements in a normal manner. There may be tremors or trembling in the limbs, slowness of movement, impaired balance and instability. It becomes even more unbearable when it is also accompanied by Dementia, where memory loss occurs.

For Harry Potts, the Dementia eventually became obvious when he would go to the local shop and bring back the wrong items, or on the occasion he set off for a walk and a neighbour found him far from home and overtired. Familiar simple tasks would go uncompleted, his sense of time became blurred, concentration lapsed, and everyday items would be put back in the wrong place. It became more and more clear that something was wrong. At its worst there was the occasion in the hallway of the bungalow when he hit penalty kicks with perfect precision and like arrows they hit the door with him thinking he was back on the football field. Then one night, racing out into the street, he relived the awful game between Burnley and Glasgow Celtic at Turf Moor which was stopped as fans poured down from the terraces, bottles were hurled onto the pitch, fencing rails were used as spears, and innocent people with bloodied heads tried to find somewhere to hide.

That Parkinson's Dementia should happen to such a man, one once so active and sporting, a man once so attractive, so accomplished, so physically fit, who had given so much to so many and had such a deep influence on so many people, made it all the more cruel and devastating and so hard to accept for all of his family.

The passage of time is unyielding and continues with an unbending obstinacy. For some, old age brings its release from mortality with dignity and a quiet calm so that even when the end finally comes we can still recognise the person we knew and loved so many years before. For Margaret's husband there was no such dignity. Only occasionally were there lucid moments when they could talk together.

When he slept peacefully, untormented by his muddled demons, Margaret, too, could then sleep, exhausted. Today she can sit and reflect on their life together, starting with the storybook way they met, their early days, the triumphs, the obstacles they overcame and above all the deep love people felt for Harry Potts. So many people who knew him still say he was just such a lovely man, a good man, a man who so often put the needs of others before his own, and it is for those simple reasons, it is time his story was told.

This book is also dedicated to all those people who have encountered Parkinson's Dementia, and for those who have carried the burden of their care. For those who have seen it at first hand and cared for sufferers, it is just as bewildering for them as for the victim.

Dave Thomas

CHAPTER ONE

A FAIRYTALE BEGINNING

HE ARRIVED at Burnley as a boyish 16-year-old in 1937. No one knew then of the horrors and suffering that would soon be unleashed on the world in just a couple of years. Ten years later we would meet for the first time in the most unusual of circumstances.

At that time I lived with my parents at Lower Trapp Farm Cottage, which was situated beside a narrow country lane, surrounded by woods and fields, set up on the hillside high above the valley. It was a bygone age of friendliness and community spirit, when everyone knew and cared for their neighbours and there'd be a cheery greeting for everyone you met walking along the lane. It was a time I remember of helping with the haymaking, sledging in winter, biking along the narrow twisting lanes and going off on long hikes over the heather-clad Pendle Hill. A car was a rarity. I remember only those owned by the mill owner, Mr Noble, who had a chauffeur, the farmer with his old banger, Mr Webster, the joiner who lived over the road, and Dr Forsythe. Our cottage was rented from the Huntroyde Estate and that meant mum had to work up at the Hall when they had a grouse shoot or a weekend of visitors and needed extra staff. When my brother Bert left school at 14 he worked on the estate farm, moved into the bothy and then worked in the gardens. It was still common for people to be in service in those days. Huntroyde Hall was a most beautiful country house, a stark contrast to the mills and the billowing smoke that poured from the chimneys in

Padiham not far away. A dwelling had existed there since 1460 and it is thought that the old hunting lodge stood where John of Gaunt would set out to hunt in Pendle Forest. The area abounded with stories of witchcraft. The grounds were filled with lovely gardens with archways made of yew trees, rhododendrons and the most beautiful elegant varieties of trees. In the summer the place was filled with roses. There were hothouses with orchids, gardenias, carnations and all manner of other plants. Fruit houses were filled with vines, peaches and nectarines. There were red squirrels, peacocks and highland cattle in the grounds and woods; it was truly idyllic. But when wartime came, and men left to join the army, the estate workers who tended all these gardens and greenhouses dwindled in number.

There were endless green fields around us, with pasture for the sheep and cattle, and meadowland carpeted with wild flowers in the spring. At haymaking time, in this bygone age, we raked the hay into rows and were all thrilled by the ride home in the great hay cart pulled by huge horses. We'd sing and laugh and talk about the day and then go back to the farm for food and glasses of milk and lemonade. There'd be walks in the woods, bluebell picking, harvesting the wild blackberries and elderberries for home-baked pies and home-made wine. We played hopscotch, skipping, 'farmer's den' and tig, games you rarely see children playing today. We'd spend weeks collecting wood and saving our pennies for a grand firework display of catherine wheels, snowstorms, rockets and sparklers for Bonfire Night. At Christmas we prayed for snow, and our prayers always seemed to be answered in those far-off days. We wrote letters to Santa, walked into Padiham or went to Woolworth's in Burnley on the bus to buy each other presents, nothing more than 6d (2.5p). We'd sit round the table laden with food in a room filled with paper chains that we had made from strips of coloured paper we fastened together.

Sometimes Granny Elliot would come to stay. She would arrive from Thirsk with a large suitcase and we would sit and wait for it to be opened because we knew she ran a confectioners from her front room and that inside the case she would have brought sweets, liquorice and those delicious chocolate walnut whips. If we visited her, the big treat was being able to open the huge cake tin she kept full of her buns and baking.

Medicine was sometimes home-made. If we had a cold, we had goose-fat rubbed on our chests, there was always a big pot of it on the shelf. Before school there was a spoonful of cod liver oil and malt and there was a big black pan that boiled away with a mixture of linseed and liquorice for when we had a cough.

Primary school days meant a long walk down the hill to the village school in Simonstone on Whalley Road. It was a walk we did in all weathers; sometimes you got there with clothes dripping wet, sometimes in winter you slid all the way down. While it might have been fun to skip all the way on a warm summer day under a clear blue sky, the long walk back up the hill was always hard work. I seem to remember it was such a tiny school, perhaps just two classes and two teachers, maybe three? They were happy days. There was Altham C of E School, and then it was on to Simonstone St Peter's. The seniors went to St Leonard's C of E School in Padiham. We'd still have to walk down to the main road but then we caught a bus the rest of the way.

How proud I was when I was still only eight and received my certificate for The Clean Hands Campaign. We had a bright orange chart to fill in and around the edge were pictures showing us how to wash our hands properly. "I have washed my hands with Lifebuoy Health Soap," it said and for four weeks you had to tick that you had washed your hands three times a day. Much more grandly, and four years later, I received a certificate of merit for my report on "Alcohol and The Human Body". What a beautiful certificate it was, so artistic, and beautifully decorated. "Sobriety aids character, citizenship and success" it announced at the top. It had a long-lasting effect on me.

One thing I remember is the day out we had. It was 'The Scholar's Trip' from Altham School to Hardcastle Craggs near Hebden Bridge. When you are only eight years old it is such an adventure to go what feels so far away even though it was only a few miles. There were three small coaches – we called them 'charabancs' in those days. Don't forget this was 1931. Thirty-seven children and nearly as many adults left the school early in the afternoon and we were all so excited. We went through Burnley and then over the moors up and along what we called 'The Long Causeway' with those little charabancs chugging and rattling away struggling like mad up the steep hills. It's the kind of bleak but wonderful landscape in which Emily Bronte set her book *Wuthering Heights*. Somewhere near a tiny village called Heptonstall, on the edge of the hillside, we left the coaches and walked for what seemed miles down through the trees to the valley bottom at Hardcastle Craggs. I thought I had never seen anywhere so pretty. There was a café, stepping stones in the river, penny slot machines and even some holiday huts.

We had tea in Greenwood's Café, ham and tongue, bread, coconut cakes, biscuits and ginger beer. We stayed there till early evening and then it was time to return. We took the long walk back to the charabancs and then the slow drive home although this time we went along the valley bottom through Todmorden and Cliviger before getting to Padiham and stopping for wonderful bags of chips. Before that, how excited we were when the driver of our bus speeded up, and overtook the adults' coach in front of us. How grown up we felt because we weren't back home till just ten o'clock. My composition about this magical day was judged to be the best by a girl and was published in the church magazine. I still have the magazine and those childhood memories come racing back when I look at the folded and creased page and read the little essay which I wrote all those years ago when I was only eight. I can close my eyes and I'm back in 1931. It seems only yesterday.

Those lovely childhood years drifted slowly by but in May 1937 there was another event when four pupils from St Leonard's were chosen to plant a tree in Padiham Memorial Park to commemorate the coronation of King George VI and Queen Elizabeth. I was one of them and there I am in the photograph I still have, smart overcoat, beret on m§y head, little white socks and strapped sandals. In July I left, ready to enter the big, wide world, my reference from the headmaster in his beautiful handwriting, clutched in my hand.

She is a girl of the highest intelligence, mentally alert, quick, reliable, very practical, and possessed of sound common sense... her character and conduct are excellent. She has a pleasant disposition, is refined in speech and manner and is a credit to her home and school...

The cottage had no electricity when we first moved in, so on dark winter months I'd curl up in a corner and read by the light of the fire or paraffin lamp, or a candle. We might play snakes and ladders, ludo and snap. In the dark, winter months we would be in bed at 6 pm. But then when we got electricity, I can't remember exactly when, we could listen to the wireless, the news and the children's programmes.

In the summer months we spent whole days outdoors playing, making dens, paddling in the stream catching tadpoles and newts or visiting the old lady in the next cottage to see her cow and hens when they came into the kitchen to be fed.

Our cottage was old with walls that seemed to be three feet thick. In the kitchen was the old, black oven range, which was kept lit all the time to warm the room. We bathed in an old tub, which was in a sort of screened off corridor, and we had to ladle the water from the boiler on bath nights. There was no flush toilet; it was down a small covered passage shielded from the scullery, and the council came to empty it once a week. Dad's job was to tear up the strips of newspaper we used, but never his beloved Sports Pink. There were just two bedrooms upstairs and a second small room downstairs, next to the living room, which we used as a bedroom when we needed to.

Mum used to make 'teas' for the people who walked around our lanes. They'd come on trams to Padiham and then walk up the hill. It was fun on the trams because the top deck was open and had wooden seats and they rattled along. We were near the bus stop and one day somebody asked if it would be possible to get a jug of tea. So mum built a little trellis shelter with tables and benches and had old blankets for children to sit on in front of the cottage for their picnic. One day friends of ours came up, the whole family, and with them was a Burnley footballer, Harold Spencer. We all watched and giggled when we saw him canoodling under the blanket with his girlfriend.

When Dr Forsythe moved into a big new house nearby, mum became his cook-housekeeper and it was he who later helped me get into nursing, writing an introduction and reference to the matron at Burnley hospital. It was the beginning of a long, long friendship and he was my doctor for many years. "You've got her up the pole all right," he said to Harry when he announced me pregnant years later and then added, "I hope you're not expecting another little footballer, it's a girl in there."

I look back on those final pre-war years with such nostalgia and happy memories. But the dark clouds of the war years came and with them a whole lifestyle changed. Those distant halcyon days came to a close and the world would never be the same. I watched the young men of Read, Simonstone, Padiham and Burnley marching away, many never to return. My mother lost two of her own family. In many ways a rural place like Simonstone seemed almost untouched by hardship, but you couldn't escape the news from the radio, the snippets of film at the cinemas, the newspapers, or the awful stories that the young men had to tell when they returned home on leave, many of them with terrible injuries. And it did touch us at first hand when we took in our share of evacuees from the nearby towns and cities that had been subjected to bombing raids or were thought to be at risk. We looked after two little girls who had come from Manchester and their mum would sometimes come to see them. My sister Doris had been evacuated to relatives in Canada and brother Bert was away in the RAF so there was a spare bedroom we could put them in.

But those terrible years were not without their lighter side. One night the local Home Guard had been up to Sabden for a drink or two. Well, actually, they had rather more than that, and coming back down the steep hill, the truck they were in crashed into the wall at the bottom of the road. None of them were seriously hurt and we talked for days about that.

A Fairytale Beginning

By the end of the war I had taken up nursing, having trained in Burnley hospital and stayed in the nurses' home. Before that I had worked in a bakery and then as a shop assistant in a ladies' outfitters in Padiham until I was 18.

Far away in India a young man was serving his country. His existence was one of which I was totally unaware but our paths were destined to converge. I would meet him in 1947.

───────────────────────────────

BY THE time Margaret Hollinrake met Harry Potts in 1947 he was already the golden boy of Burnley Football Club. Season 1946/47 had been a marvellous one, resulting in the 'double' of promotion back to Division One and the FA Cup final at Wembley, although they lost. There is no doubt that with his good looks and golden hair left to grow slightly longer than the standard, obligatory, convict, short back and sides of the day, and with his comb always in his pocket, young Harry Potts was a Beckhamesque figure amongst the cobbles, terraced rows and mill chimneys that belched out endless smoke in an immediate post-war Burnley, a working-class place of low wages, drab buildings, shortages and rationing, and which even at best could never be described as picturesque until you reached the villages and countryside which surrounded it. The words 'golden boy' fitted him beautifully. He was the all-round dream player a whole town, previously starved of success and colour, could look up to. Harry Potts seemed to transcend the image of a time when footballers were working-class men who appeared every Saturday afternoon to perform before other working-class men.

The team of 1946/47 with Potts the goal-scoring general covering every inch of the pitch was seen as one of the best produced at Turf Moor. Manager Cliff Britton, capped many times by England, and trainers Billy Dougal and Ray Bennion, the latter two seemingly at the club since the time of Noah, along with the inspirational iron-man captain Alan Brown, had produced a team that was unbeatable in spirit and almost impassable in defence. If it was dour, it

7

was not entirely dull; if it was mechanical, it was not totally without flair, and that flair came from Harry Potts. He was the leading scorer in the League with 15 goals; in the cup final he had hit the crossbar. The late author Jack Rosenthal, writer of many television scripts, including the very first *London's Burning,* was a boyhood Burnley supporter, and once wrote that he was convinced that Potts preferred to hit the crossbar rather than score, he did the trick so often.

Potts was the son every father wanted, he was the footballer every young man who ever dreamed of playing for Burnley wanted to be, he was the young man every mill girl dreamed of. He had that indefinable star quality – glamour.

At the beginning of that season no one could possibly have imagined the success that was heading Burnley's way. The first three games were in no way impressive although they included a couple of victories; games four and five were both lost. In one of the opening games the team was described by Henry Rose in the *Daily Express* as "ten comedians and an amateur, Peter Kippax." (Kippax would later be the inspiration for the title of a Jack Rosenthal play, *P'Tang, Yang, Kipperbang.* Rosenthal and his boyhood pals had somehow played on the name Peter Kippax, one of their favourite players, and changed it into *P'Tang, Yang, Kipperbang.* It then became their secret password. For years people have wondered how this play got its name. Peter Kippax never knew either.)

But then Potts scored his first two goals in the next game against Newcastle and from that game on the machine-like precision of the team with the iron curtain defence lost only four more games, conceding a total of only 29 goals. Indeed the team seemed so impregnable that at one stage nearing Christmas there were hopes that the 30-game unbeaten record of the championship team of the legendary Halley, Boyle and Watson era would be emulated. It wasn't, but for one wonderful spell of 37 games there was only one defeat with Potts controlling game after game with his skills, goals and adept passing. He was its hero and adulation was heaped upon him.

Archie Ledbrooke in the *Daily Dispatch* said Burnley were: "... go ahead, business like football ... crisp passing, swift and understanding, interchanging of positions... certainty in the tackle ... and two goals from Potts".

Another report from the home game against Newcastle summed up the team beautifully. "Burnley played first-class, workmanlike football, no frills, no flounces, the complete get-on-with-the-job team. They are like a well-drilled platoon, each seems to know exactly what to do, whatever situation the run of play throws up, a wonderfully well disciplined turn out. If ever a team looked capable of the double it is Burnley, the team without a star, but every man is a complete cog in a perfect piece of football machinery, the defence is just about as watertight as they are made." Other reports describe "the ball going from man to man with machine-like precision... sheer methodical soccer played at top speed... thoroughly schooled in football tactics... their defence the nearest thing to rock... difficult to fault. There is a sweetness of movement and understanding about the team which radiates confidence."

And boring? In the cup games they got to the final with "a song and a smile." At West Ham, "it was a magnificent exhibition of splendid ball control making this Burnley team superior to two thirds of the First Division."

As if to make the success even more remarkable, that winter was one of snow and freezing conditions. Margaret Hollinrake's father had walked on top of frozen snowdrifts to get to work in Burnley where he was a Co-op grocery manager. Games were postponed; others were played in the most difficult and dangerous of conditions. The 'big freeze' lasted from January till March and was at its worst in February. For a period of two months Burnley players never saw green grass but nobody thought twice about playing on snow. The season was extended long after the cup final so that when Burnley finally achieved promotion in June it more than compensated for the April Wembley defeat. A total of nine cup games were played with Potts scoring two of the goals along the way. The semi-final against Liverpool was a tense affair with the first game ending in a 0-0 draw and the replay was won 1-0 at Maine Road in front of 72,000 people. It was a marvellous victory and a measure of Burnley's excellence that Liverpool then went on to win the First Division Championship.

Times were difficult, though. Burnley had to put out an appeal for coupons to buy new boots for the players. The result? "… are being received from all parts of the county and officials are very gratified with the response."

Promotion was clinched with a 5-0 trouncing of West Ham in London with Potts scoring twice. The final game at Millwall was drawn but it didn't matter and the celebrations were long and loud. For Cliff Britton it was especially sweet; it was his first year at Turf Moor.

One person who was especially delighted was Margaret Hollinrake's father, a dedicated fan who had watched Burnley since the age of ten. He had travelled to Wembley for the final. The match went into extra time with a goal from Charlton's Chris Duffy settling it. Ironically, as Albert Hollinrake groaned and despaired when Potts hit the crossbar, his daughter Margaret was listening to the radio commentary at home. Rosenthal and his pals were listening to the radio too. When Duffy scored six minutes from time "that was the moment I grew up", wrote Rosenthal later.

It didn't dawn on Margaret that when the name Potts crackled over the airwaves, it was the same young man she had already met in the most unusual of circumstances.

I'D BEEN to Port Talbot in South Wales to see the parents of a friend and was coming back by train. I loved train journeys but have you any idea what a long-distance train journey was like in 1947? There were no motorways; hardly any long stretches of fast dual carriageway roads, and in any case very little petrol. The war had finished but the shortages remained. Nobody would have dreamed of driving from South Wales to Burnley. You journeyed by train – they were steam trains, often with unheated, freezing cold carriages – as did all the football teams at that time, unless the game was nearby and a coach would suffice. And on top of all that it was a dreadful winter and a grim post-war age when central heating was virtually unheard of. Of course, I was living at home quite a way out of Burnley with my parents but my mother's side of the family were country people and came from Thirsk in North Yorkshire where my grandfather was a blacksmith and a local Lay Preacher. They were strict Wesleyan Methodists. My mum used to tell me that when she and dad first met, my dad was still a soldier, and the first time he went in the house his newspaper was taken off him and he was asked to read the Bible. While staying there I, too, had met a soldier, a Welsh Guardsman who happened to be from South Wales. So that's how I was staying in Port Talbot. I'd been to see him; he wanted me to meet his parents and family.

Eventually, after what seemed an endless journey, the train reached Manchester where I was supposed to change to the bus for Burnley. All the while back I'd chatted to another passenger, another soldier, and at Manchester he jumped out with a "cheerio" but then came running back down the platform to tell me somebody from Burnley would give me a lift the rest of the way. He must have told them about this girl from Burnley he had been talking to. Of course, in those days railway stations, especially the big ones in Manchester, were places of noise, smoke and steam billowing upwards. They were busy, crowded places.

Then another chap approached me and asked if I was the young lady who wanted to get back to Burnley and would I like a lift? Somehow I thought I had seen his face before. But thinking this was not possible, I refused the lift, thinking about the snow on the hilltops. I didn't want to get stuck in a car with a total stranger. I had a bus ticket for the rest of the journey and was just explaining that when another gentleman walked up and explained that they were with the Burnley football team. They were on their way back from Swansea, and had a coach to take them back to Burnley from Manchester. Eventually the two men introduced themselves as Mr Britton the manager, and Mr Kay, one of the directors. Both of them must have been thinking they had a right little Eliza Doolittle here. I was lucky that Mr Kay knew me. Allowing a young lady onto the team coach was not normally something the manager Cliff Britton would have allowed.

Once I realised that I would be safe and well looked after, of course I accepted. Believe it or not, Mr Kay had recognised me because he too lived in Simonstone. Then, of course, I put two and two together and realised why I had thought I had seen him before. That was it, we all walked out to the coach and I was offered a seat at the front, very politely and courteously.

Well this was amazing; what would my father think, I said to myself, knowing how keen he was on the fortunes of Burnley Football Club, remembering that he had been to the cup final, and was always talking about a grand young footballer called Harry Potts who had come back from India and was now the star of the team. He would never believe my story when I got home, I told myself a dozen times until I had the bright idea of getting all the players to sign their autographs. All I had in my bag was my Royal College of Nursing Certificate so I asked Mr Britton if he would pass it around and they all signed it on the back.

But it wasn't actually Mr Britton who took it round the coach, it was one of the young players, who, I just happened to notice when he brought it back to me, had blonde hair. He didn't say who he was and I didn't ask him. He just smiled, and said hello and here were all the signatures. Just one was missing, that of Peter Kippax. It was only later that I found out the other players had sent Harry round because he was one of only two players who weren't married and they thought it was a good chance for him to meet a nice young girl.

And that was that, I thought, at the end of the journey home. I was actually dropped off in Simonstone. I proudly showed dad the signed certificate and when he looked at it and heard my story his eyes just filled up with tears of wonderment and amazement that his daughter should be given a lift back to Burnley in the team coach.

"So who was the lad you spoke to, who was the lad who took the certificate round and brought it back to you?" he asked wide-eyed. All I could tell him was that he was young with bright, fair hair and he'd told me they'd won 2-0. "That's Harry Potts then," he said with continuing astonishment, "that's Harry Potts".

A Fairytale Beginning

He was truly astonished. He was Burnley mad. Later it was me who'd get him the ticket for the cup final from someone I knew at the factory, Platers and Stampers, where I was the factory nurse. Arthur Woodruff, who was a Burnley player, had a relative who worked at the factory and it was from her I got the ticket, paying her three guineas for a three-shilling ticket. My dad was ecstatic; he'd already queued unsuccessfully at the ground when the queues stretched for a mile. Of course, I didn't know then that players weren't supposed to sell their tickets for a profit and I suppose Arthur Woodruff would have been in big trouble had I told anyone. It was at this same factory that later, when the Burnley team toured the town in their coach after the cup final, I came out with all the workers and waved like mad at the players and the coach. I'd given no more thought to Harry Potts and the coach ride back from Manchester, and him handing over the signatures with his lovely smile. In fact, I'd decided to apply for a six-month Sister's post in Port Talbot. So I certainly wasn't interested in this golden-haired star player who had just come back from India.

But then a letter arrived from him with the club address at the top.

Dear Margaret,
I hope the signature of Peter completes your list and I think if he had been present in the bus when you were listening to our chants of 'Nursey' he would have been in the same opinion as the rest of the team i.e. he would take a chance of recovering if Nurse Hollinrake was in charge of operations!
I caught him just before he went away for a few days rest, and we are hoping he will soon be back to his normal self again. I was just thinking you seem to do very well for holidays. However I hope you are having an enjoyable time, if you want a partner for golf any time just let me know.
Thanks a lot for your good wishes, which I conveyed to the rest of the boys.
Yours Sincerely
Harry Potts
P.S. Pulse normal at present.

When my sister Doris saw the letter she was very excited.

Doris used to go to Burnley matches and knew very well who Harry Potts was. She had been evacuated to Canada during the war and she still had a Canadian accent. "Gee Sis, I'll caddy for you," she said.

And then the phone calls started near the end of the season. We had a phone, unusual in those days, but only because we had taken in the evacuees during the war and been allocated one on account of something to do with that. Of course we kept it and it really was very unusual in 1947. "There's been a Harry on the phone for you... several times," my dad said early one Sunday afternoon when I arrived home from visiting my convalescing brother, a Warrant Officer who had been de-mobbed with severe chest problems.

The penny didn't drop, I didn't know any Harry; I certainly didn't connect it with the Harry on the coach from Manchester all those weeks earlier and neither did my father. As we spoke, the phone rang again and it was Harry again, asking could he come and see me? This time he explained who he was, that he was the chap who had got me the signatures on the coach. By this time my dad had twigged and was muttering excitedly, "Harry Potts, Harry Potts" and pulling faces at me.

"Not very convenient," I told him as nicely as I could. The very next day I was due to travel to Port Talbot to take up the six months holiday relief nursing post I had applied for, the trunk was packed, the tickets bought, the arrangements made. "And anyway, it's Sunday, there are hardly any buses. How are you going to get here?" I asked. "I'll get a bus to Padiham if I can and walk the rest," he answered.

I had just returned with my sister-in-law from seeing my brother Bert in hospital. He'd been a wireless operator/air gunner in the RAF and had only a part of the lobe of one lung fuctioning properly. I had just been told he had only six months to live and I needed to be on my own to think what I should tell my parents (as prognoses go that wasn't the best. He lived until 1980).

I needed some fresh air so I decided to go for a ride on my bicycle. Off I went down the lane and there was Harry walking towards me. I passed him, he stared at me, and I stared at him, not quite recognising him, for it had been weeks since we had met on the coach back to Burnley. We said the obvious. "I suppose you are Harry?" I asked. "Yes, and you must be Margaret," he replied with that same lovely smile. So, having met on the Lane, Harry and I walked and chatted for a while, strolling all the way round Bluebell Wood, Whins Lane and round the top roads with the views of farms and countryside everywhere you looked: Harry all the while explaining that he hadn't got in touch until now because there had been so many matches to play because of all the postponements caused by the terrible winter, then there'd been banquets and celebrations and he had been so busy. I invited him back to our cottage.

My mother, of course, was a great cook and baker. She always baked on a Sunday afternoon so the scones and the Anzac biscuits were coming out of the oven as fast as you could count them. On the other side of the kitchen dad would sit, polishing all our shoes ready for the week's work.

And my dad's face, when we eventually walked back into the cottage, was a picture. So when we came back and went indoors out came the cakes and biscuits and orange and Harry, famished, was in his element, chatting away to my parents and tucking into the food on the table My dad was in his element having been a Burnley fan for so long and he really believed that this team of Harry's was as good, if not better than the great championship team of 1920/21.

So that was that, a lovely long afternoon, but the next day I was due in Port Talbot and Harry told me, "I don't want you to go." He was clearly smitten and from that day seemed determined to make me his. But I had to go, so we parted late that day, agreeing to write and keep in touch, with me never thinking that this would lead to something permanent. By the time he left he knew pretty much everything there was to know about me and my nursing, that we were very much 'country' people who attended the local chapel, loved the outdoors, the garden and animals and he was clearly at ease with all of the family.

I watched him walk down the lane early in the evening and at that point realised how much I had enjoyed his company.

HE WAS born in Hetton-le-Hole, a mining village in the north-east just north of Sunderland, in 1920, the only son of Harry and Mary, a mother who was totally devoted to his needs. It was an age when mothers did exactly that, especially when they had sons who were good looking, accomplished, and clearly had a wonderful future ahead. Harry was her pride and joy and she wanted everything that was best for him. His father was a Co-op salesman and he rode round the area with his horse and cart selling groceries. His stock phrase was "why worry? Worry gets you nowhere at all". It was a trait that Harry junior would not inherit. Though they weren't miners, they lived in a tiny terraced house typical of the area; the front door opening out onto the street; front step immaculately clean, a small backyard with an outdoor toilet and a tin bath hung on a peg on the wall.

After Margaret made her first visit she reported back to her father that he needn't worry, they weren't posh and had to go "up the yard" to the outside toilet whether it was raining, snowing or blowing a gale. Outside the backyard was an unmade dirt road and alongside that one of the colliery railway lines. Gaslights lit the streets at night. Smoke from the engines billowed over the houses throughout the day. In the kitchen, his proud mother cooked and baked on an old-fashioned gas oven. Small the house might have been, but in it Mary Potts fussed and bustled and made it a happy place to live.

If Harry Potts Senior was a quiet, unassuming man, then the matriarchal, sometimes domineering, Mam Potts more than made up for that, and this was to influence her son for the rest of his life. Next door but one lived Robert and Alice Paisley, the aunt and uncle of Bob Paisley, a lifelong friend of Harry, who went on to become a great Liverpool manager. They were inseparable as boys and later in life became known as "the likely lads". They played snooker together as often as possible and afterwards Mam Potts would make piles of chips which were heaped into one of the paper bags his father made for the foodstuffs sold at the Co-op.

At school, it was football, football, and more football of course; few boys were not football daft and there was the old saying that if you whistled down a Geordie pit up would come a procession of footballers.

In his schoolwork at Hetton Boys 'School, Harry was diligent and conscientious, receiving a glowing reference from the headmaster, Mr Brittain, who described him as hardworking and always doing his best. It was the same headmaster who eventually advised him to make a serious decision, that he should choose between football and a career because he couldn't do both. Harry was a regular churchgoer from childhood, and the Reverend Gibson Salisbury described him as one of the finest boys in Hetton, honest to a degree, upright, strong and sports loving. The vicar was a good judge of character and had deduced very early that Harry had no wish to pursue further scholarship and would rather be at work – which for Harry meant football.

There is no record of who recommended him, or how Harry was first directed towards Burnley, but he was one of the very first of the Burnley youth system whereby young footballers from all over the country, but mainly the north-east, were invited to Turf Moor, were placed in digs, and were determined to seek fame, if not quite fortune.

There were no great sums of money to be made by footballers in those long ago days. This was a time of the retain and transfer system and the maximum wage which was lower in summer than the playing season. A club owned and controlled its players and some clubs treated them scandalously.

Harry first turned out for Burnley in a midweek junior game against Blackpool. His mother was heartbroken that he should choose to go so far away from home. He was impressive in that game and, continuing to make good progress, joined the ground staff on his 17th birthday. Two men already there were the trainers and coaches, Ray Bennion and Billy Dougal, and they were instrumental in getting the youth policy off the ground. They would still be there years later when Harry returned as manager.

By the outbreak of war in 1939 he was an established player in the reserves but had yet to make the breakthrough into the first team. The war altered everything though, as Harry joined the RAF and served in India for much of the time as a sergeant and physical training instructor. Before actually travelling to India he guested in a few games for Sunderland and Fulham.

Guesting was a common occurrence in the war years when football was played on a regional basis and more often than not a team was only finalised with a couple of days, in some cases just minutes, to spare. In some games loudspeaker announcements were made for players to step forward to complete the team. Old timers frequently came out of retirement to make up the numbers. On the other hand, a team like Aldershot with its huge Army camp had an embarrassment of players. Brighton, however, faced one game with just five players from which to choose. They filled the team with soldiers on leave and lost 18-0! Interruptions to games were also frequent when the air raid sirens sounded and in single page programmes, when they were printed, it would be announced:

IN THE EVENT OF AN AIR RAID WARNING BEING RECEIVED THE POLICE WILL INSTRUCT THE REFEREE TO STOP THE GAME WHEN THEY DEEM IT NECESSARY AND THE PLAYERS WILL LEAVE THE FIELD. SPECTATORS MUST TAKE SHELTER AND REMAIN UNDER COVER UNTIL THE 'ALL CLEAR' HAS BEEN GIVEN.

Exactly where spectators or players should take cover was not quite clear.

In India, Harry Potts toured with Denis Compton's side, playing in exhibition games against other service teams, did his PTI duties, and met a whole host of other sportsmen including world light heavyweight boxing champion Freddie Mills.

Harry Potts' journey home by troopship in 1946 took six weeks and with Burnley having retained his registration he was called into the first team at the back end of the 1945/46 season just a week after embarkation. He had a stinker of a game, having totally lost touch with properly competitive football. Spectators at the game wondered what on earth was this player doing on the pitch. One wrote later:

> *"My friend and I had just started going to Turf Moor and we knew very little about football. So when the crowd shouted so did we. Harry Potts miskicked the ball and the boys at the Beehole End were calling him anything but a footballer. My friend and I not wanting anyone to know we had very little knowledge of the game joined in the barracking of Harry Potts – much to our regret. A lady in front of us turned round red with rage and said: 'Leave the lad alone, he's just come back from India'. My friend retorted: 'Lucky for him. My brother's still there.' "*

It was against Sheffield United, the last game of the season and Burnley lost 1-0. There was little to suggest to the average fan that the following season Harry Potts would be such an integral part of a team which was to do so well, when one minute he would be defending in his own penalty area and in the next accelerating upfield to finish off an attack he himself had started.

But Bob Lord, then aspiring to join the club's board, showed what made him such a success in football administration. As he put in in his book *My Fight For Football*, "He looked to me head and shoulders above them all, clean and immaculate. Potts stands out in my mind. He wasn't physically fit for first-class football that day but his enthusiasm for the club made me think. Before the match had finished I was thinking: 'This chap's above average type.' Soon after, I met him and these impressions were confirmed."

BY THE time we met at Simonstone on that Sunday afternoon, he was an established star and really I had just no idea how famous he was in the town. From that point we kept in touch by letter and he would urge me to come back which, of course, I couldn't do until my contract ended. He would write that he was earning £8 a week and that was enough to support me. Occasionally I would get back home for a few days but by saving up my days I was able to return to Burnley in November and by Christmas we were engaged. I suppose we realised it was serious the first time he stayed for the night at Trapp Cottage.

One day his father arrived on our doorstep. He had stayed at Harry's digs for the game and afterwards Harry brought him up. Burnley won 4-0 and Harry scored twice. How proud we felt. Harry took his dad, who really enjoyed the visit, back to stay in his digs with Mr and Mrs Livsey, his landlord and landlady, and then came back to spend the evening with us.

During the weekend in early December when we became engaged it was his mother's turn to arrive at Trapp Cottage. She, too, had stayed with the Livseys and Harry brought her up after the game. There were a number of people there who had come to congratulate us; friends, neighbours, relatives but Harry's mother's remark as soon as she arrived upset us all greatly.

"A pity – such a lot of nice girls our Harry could have married," she said.

Perhaps she was shocked by the speed at which we had become engaged, perhaps it was our cottage and rural location, so different to what she knew in Hetton, perhaps it was my personality she didn't like: outgoing, bubbly, chatty and sociable, not quite the "dutiful wife who should be seen and not heard" type. Maybe she thought I wasn't good enough for Harry and he could have found someone better. We were all upset; my parents thought perhaps we weren't posh enough for her. I suggested to Harry that we should wait a while. I tried to give the ring back but he wouldn't take it, saying that everything would be fine.

He insisted he did not want me to go back into hospital nursing, which would have meant living in a nurses' home. So I managed to obtain a post in Burnley as a school nurse, the 'nit nurse' to be precise as we were known for many years, and there was one occasion I remember so clearly when Harry came looking for me after training had finished. There I was doing the medicals with the doctor at Rosegrove Boys' School, and I have this recollection of the room being at the top of an iron staircase and all the boys were lining up. As I walked up there were quite a few wolf whistles. Then, once I was in the room and ready, I heard such a commotion and a stir as voices started whispering, then getting louder, saying, "it's him, it's him, it's 'arry Potts, 'e must be coming to see 'er." Meanwhile I was going as red as a beetroot. Then, at the moment Harry came in the room, there was a young lad called Albert Cheesebrough waiting for his medical. So, of course, Harry chatted to him and asked him what he wanted to be when he grew up and Albert replied straightaway, "a footballer."

And, of course, he did. He went on to join Burnley Football Club and become one of their best young players. I think back to that day and smile. Can you imagine that happening now, a star footballer walking into a school unannounced to look for his girlfriend? There'd be mayhem and a dozen photographers traipsing after him. But the headmaster, and the teacher who was supervising all the medicals on that day, just accepted the interruption with a smile. They were probably as excited as the boys to see Harry and what a lovely story the boy would have to tell his family at home.

So we saw each other as often as possible. He talked very little about his time in India or Burma where he was also in service. About the only thing he ever said about his very early days at Burnley was that a lot of training time was spent mixing concrete for some of the terracing. He'd always laugh as he told me that and then that he'd been in digs on Thurston Street with Mr and Mrs Livsey and they were very nice and it was ever so homely so he was perfectly happy there. Some of the other young lads did not fare so well and they were barely even fed properly.

Having got engaged in December 1947, Harry decided there was little point waiting much longer to get married. If we married before April he said there'd be a tax rebate. Of course in those days there were still shortages of just about everything, there were dockets and coupons and rationing, and utility furniture and half the male population were still walking around in their demob suits. I'm sure Harry still had his hanging up somewhere. Maybe a factor in his decision to go ahead so quickly, and my acceptance, was that both of us had already had broken engagements. During the war I had met a Burnley lad but one day he came home on leave while I was at work, arrived at the cottage and asked for his ring back and even a little table he had made!

I learned from his mother later that Harry's first fiancée was from a rather well-to-do family. But it was she who broke off the engagement when Harry was away for so long in India.

We were married on Wednesday March 31st 1948 at St John's Church in Read and Burnley's captain Alan Brown was the best man. Harry, being Harry, had officially informed manager Cliff Britton and his response was disappointing to say the least. He told us he thought we were rushing into things. There we were, I was nearly 25 and Harry nearly 28, and he was telling us we were rushing into things. I suppose all these years later I realise he meant that we had only known each other for such a short time. We'd been seeing each other properly only since the previous November.

The wedding had to be on a Wednesday, and Burnley were at home at the weekend. The star player was needed, married or not. I learned an early lesson: football always comes first. Our friends and relations rallied round with coupons for this and coupons for that, so that I could get the satin I needed from Pooles' Silk Shop in Burnley to make my dress. We improvised in those days with all kinds of odds and ends of pieces of material. Nylon stockings, too, were hard to find so that women still painted black lines down the back of their legs or stained their legs brown. We married against a background of shortages of everything; petrol was still desperately hard to get, meat, sugar, sweets and dozens of other items were still rationed. For some things there were even worse shortages than those experienced during the war and some rationing was actually more severe. The dark bread that some people had to buy was horrible because there wasn't enough white flour to make good bread. Evenings were spent by candlelight and newspapers were reduced to just four pages. Fortunately, by the time of the wedding, the worst of the dreadful winter was over. Previously burst pipes had made homes waterless, farms and villages had been cut off, buses had been buried in snowdrifts, coal was almost impossible to buy and there were endless electricity cuts. The local newspaper said it was so bad that on one day, a hearse found the roads impassable on the way to a funeral and the coffin was pulled to the church on a sledge.

My parents organised the reception for forty people at the Simonstone Hotel. It was all they could afford and on top of that there were all the shortages. The Smith family, who ran the hotel, were friends and I had been friendly with their daughters since schooldays. One tier of the cake was decorated with a football scene and goalposts; another tier had a little hospital bed and the figure of a nurse. On the table were football boots filled with tulips. My sister was organised to be the bridesmaid. All Harry's football colleagues were to be at the church and a thousand Burnley mill girls were upset and jealous that their pin-up Harry Potts was jilting them all. And then Mam Potts intervened. She wanted more bridesmaids from her side of the family, all her nieces, and she wanted more people from County Durham. It was the first indication of her interference in our lives, which was to go on until almost the day she died. Princess Diana always said there were three people in her marriage. There were three in mine as well and one of them was Harry's mother.

I had seen the signs of impending problems at the first football match I went to see Harry play in and the first time I had met his mother. It was a game against Sunderland sometime late in November just after I had come back from Port Talbot. As ever a coach load of Harry's friends and relatives came down from the north-east. Harry had given me a little book with tickets in because he said all the players' wives sat together and I could get to know them. In I went, sat down full of expectation and excitement amidst all the buzz and noise from the crowd that was building up, and after just a few minutes who should walk up but a very formidable looking lady who announced that I was sitting in her seat.

"Do you know who I am?" she announced as she stood at the end of the aisle. "I'm Harry Potts' mother and that is MY seat."

The steward sorted it out. "Lady," he said, "I don't care who you are, this ticket is for this seat." He took her away to another seat and when I saw the indignant look on her face I realised that this was not going to be an easy relationship. Up until that moment I can only suppose that she had been the one who accompanied Harry on trips and visits, had taken centre stage and had enjoyed all the attention and limelight of being the mother of the team's star player. She had been to the cup final and all the ties leading up to it. She had attended all the social events. She was proud of him and rightly so but had a possessiveness that wouldn't allow her to let go of him.

The snow might have disappeared but the rain came down with a vengeance. It was so bad that the car was allowed for the first time ever to drive down the path right to the door of the church where a huge black umbrella held by Bob Johnson gave some shelter as I got out. The choir was bigger than usual; children wanted to take an afternoon off school to see Harry Potts' wedding. One of the present sidemen at the church today was there in the choir all those years ago. The reception, now doubled in size from one to two rooms at the hotel, went well enough when a private room upstairs was opened to accommodate all the extra guests brought by Mam Potts. In addition to the decorated cake made by the hotel there was another one, a gift from Oddies the bakers. Rationing or not, we did not go short of cake.

Needless to say, the honeymoon was wet. Alan Brown and Bob Lord, who was not yet on the board of directors at Burnley but was a friend of Harry's, took us to the station at Preston. We had just a couple of days at the Storrs Hotel in the Lake District. It was my first experience of luxury and when the waiter came over with a white napkin over his arm and asked very grandly did I want black or white coffee, I was quite speechless and as he walked away very ostentatiously I had to cover up my giggles.

Our first home was on Deerpark Road in Burnley but we had precious little furniture. In those days there were no plastic credit cards, you saved up for whatever you wanted. The occasional special item you might buy on what was called hire purchase. Harry sold his car so that we could buy carpets and curtains. So soon after the war, furniture, indeed all household goods, was in short supply. It was known as 'utility' furniture and it was functional, cheaply produced as quickly as possible. No one could say it was stylish. For quite some time we sat on planks balanced on piles of bricks in the lounge. The first furniture we bought was for the dining room and the bedroom and then once the lounge was furnished, the visits began from Mam Potts who took great delight in bringing relatives with her to see Harry in his grand new semi-detached house. This, plus carpets and new furniture, was something to tell her friends about back home where only the doctor, the parson or, perhaps, the schoolmaster lived in anything bigger than a terraced cottage. But Harry didn't boast about it; all he could do was worry about the £1,100 mortgage, which he thought was a noose around his neck on his wage of £8 a week plus £3 for a win. Mortgage worries bothered him continually. Of course, it was a huge amount of money, way beyond the reach of the average working man who scrimped and scraped on low wages to make ends meet, that is if they had work at all. For the unemployed, the hardships and shortages were often appalling. But our house was a status symbol in the eyes of his mother.

For her first lengthy stay, she and Dad Potts arrived with two suitcases for two weeks holiday. It was September 1948, and they arrived totally unexpectedly. I had no idea they were coming. Before they had even set foot over the doorstep Mam said her piece: "When we come to Burnley we want a big welcome on the mat. What's our Harry's is ours, always has been, always will be and don't you forget it."

And then Bob Lord came more into my life. Harry had been friendly with him, his wife Hilda and their two young daughters Barbara and Margaret, for a while and he had already taken me to meet them before we were engaged. Harry used to give books to the girls for Christmas and Harry's parents already knew them. Bob was a throwback to Victorian days, complete with centre parting. He was a butcher in Burnley, climbing rapidly up the business ladder, and was besotted with Burnley Football Club. Bob and Hilda came to visit us at the new house. Bob had already advised Harry that it was a sound property and a good price, and they bought us a vacuum cleaner as a wedding present plus a basket of meat, butter and bacon. Of course, it was no trouble for Bob Lord to get hold of this kind of food with him being in the business. I can still see him sitting on the planks resting on the bricks in our otherwise empty front lounge and Harry admiring the vacuum cleaner. Of course, we couldn't try it out. In those days things didn't come with a fitted plug. Harry and Bob's relationship was lifelong and though it may have had its ups and downs it lasted for many, many years.

Something else Bob Lord did was give meat to the players and the Christmas after we were married he gave us a huge turkey. When the club gave us one as well, we just stood and stared at these two huge birds in the cold pantry – there were no fridges in those days – and I felt overcome by our good fortune. A cold pantry was just a small walk-in cupboard in the kitchen with stone slabs for shelves, which stayed cold all year round. The turkeys were well appreciated by all our friends and family. There were certain bonuses to being a footballer's wife.

Once married, Harry became determined I should no longer work. He was adamant that it would reflect badly on him if it looked as though he could not support his wife. Back in the north-east, he had been brought up in a culture which decreed that a miner's wife certainly did not work – she stayed at home washing, mending, cooking, bringing up the children, and was at home in the kitchen with his bathtub in front of the fire and his plate of food in the oven, ready for when her man returned from his day down the pit, or the jar in the pub on his way home. A woman was expected to occupy second place in the home. It was as simple as that. It was as if a woman should be seen but not heard.

That was fine by me, except for the "seen but not heard" part. I certainly loved the housewife bit. There was the house to look after and I loved gardening – a love that had been developed at Trapp Cottage by my mother who was a wonderful gardener. I made a lot of my own clothes and loved to knit. Many of us were still in the wartime 'Dig For Victory' state of mind. My mother had persuaded the farm next door to let her have a patch of land next to the cottage in the war where she grew masses of fruit and vegetables. She kept it for several years afterwards and gave me so much help with my garden. The 'housewife' role remained for the rest of our married life. It was perhaps as well seeing as Harry, bless him, didn't know how to change a fuse or even a light bulb such was his preoccupation with football. He had been spoiled at home by his adoring mother, then in digs by the Livseys. As a footballer, his day was organised for him and in some ways it was not his fault that he was unused to doing even the simplest tasks. Many years later there was one truly momentous occasion when he actually washed the car.

Our life in those early days was basically quite simple. He trained, he played, I cared for him, even massaging his feet with surgical spirit to toughen them up. We would make toast over the open coal fire with the bread on the end of a long three-pronged toasting fork. Toasted crumpets were even better. In the evenings we would listen to the radio – Dick Barton was a favourite – or records on the gramophone. There was a cup of Ovaltine or cocoa for supper and we were nearly always early to bed for 9 o'clock – he needed a lot of sleep, his mother said. If there was a match on Saturday there was no sex after Thursday. Then on a Saturday his match preparation was a slice of toast and an egg in sherry.

In the summer of 1948 there was a club tour abroad somewhere after the season had ended and one afternoon mum and a friend turned up with a huge, heavy suitcase she had lugged along on the bus. Lo and behold, when she opened it out in the back garden it was full of turf she had dug from her garden so that she could lay down a patch of grass for me "so that Harry would have somewhere to put his deckchair" when he came back. Of all the things my mother did for me that was the most extraordinary.

When Harry went on that tour it was the first time in my life I had ever been really alone somewhere in a house for a lengthy spell. Trapp Cottage had been full of constant life and laughter. While spending years in Burnley training to be a nurse, I lived in the nurses' home and as a Sister in Port Talbot I was in a home with lots of company, so being in that house for the first time on my own, with other empty and unfinished houses around, came as a huge shock. But Cliff Britton and his wife lived very close by and Mrs Britton arranged for me to have telephone calls at a certain time from Harry in her house while he was on the tour. I still keep in touch with her nearly fifty years later.

When the tour ended and they all returned for the 'close' season we had our first real holiday in the north-east with all Harry's family. Before we were married I had been there one weekend to meet them. His mother fussed all over me and insisted on bringing me a huge bowl and a jug of water to my bedroom (Harry had to sleep on the sofa downstairs) so that I could wash in private instead of in the kitchen sink. They'd seemed determined to make me welcome. As Harry no longer had a car he borrowed a van and I can still remember the journey today: it was so long and up hill and down dale. For long spells no road ever seemed to go in a straight line. It was so uncomfortable and I was so car sick it was dreadful. But get there we did and after a few days with them we then went on to Butlins Holiday camp at Filey just down the coast.

In later years one summer we went to Seaburn near Sunderland every day and Harry's dad would set off on the bus early to the beach to make sure he could hire a tent that he would set up on the sand. Then we'd all follow on, a great gang of us, Mam, neighbours, aunts, children, with all the picnic bags and the baking Mam had done the night before. There was something marvellous about that; she was such a good cook and must have stayed up half the night to prepare it all. And we'd do this not just one day but several and had a wonderful time during that summer. This was the life and role that Mam Potts loved and her energy was enormous. But she always needed to be in control and to try to keep Harry to herself long after he had left home.

CHAPTER TWO

ON THE MOVE

THERE WAS a holiday spirit at Turf Moor on the morning of Friday March 7th 1947. As the seasons come and go, the triumphs and successes of a football team can be fleeting. 1946/47 at Turf Moor had been a rebirth and nobody wanted to see failure following on behind. Could success be continued? Would they cope against the top sides of the First Division? They had no need to worry as the football club once again assumed a prominent position in the life and fabric of the town, giving pride and a sense of success in a place characterised and shaped by its cotton and coal industries, although in the case of the cotton factories the embryonic seeds of decline had already been sown. As post-war rationing and all manner of shortages continued, Turf Moor stood out as a place of achievement as this provincial, small-town club defied the strength of mightier names.

Harry missed just a handful of games at the back end of the season. To the amusement of spectators he became skilful and adept at falling over just at the right moment in or just on the edge of the penalty area. There is nothing new in the art of diving to win penalties. The difference, however, is that today they are shown over and over again in TV replays.

Jack Rosenthal remembered Potts well: "Harry Potts, blonde hair shimmering in the sun, running like an athlete in training, his forearms held parallel to his shoulders… Potts careering off on long solo runs, beating everybody, beating the goalie, then with long-perfected precision, smacking the ball against the crossbar…"

He was adept at running craftily alongside an opponent and surreptitiously tugging at the other player's shirt. When the opponent reacted furiously Harry would look quite innocently at the referee as if nothing had happened. One spectator likened his dribbling style to a kind of shuffling movement. One of his best ever goals was a thirty-yarder in a game against Arsenal. This was no mean feat in those far-off days when a wet leather ball seemed to weigh as much as a lump of concrete by the end of the game.

He scored 14 goals, when all eyes were watching to see if Burnley could consolidate their new position. They did so comfortably and finished third on the same number of points as Manchester United who had a better goal average. Arsenal were the champions. Burnley's iron curtain defence was again the foundation of the side, conceding only 43 goals of which five came in just one game against Manchester United. But they found it difficult to score – with only 56 goals coming in 42 matches, compared with Arsenal and Manchester United who each scored 81. Burnley won seven games 1-0 and Harry scored the only goal in five of them. It increased his importance and his status continued to soar.

Albert Maddox, who became assistant secretary at Turf Moor in 1947, remembers seeing Potts play. "In those days he was what we would call the 'general' of the side, that is to say the player who made the others tick. He wasn't a hard player, again to use an old-fashioned term he was the 'ballplayer', skilled and brainy, not particularly fast but with the knack of being able to find space and a good pass. He was the engine room of the team. And, he was known for his ability to fall over just at the right moment. He won quite a few penalties doing that."

Potts Does It Again said one picture caption. The writer added: "All in a flash, Potts took the ball on the run at the edge of the penalty area, cut in, and from an acute angle let fly." At the end of the season in April he was called up to play for The Football League XI against Northern Ireland at Deepdale. By now he was paid £12 a week during the season if in the first team and £10 a week in the summer. His contract mentions nothing about bonuses.

It had been a truly magnificent season for everyone and at one stage Burnley had high hopes of the title. The moment of truth came in February when Burnley went to play Arsenal at Highbury, but lost 3-0. Joe Mercer, Jim Logie, Don Roper and company were just too good but still Burnley were in second place with a game in hand.

The following season produced fewer goals for Potts but he played in 36 games and was still an essential part of the machine. Although with a 15th place finish and more losses than victories, it could be said the machine was running less smoothly. Manager Cliff Britton left the club that season to join his real love, Everton, at a higher salary. It was an important move for Potts, too, for one day he would rejoin Britton at Everton. But if the team struggled a little and was no longer the real force it had been the previous season, Potts was still widely respected. His flicks and other clever touches appeared effortless and almost part of his running style. The ground he covered, his defensive and attacking play, his astute finding of space, and his ability to be in the right place at the right time earned him excellent reports and reviews. He was, in short, a very accomplished player, full of subtleties one minute, then bursting into the penalty area the next. One described him as the most deceptive inside forward playing and so natural that even his little tricks appeared to be just part of his normal play.

But for all that he was Burnley's lynchpin, he remained on the same wages. It was to become a sore point and understandably so.

In season 1949/50 Potts did not miss a single game out of 42 and he scored 11 goals. Only one other player was ever present. He was still the general. He scored a hat-trick against Everton at Turf Moor. Cliff Britton did not forget the master show put on by Potts. His third goal was stunning. He beat several defenders in a race for the ball and put it past Ted Sagar in the Everton goal. His record did not seem to matter to manager Frank Hill or the directors. His wages remained the same for yet another season.

The writing was on the wall and a dissatisfied Harry Potts refused to sign a new contract until the very last minute on August 19th 1950, the beginning of his final season at Turf Moor. The first game was on the 20th. His reluctance to sign made no difference; a stand by any player was futile. Such was the system a club could simply leave a player on the sidelines, retain his registration and pay him nothing, or transfer him. It is not unreasonable to assume he must have been deeply unhappy with the apparent lack of reward for and appreciation of his services. He would play just nine more games.

I KNEW Harry had been on £8 a week before we got married but after that I never ever knew what he was earning. He used to give me £3 a week for housekeeping. I learned very early on that Harry would not be the kind of husband who confided in me or who brought his problems home to share. In the past at home he had turned readily to his mother and father. At Burnley he turned to Bob Lord.

Life went on, Harry the footballer and me the housewife. In the summers we would go to Butlins holiday camps where Harry would do football training and coaching. Our daughter Linda was born on April 23rd 1949; it was a difficult forceps delivery. Mam Potts had already been staying with us to help for what seemed weeks. "Oh let her come," said my own mother, but she'd have come whether she was asked or not. She took over the house, the cooking, cleaning, the kitchen, everything, and even painted. Just about everything we had she painted white.

On the day Linda was born, Harry was playing at Sheffield Wednesday. When he arrived home he leapt straight over the garden wall because when he had left in the morning he knew something was imminent and raced upstairs to see if anything had happened... and it had... there was Linda. Oh, the joy and pleasure on his face was wonderful and that was the beginning of all the years he spent being such a good father and family man with his children.

I confided my worried feelings regarding his mother's possessiveness to Dr Forsythe. "Don't worry," he said, "it's just mother-in-lawitis, and she'll soon get over this." She never did.

After Linda's christening on Whit Sunday 1949, I walked into the room after my family and the Lords – Hilda was her Godmother – had gone home and found her, holding Linda, and Harry sitting on the sofa. She had her arm across Harry and she looked at me and said forcefully, "Harry wants a divorce, our Harry's not happy." Harry didn't look at me; I was struck dumb and left the room. A gust of wind blew the lounge door shut with a bang. "No need to slam the door," she said.

He promised for the first time of many that he would speak to her about things. He said it was her talking and not him. But nothing else was said and the situation remained unresolved until later in 1958 when I was in hospital and Harry, worried about my health, told me he couldn't do the job without me. She never ever did let go of him.

But Mam Potts was by now a problem. She was the classic overbearing matriarch and he was still her Harry, the blue-eyed, golden-haired boy who had left home to go to war. She could not let go even though he had come back a man. Linda was her grandchild first and my daughter second. There were times when she would come and stay and then could not bring herself to leave. On the first occasion she was leaving, on her way down the garden path with her suitcase, she threw herself on the ground and said she was having a heart attack.

"Do something," Harry shouted at me in panic. "You're the nurse, do something."

We got her to her feet and two aspirins and a cup of tea later, with Linda back in her arms, she was fine, although Bob Lord's chauffeur had to give her a lift back to the north-east.

Harry was so worried after that and insisted she had a bad heart and mustn't be distressed. He needn't have worried; she lived till the age of 95, but she would continue to worry about her bad heart.

When Harry wasn't there to hear, she'd tell me that Harry was the son-in-law Bob Lord always wanted. But Bob's daughter Barbara says that what her father used to say was, Harry was just the son he would have liked.

Money worries haunted Harry and the mortgage hung constantly over his head. Though he said nothing, I knew he was worried about bills and Linda and all the extra costs. There were stories that in his last few games he wasn't playing well, that supporters were grumbling at him, and that there was ill feeling because he had refused to sign until the last minute. When the transfer was granted it was obvious what had happened even though he said nothing to me. I learned much later that he had been on the same wages for how long… three years… four years and here we were with an extra mouth to feed and this worrying mortgage hanging round his neck. It could only be that he asked for more money, was refused and was put on the transfer list. It was reported in the papers that it was he who had asked for the transfer. Today, I wonder if, when they refused to increase his wages, he saw red, which he was prone to do every now and then throughout his career, and angrily demanded to be transferred. I saw one newspaper report where he himself said he was not playing well, that the crowds were now against him, and the reporter said he thought a change would do him good. But it was from newspapers that I learned all this, never from Harry. It was the pattern for the rest of our life, whether it was football or money or domestic worries, and it was such a shame because I could have talked to him. I shared his anguish, for anguish was what it was when he came home that day and said he had been put on the transfer list and he was so deeply hurt and upset.

I wasn't worried though and said to him to do what was best. I'd been told by lots of people that other clubs wanted him because he was such a good player. I told him I'd go wherever he wanted, but not the north-east. Somebody said to me, "I hope he goes to a club that has to play Burnley and he shows 'em what a good player he is."

He ended up at Everton with Cliff Britton again and that didn't surprise me. I went with him gladly and I happily encouraged him to be positive, to see it as a good thing. But it was funny how it happened. There were a lot of interested clubs, including Liverpool, but agreement was reached between Burnley and Blackpool at a price of £20,000. Now, not for one minute did Harry say to me he didn't want to join Blackpool, but we went over there to meet the officials who were going to show us a house. Maybe Harry knew something was in the offing with Everton and Cliff Britton because all the while he was telling me to say the house wasn't suitable, to say no to the house thus giving Harry his excuse to delay things, to talk to Everton and not sign for Blackpool.

So Everton it was for £20,000. He was pleased because he had some benefits to come and Burnley Football Club bought the house from us. And, of course, there in the background as ever was Bob Lord advising him. What would he have done without Bob to turn to? It was a real and deep friendship and by then Bob was getting more and more successful and prosperous with his meat business and more and more determined to become a Burnley director. So Harry was pleased and I was delighted but I learned quite soon, though, that the extra miles didn't decrease the visits from his mother.

––––––––––––––––––––

THE £20,000 fee was a record for both clubs when Harry signed for Everton on October 16th 1950. At Burnley, where the war robbed him of six years of his career, he had played 165 games and scored 50 goals. Surprisingly, he left for the same pay, with the addition of bonuses "according to League regulations", said his new contract. But to his great advantage was the fact that he moved into an Everton club house at a rent of 50 shillings per week (£2.50), the arrangement modified so he would only pay 30 shillings (£1.50) of that while an employee of the club. Having sold his house in Burnley and paying such a low rent for what was a lovely house in Crosby, one of the better areas of Liverpool, plus bonuses, he was much happier financially.

Supporters and Press were clearly excited at the signing for such a fee. At the age of 30 Potts was at his peak and had a glowing reputation. One Liverpool paper described him as a great signing and one of the finest players in the country. The pre-signing discussions were brief; he had clearly already made up his mind. "It's a treat to be back again with Mr Britton and I will feel at home under his management," he announced.

If he had a house to look at in Blackpool, at Everton there was no house waiting for him but that didn't bother him for he knew Britton would find something. "We are quite pleased to leave that to Mr Britton," said Margaret Potts. Harry was certainly pleased to rejoin Cliff Britton, and acknowledged the high expectations. His reputation for consistent play and a fine tactical awareness preceded him.

As far as housing went, he was quite prepared to travel by car from Burnley every day for training until things were sorted, a two-hour journey even with the relatively fast East Lancashire dual carriageway for the second half of the journey between Manchester and Liverpool. According to newspaper reports, a host of other clubs were after him but he had eyes only for Everton.

If his first season at Goodison Park was a personal success with 28 appearances and five goals, for the club it was a disaster. They were relegated. Manchester United trounced Everton 4-1 on his debut. In the final game they were humiliated 6-0 at Sheffield United. They won only one of the last eleven games when Potts scored the only goal at Derby. The poor season was not for lack of effort on Harry's part and in a 2-0 win over Liverpool in January he was described as "ranging the midfield spaces, converting every loose ball into a delicate thrust or a long defence-splitting pass, and proving to be the key man."

But when he arrived they were in a lowly position. It would have taken far more than an injection of the Potts magic to save them.

WE TRAVELLED to Manchester for the signing. Little Linda and I went as well in our smart outfits. Linda had a lovely little blue bonnet and I wore a 'new look' corduroy coat. After the restrictions of the war years, new fashions were at last beginning to emerge. There were a few photographers and reporters but nothing like there would be today. There were no TV cameras and that kind of thing and as far as I know Harry didn't make anything out of the deal, not like modern players can make.

I really enjoyed being at Everton and we were there for quite a few years. The rented house we had, semi-detached and in the corner of a leafy cul-de-sac, was in a lovely area in Crosby and nearby was Blundell Sands. You could get a train to Ainsdale Beach. Linda and I loved these trips. There were electric trains going into Liverpool, shopping, the ferry to New Brighton. There were some lovely stores in Liverpool and I used to enjoy going into some of them where you could have afternoon tea. In one of them, models would parade in all the newest fashions. Very close by was a park with picnic areas and a large pool where children could sail their boats. Linda joined a nearby school and Ken was born while we were in Liverpool.

There was every kind of shop you could think of just down the road. Don't forget this was an age of corner shops and little shops and in one street you could find every kind of shop you needed so you got to know the shopkeepers so well. They'd greet you by name. It was, "Hello Mrs Potts, how's Harry, did he score?" It was all so friendly. I feel so sorry for those people who never experienced anything like that and shopping for them is always in some huge giant supermarket, pushing and shoving your way up and down the aisles and where the girls on the till have no idea who you are. I'm still lucky today, living where I do, where there are still some small shops and nice shopkeepers.

I loved it. So did Harry's parents and they visited just as often as ever.

We had a quite elderly next door neighbour who used to be always quite concerned that I would be chopping firewood and carrying coal into the house. But one day when both Potts were visiting us, Dad Potts did the job. "Who was that stranger chopping your wood?" asked the neighbour who had never seen him before and thought that Mam Potts was a widow who lived with us permanently, she was with us so often.

Then the 1940s became the '50s and you were pleased to be rid of that decade. You wanted to look forward because you wanted to forget the war years and all the hardships everyone had been through. You wanted to think how much better the '50s would be and you looked to the years ahead with hope and high expectations. But, believe it or not, there was still rationing of some items. There was a general election in 1950 and Labour won again although they were not so popular as they had been. In fact within a year the Conservatives and Winston Churchill had taken over. The Festival of Britain in London was supposed to cheer us all up but not everyone was excited, especially those fed up with continued meat rationing.

We were lucky; the house we rented had once been owned by Cains, the Liverpool butchers. Fortunately for us he was an Everton fan so we never went short of best meat, including the fillet steaks we had when we had visitors. But whereas Bob Lord had often given us meat, I now had to pay for it, and still on £3 a week for housekeeping. In exchange Harry would arrange tickets for matches.

It was later in the '50s before things began to get a little easier, less gloomy and drab. At last you could buy fridges, washing machines and televisions but we never had a telephone while we were at Everton. You had to go on a waiting list to get one of those. We had no TV of our own but I saw my first one in a friend's house.

Harry kept the football side of things much to himself. I know he was so miserable at the end of his first season when Everton were relegated. He knew they were struggling when he arrived but he couldn't help blaming himself for what happened. I could tell that even though he said little, he was clearly unhappy about it. Then, when Everton were promoted back into the First Division three years later, he wasn't part of it. He accepted that because by then he was getting into his middle thirties and he'd had a cartilage problem. Linda called him "the old man on crutches". He was playing fewer and fewer games. By then his playing career was coming to its end and he must have known that. I could tell he worried about it because football was all he knew and just on a rare occasion he would let slip that he was concerned about what to do next. But still, as ever, he said no if I suggested going back to nursing.

He had been doing a lot of coaching, and had taken various official coaching certificates at Lilleshall. While he was at Everton he coached at the Stork Margarine factory. I suspect he hoped that Cliff Britton would have kept him on as a coach but there was no offer. I remember asking him why he did not go abroad to coach, but he replied that was only for failures who couldn't get a job coaching in England. He remembered Bob Lord telling him within five years he'd be on the board at Turf Moor and he would have him back at Burnley but that was no good if there was nothing in the pipeline during those five years. One thing I did say was that there was no way we were going anywhere up in the north-east like Sunderland, which was too near Hetton.

This was when he missed Bob Lord being close by in that father, or big brother, relationship, always there to give advice and a shoulder to lean on. Bob and Hilda visited us a number of times at Crosby and Harry and Bob would quietly go off somewhere and talk for an age. Sometimes we would go over to Read just outside Burnley and visit them. I have always assumed they talked about Harry going back to Burnley as soon as Bob had some influence there, which he eventually got when he became chairman.

When Ken was born in June 1954 it was another worry for Harry. He was hardly in the first team, which, of course, meant a lower wage. Ken's birth was not without its problems. I was taken into a local nursing home when things began to happen. The place was run by nuns. Of course Harry, being Harry, was in total panic and we dashed to the nursing home in a taxi. The rain was lashing down, I was in agony, the nuns took me in and then left me on my own. Harry came back later, saw me in agony and was distraught.

He phoned immediately for our lady doctor. She was incensed with the nuns whom she had told earlier to contact her immediately anything happened. But they hadn't. Out came the forceps but Ken was on his way before they, the doctor, or the forceps were even ready. The poor wee baby was black and blue, I didn't see him for two or three days and Harry was going berserk with worry. Eventually we returned home with me looking forward so much to seeing Linda and showing her the new baby.

HARRY PLAYED only four games in 1951/52 because of injury. But on his recovery the following season, "the return of Potts to the side seems to have made all the difference," said one reporter. He was warmly welcomed, playing 19 games and scoring eight times. In his first game of that season he earned rave reviews and "enjoyed a field day," as another reporter, William Greatorex, put it. He scored two goals in a 4-2 win at Brentford when his performance swept aside the opposition who were led by the legendary England centre forward Tommy Lawton. "Potts is a good general, his work behind the line has always been sound, but he has been able to score goals when the opportunity has arisen." His perfect pass resulted in the fourth Everton goal.

But after that season there would be few games in which he displayed such quality. In 1953/54 Everton were promoted back to Division One but Harry played just one game towards the end of the season, a 0-0 draw against Fulham.

In 1954/55 he played only four first team games. There was the ultimate ignominy in a reserve game when he was sent off for constantly niggling and complaining to the referee who reported that he had grumbled at every tackle made on him. The club report did not agree with the referee and spoke of Harry in glowing terms, "one in whom we have a very high regard as a player and a man".

In his final season he played only three games. His time was running out. Ironically one of these games was at Burnley as Everton won 1-0 with a penalty given after Potts was brought down. The report described him as the brains and the general of the line. After just two more games though, his day was done, his playing career over. He was 35. According to Margaret, he made few close friends at Everton but significantly two of his playing colleagues were Harry Catterick and Maurice Lindley. Lindley and his family were regular visitors and they went to Ainsdale Beach together. The Catterick and Potts paths would cross again in the '60s, when Catterick incensed Potts with a comment he made about Willie Irvine's broken leg during a roughhouse FA Cup replay at Goodison Park. Maurice Lindley became part of the backroom team at Leeds United with Don Revie and the confrontations between Leeds and Burnley were frequently dreadful affairs.

In total, Harry Potts played only 59 league games for that record fee, due mostly to the serious knee injury he suffered. In fact doctors advised him to give up playing, but manager Britton went on record as saying he had no regrets about buying him. He then went on to acknowledge his presence and influence in the reserves. But there was to be no offer of another position at Goodison, either playing or coaching.

The letter, dated 25th April 1956, was formal and brief.

In accordance with the regulations of the Football League, I have to inform you that my Board do not intend to retain your registration for next season, 1956/57. You have been granted a free transfer.

Though he knew it was coming, reading the words had the same effect as the cut of a knife. He knew he had nothing in the pipeline to go to, was living in a rented house, and had a wife and two very young children to support. When his P45 and Insurance Card landed on the doormat in June it was the final confirmation.

HE CAME home one day and Linda and I were in the garden. He went into the kitchen and started throwing things around. Hearing the racket I ran back in to see the breadboard hurtling against the wall. My first thought was that I had done something wrong, hadn't got his meal ready or something like that but then I realised it was only mid-afternoon. They had finished him, told him they wouldn't be keeping him on. I knew he had been hoping for a coaching role because he had spent so much time with the reserves, bringing them on, and it seemed this was his official role. When he calmed down he still told me very little but enough to make me realise that our situation was shaky to say the least, especially as we would have to leave the rented house, which I loved, or if we could stay temporarily, would have to pay more rent. How do you pay more rent with no wage coming in? He told me so little about what money he was earning, he was 'in charge' of finances and I had no idea if we had anything in the way of savings.

But, as they say, every cloud has a silver lining and to his credit Cliff Britton told Stan Cullis at Wolves all about Harry. It's a very small world, this collection of football people, for only a few years later when Harry was at Burnley, Stan Cullis and he became great rivals. But for now Harry was offered a coaching job at Wolves which was a great honour because although my football knowledge then was small I did know they were a great name and very powerful and that Stan Cullis was one of the great managers of his day.

So all his previous coaching experience, whether it was at Butlins or local factories or with the Everton reserves and the Football Association certificates he had taken for the last three summers stood him in good stead. Of course he had been a PT instructor in the RAF so he knew all about fitness and training.

He'd coached at the Butlins camps at Filey and Pwllheli, and those were the days when they were really popular places and crammed with holidaymakers. We'd be there for three or four weeks and, of course, there was the extra pay as well. After that we'd treat ourselves to a little holiday in somewhere like Blackpool or at Morecambe in the Midland Hotel. What a beautiful hotel that was, so grand and elegant. There was a really grand staircase and I would feel like a VIP just walking down it from our bedroom.

We were in tears when we left Crosby. So many neighbours

came out into the street to wave goodbye. They had all come to love the children and thought a great deal of Harry of course. I don't remember much about the move to Wolverhampton. I know Harry took out a £3,000 mortgage which looking back was a huge amount of money. The worry lines on his forehead doubled overnight. We found a detached house with a garden all the way round, although there was some fuss about getting the mortgage because there were repair jobs to do first. Our new neighbours, never as friendly as Lancashire folk, told us they used to call it the 'frumpy' house but the Potts family filled it with life and noise. From here we could visit Dudley Zoo, Stourport, and Sutton Park. The club had offered us a rented house but it was too small, certainly not big enough for two children who would need a bedroom each before long. I can remember Stan Cullis's words when I mentioned there'd be "in-laws" coming to stay as well. "We don't cater for relatives," he said quite abruptly.

It was in this house I got my first ever fully automatic washing machine and there was one occasion when there was about five weeks of Harry's washing to do. He had done a three-week residential coaching course, and the minute he was home we were off to Bournemouth for a holiday. The washing machine went on quite noisily at 7 am and down came Mam Potts, still with us, of course, even though they had just had the two weeks in Bournemouth with us. Goodness, didn't she go mad, saying I shouldn't be disturbing Harry's sleep and it was Sunday morning, what on earth was I doing? And this was after I'd taken them all a cup of tea upstairs so I knew they were all awake. And anyway, she went on, these machines were a waste of time. There was only one way to wash clothes properly and that was by hand, boiling and scrubbing them.

It seemed such a short stay there at Wolverhampton because quite quickly Harry was off to be manager of Shrewsbury. That didn't involve another house move because he travelled from Wolverhampton every day. At Wolves I saw even less of him than I had at Everton; the hours were longer, the duties quite strenuous, whereas as a player there was a lot of time off. As a coach there certainly wasn't.

The huge personal shock came, though, when Harry was

in bed for a spell, quite ill with Asian Flu. It was a really bad attack and I had to nurse him through it, constantly sponging him and changing his pyjamas. And at the same time Ken was teething. With Harry laid up, it was me who had to pay the decorator who had been working in the house. Harry did all that kind of thing and when the bill wasn't paid the decorator came round to ask for his money.

"There's money in the tallboy," said Harry, and while looking for that I came across a pile of letters in Mam Potts' handwriting, some in his dad's. I had never seen these before as they had been addressed to him care of the club. I read them and was shocked to find out that most went on and on at Harry to leave me and return home to his mother with the children. With Harry in bed ill there was nothing I could do. I could not tackle him immediately about it. It never was resolved, except that I took the whole lot to a solicitor who said that if he could divorce all young couples from their mothers-in-law he'd be a millionaire and retire. Then we talked about having a good marriage and it must be a problem being married to a footballer who was away so much and open to temptation such a lot, which is true enough. Later, when Harry was better, I did tell him what I had found. "Well, everyone's entitled to their opinions," he answered, shrugging it off, and that was the end of that. The big problem for me was having no one really close to talk to in Wolverhampton, no one to confide in.

Any early resentment about Harry insisting that I should not have a job was well and truly ended. When we were on our own, I loved the life, being at home, gardening, looking after the children. I never got to any games but that didn't bother me. I was pleased that his career seemed to be secure and going somewhere and all the time in the back of our minds was that promise by Bob Lord, "just give me five years to be on the board and I'll have you back as manager."

When Harry was invited to take the manager's job at Shrewsbury after not much more than a year at Wolves we knew that everything was on track . This was just the kind of job he could do well. He'd be his own boss, he could use his own ideas and make all the decisions. It was ideal for me, too, as we would stay in the same house in Wolverhampton. He used

44

to love to tell me that one job there was to fish footballs out of the nearby River Severn when they had been kicked out of the ground. And that a man was employed to sit in a special little round boat called a coracle and collect them during a match.

I have just one memory of Shrewsbury and that was receiving a scabious plant from Percy Thrower, that most wonderful of gardeners. He met Harry at the ground and Harry told him how fond I was of gardening. Some time later I met Percy Thrower at Southport Flower Show and thanked him.

Of course I treasured the plant and when we moved house again back to Burnley, I transplanted it. Some time later Harry, in a rare gardening and helpful mood, dug it out and threw it away thinking it was a weed.

HARRY TOOK over from George Poyser at Wolves. His appointment was considered to be a rare achievement for one so young, bearing in mind the tradition of the club and its dominant position in the game. But Potts, in spite of all his worries about having an uncertain future and the possibility of unemployment, was highly thought of throughout football circles. He had also received an offer from Raich Carter to take up a coaching post at Leeds United. The letter he received even invited him to reverse the charge for the telephone call should he decide to make one. How different things were when you made a call in those days through a telephone operator in a central exchange. He declined the offer but it is certain that the course of football history at both Burnley and Leeds would have been hugely different had he accepted.

Although he did not stay long at Molineux, Harry worked with great players such as Billy Wright, Peter Broadbent, Eddie Clamp, Ron Flowers, Norman Deeley, and a strict disciplinarian manager in Stan Cullis. That their fitness was outstanding was very much due to Harry's contribution. It could never be said that Harry was the greatest coach in terms of complicated tactics, as many of his players testify, but Wolves had such outstanding individual players who were fit, powerful and athletic that sophisticated tactics were hardly necessary.

Wolves simply steamrollered and powered their way to victory with a brand of power football that was fast, direct and without frills. Their 'friendly' games against European opposition were a feature of the 1950s. Moscow Dynamo, Spartak, Honved and Real Madrid all went to Molineux and were beaten with the nation rejoicing that we could show these continentals a thing or two. That Potts should be invited to join Wolves at such a wonderful time was a compliment to his ability and character.

In the summer of 1957 he was invited to apply for the manager's post at Shrewsbury, although he had never seen them play, and Wolves placed no obstacles in his way. There were twenty-five applicants. At the age of 36 he became one of the youngest managers in the League. It didn't take the directors long to make up their minds. After interviewing him on a Friday, he was offered the job the following Monday. On accepting it he made all the appropriate noises: he would not be able to guarantee success but he would give 100% and if he failed it would not be for the want of trying. There was a clear policy of encouraging local youngsters from the area and that he vowed to continue. Training began with 16 full-time professionals and 20 local amateurs.

The chairman, in no way different to any chairman today, was concerned about finances, hoping for better attendances and a good cup run so that the club could break even.

Amazingly, within three weeks of Potts joining Shrewsbury, his name was in the news when the manager's post at Burnley became vacant because Alan Brown left Turf Moor to take over at Sunderland. However, nothing came of the speculation about Potts rejoining Burnley and trainer Billy Dougal took over. It is fair to surmise that Bob Lord, by now chairman, decided to leave him at Shrewsbury just a little while longer to learn his trade. Potts was certainly interested. The idea of going back to manage the club with which he had such close ties and where he had spent so long really appealed to him. He had yet to sign a contract at Shrewsbury so there was nothing to hold him back. The Burnley boardroom was split, however, with the names of Cliff Britton, Raich Carter and Freddy Cox mentioned. But the club wanted a manager they knew would settle. Potts was certainly favourite until Dougal's appointment. In some ways this was a strange one, even though Dougal had been at the club so long. It all added to the view that he was simply keeping the seat warm.

Dougal suffered from ill health and in January 1958 had to resign from such a demanding role, although he had steadied the ship and improved results since the first few weeks of the season. The club, to its credit, offered him a salary for life and appointed him physiotherapist.

In the intervening period, Potts spent several months at Shrewsbury, losing just 10 of 30 games. When Dougal had to resign, Bob Lord's mind was made up. Potts was his man; this time he would be offered the job, thus fulfilling the promise, "give me five years and I'll have you back at Burnley."

While the press pondered the name of the next manager, with calls for careful assessments of the needs, speculation was rife. But Lord knew exactly who he wanted and was powerful enough to have his own way. There was never any question that this time Harry Potts would get the manager's job at Turf Moor. Bob Lord knew he could get on with him and that he would not have the same problems and differences he had occasionally experienced with Alan Brown. Alan Brown was his own man with forthright opinions, just as strong as Lord's. Potts was Lord's man. They shared the same dreams and plans and their relationship went back a long way.

What few people know, however, is that because of an illness suffered by Margaret, the move to Burnley very nearly never happened. The subsequent history of Burnley Football Club and indeed Bob Lord might have been very different.

CHAPTER THREE

RETURN OF THE FAVOURITE SON

HARRY, BACK at Burnley, was living with Mr and Mrs Livsey again, near the club. At the same time as starting his new job he was trying, as and when he could, to find a suitable house for us. There were few new houses being built in the area at this time and just two on the books of Pettys the estate agents which were suitable. Mam Potts had taken Ken back to Hetton while Linda and I, back in Wolverhampton, began to prepare for the move.

My own dad was by now retired, crippled with arthritis, and he and mum were living at Mellor. It was arranged that Linda and I would stay with them over Easter so Harry and I could look at houses.

Shortly after arriving, I began to feel ill, dreadfully ill in fact. I was dizzy, had vertigo and headaches and was unable to keep my balance. At the same time dad had a really bad dose of flu but it was clear that with me it was something more serious than that. My mother called the doctor who immediately said I should go to hospital. By then I couldn't tolerate light, was unable to speak, and couldn't walk. A hospital in Blackburn was the last place I wanted to go but living in Mellor it was not possible to be taken to Burnley hospital.

With mum having to stay to look after dad and Linda, there was nobody to accompany me and when I was admitted, unable to speak, I couldn't give them any details. By now I was unable to move anything down my left hand side, with no feeling at all in my arm and leg. Three different doctors discussed "this strange case". A staff nurse began to explain that they would begin tests including a lumbar puncture, blood tests and X-rays. There were no scans in those days. Somehow, I managed to indicate that I wanted to write down some things and give them some information, for example that I was a nurse myself.

Meanwhile, my mother had managed to contact Harry at the club and in he came, looking so worried and tired. Gradually over the next few days I was able to talk but I had been told I would probably have to live my life in a wheelchair. Harry brought the club doctor, Dr David Iven. Matron Culpan and Sister Newlove, who I knew from Burnley hospital, began to visit. The consultants discussed meningitis, or a brain haemorrhage, and I had to continue to lie flat otherwise the vertigo would return. I was moved to a quieter side ward.

You do a lot of thinking in a hospital bed and the one thing I thought about long and hard was the situation with Harry's mum and our future as a family. One staff nurse with whom I had become very friendly had listened to me and like many friends advised me I must tell Mam Potts to stop her interfering.

I thought to myself that if I was to be a semi-invalid, it would suit Mam Potts perfectly. It gave me a determination to walk properly again, to be able to run with Linda and Ken, kick leaves in the woods, and go on walks and picnics. No – somehow I had to walk properly again. I had two things, prayer and faith.

I also had penicillin. This was the new wonder treatment, having been used in the Forces, and was only just being introduced in some hospitals. The injections every six hours had good results and by May 9th I was beginning my 'walking lessons', which involved walking along a white line on the floor. The sweat poured out of me.

There was one particular evening, however, when Harry came in looking even more tired and anxious than usual and it was then I realised that I had to make him understand the seriousness of the situation. I told him I thought he would be better off without me; his mother had never approved of me or liked me. Unless he could do something about it before we moved into a new house I wasn't prepared to put up with it any longer. I suggested we start living our own lives unless he would do something to stop her interfering with our marriage. It was exactly ten years since we had married. He buried his head on my chest and cried, really sobbed. I felt dreadful but I'd had ten years of upsets with her and I thought again of the letters I had found in the house at Wolverhampton.

"In that case," said Harry, "I'm not going back, I can't do it without you." He continued to tell me that he missed the children and me, and how unhappy he was and that he would resign from the manager's job at Burnley.

I told him, "Tell your mother that. The longer you leave it, the worse it will get. Your parents have their health and their faculties and each other. They are welcome to visit but within reason."

Poor Harry, though, he never did tackle her. He was a man of so many loyalties; to me, to his family, to his mother, to the extent that he could not do as I asked. He was a man who never wanted to upset anybody and nothing was said or done.

My recovery continued and I was discharged on May 18th. "You've done it yourself," said the consultant. Me, plus penicillin perhaps. They told me their diagnosis was "Vestibular Neuronitis" and they had kept meticulous records of the case because it had been so unusual.

My parents had moved to Crawshaw Hall where mum had a new position as cook-housekeeper to Miss Brooks. Linda and I spent time with them in their flat as I convalesced, or at Harry's digs with the Livseys. I could walk unsteadily but did short trips to the shops with mum for help. And one thing I remember vividly, even after all these years, was a beautiful huge cherry blossom tree outside my bedroom window. It was almost inspirational in its beauty.

We found a house in Brierfield at Hillsborough Avenue and the Wolverhampton house was sold. Neighbours did all the removal work and packing down at that end and a new neighbour helped unpack at the Burnley end. To this day I remember watching and her asking me why there were so many half-eaten jars of jam and marmalade and wondering why they hadn't just thrown them away at the other end.

That time was a blur. I don't know how we did it or even who did it.

Harry continued with the Burnley job but it so nearly didn't happen. I don't know how he coped with those first few months at Turf Moor. His mind must have been going haywire; new job, living in digs, and his wife ill.

Of course, Bob Lord was there to advise Harry about the house and reassure him that he could afford another mortgage of £3,000. Bob looked at the house with Harry and pronounced it good, solid and eminently suitable. With a salary now of £1,650 a year and other expenses paid as well of course we could afford it, but still Harry worried. For the first time we had a telephone and then a fridge. All these things that we take for granted today came less easily all that time ago.

For ten years I had endured Mam Potts while Harry simply either tried to brush it off or said that he would do something about it, as he put it. Of course it had produced tensions between Harry and me. Bob Lord was aware of the situation and my feelings. Something prompted me to talk to him about it, probably the reply he sent when I wrote to him while I was recuperating thanking him for giving Harry the job. In his reply he talked about team spirit and how it was needed right from the top to the bottom. We met and talked and it gave me the chance to tell him what I thought, that I was fully prepared to be part of that team spirit but others must play their part too. I told him the problems weren't between Harry and me, but they all stemmed from his mother.

I can hear Bob's words today: "I might be a bit hard of hearing lass, but there's nowt wrong with my eyesight... you'll do for me. But we can't rock the boat." It made me think Bob would be someone that not just Harry could turn to, but me as well, especially as Mam Potts' latest words were still ringing in my ears.

"I have got our Harry this job – and mind you don't let him down," she said to me. How desperately unhappy those words made me feel, thinking how awful it was for her not to give Harry the credit.

Dr Iven was a great support and he made a comment about Harry's mother, "She comes too often and stays too long but time is on your side, Margaret." Sometime in the 1980s when she was still causing upsets, he made another comment. "I got it wrong, didn't I?"

But in the next year I learned to drive and what a difference that made. Ken and Linda were now so much older and I could drive them to school with my good friend Connie Roberts sitting with me. At Brierfield, Connie and her husband Cliff were so helpful.

I was able to become more and more involved in the football club now that we were at Burnley. At Wolverhampton and Shrewsbury I felt apart from it, as though he just had some kind of distant office job with long hours and then came home in the evenings for his meal. At Burnley there was just no getting away from it. Suddenly it was as if we were high profile and I felt like I had been thrown in at the deep end just as much as Harry. If there was one thing that brought it home to me just what sort of a life this was, it was the telephone that was now in the house because it was just so essential to his job. It never stopped ringing day and night and more often than not it was me who answered.

Sometimes I had to say no he was not in, even if he was sitting in the next room. There was the day we laughed so much because Ken picked it up and, without thinking, shouted, "Are you in, Dad?" The media phoned the club or the house and they didn't care what time they rang. The worst person was Bill Shankly from Liverpool in the early days of his career. If I had a pound for every time he rang at any hour of the night to talk to Harry for advice or help, wanting "just a wee chat about this laddie", I'd be a wealthy woman.

WHEN HARRY took over at Burnley FC, he inherited much of the team that would win the championship in 1959/60, a training centre initiated by Alan Brown that was way ahead of its time, an outstanding youth policy producing a steady procession of outstanding players, and a chairman who was determined that Burnley Football Club would rival any of the other teams in the land.

There might be those who would ask, how could he fail? Or make the comment that it had all been done for him. But that would be to seriously underestimate Harry Potts and to make no recognition of his true abilities. The wrong man might have ruined the whole set-up, but the right man, that is to say Harry Potts, simply brought his own talents and skills to the mix. Burnley FC flourished, as it had never done before; he was the right man in the right place at the right time. There was nothing to fix, so he didn't fix it. Someone else might have done things differently.

His appointment marked a reunion with those two wily old birds, Ray Bennion and Billy Dougal, who seemed to have been there forever. Margaret Potts smiles at the notion that the famed Liverpool 'bootroom', where all the plotting and planning took place before a game, and all the analysis afterwards, was the invention of Bill Shankly. Jimmy McIlroy remembers Burnley's 'bootroom' as well in the 1950s and how Dougal would take players in there to talk about their contributions to the match they had just played.

HARRY, BILLY and Ray had a bootroom of their own long before Bill Shankly ever thought of it. Just a small working room where apprentices cleaned and repaired the dozens of boots kept on shelves or on pegs. When Harry took over there were just the three of them and Harry had to cope with just about everything at the club – and no mobile phones, faxes or emails in those days either. He didn't have his own personal assistant, his own secretary or an assistant manager like they do these days. They'd spend hours in that room thinking, talking and discussing things. Billy and Ray had been there since before the war and my dad used to talk about young Tommy Lawton who was at Burnley as well and that he was coached and looked after by Billy and Ray. They were like part of the furniture.

THEY HAD joined the club in 1932, and, according to Bob Lord, had become the finest servants any football club could possess, jewels in their training and coaching roles. Both knew Harry Potts from his earliest days as a 16-year-old, and then as a post-war player. They were thinkers and the development of many of Burnley's famed free kicks, short corners and passing moves were their ideas. Harry Potts, in a late 1970s interview, explained that in his younger days he had sat at Billy Dougal's feet after training had finished late into the winter evenings, long after the others had gone, soaking up his beliefs and listening to his theories. On his first trip to Old Trafford as manager Matt Busby saw Dougal with Potts and chuckled, commenting, "Don't tell me you've still got that old so-and-so with you." They were an absolutely integral part of the club and essential to Harry Potts.

Jimmy McIlroy today still pays tribute to Billy Dougal. "He had such an influence on both myself and Harry. What he didn't know about football wasn't worth knowing. He was full of wisdom and knowledge and always telling us to look for the perfect ball. His simple philosophy was always do what the opposition don't want you to do. And when Harry became manager he turned to Billy Dougal such a lot. Dougal often knew what we were thinking before we even thought it and is one of the great unsung heroes of Burnley Football Club."

Not only did Potts inherit the two old-timers, he was also bequeathed what was largely previous manager Alan Brown's team. Brown, too, was a thinker and had devised all manner of training and passing routines. It was Brown who had approached Bob Lord, then a director, about the possibility of buying a training ground. Lord purchased acres of land at Gawthorpe on the edge of Burnley and for years the training facilities there were the envy of the football world. While Manchester United played practice games under the framework of one of the main stands, Burnley had full-size grass pitches, an all-weather pitch and

Harry Potts in his first pair of long trousers.

Harry with his father, also Harry, and mother Mary 'Mam'.

Harry Potts senior was a salesman for the Co-op and is seen leaning on his cart.

Harry (front row, far left) at 16 in his local football team.

Harry served in the RAF as a sergeant and Physical Training Instructor.

Also in India with Harry was the legendary England cricketer Denis Compton. His message reads: "All the very best Harry. Hope we soon meet in Blighty".

World lightheavyweight champion Freddie Mills also served in India with Harry.

Denis Compton's RAF team in India. Harry is front row, third left, with Denis on his left.

Burnley in the late 1940s. (left to right) Frank Hill manager, Reg Atwell, Arthur Woodruff, Jimmy Strong, George Bray (in suit), Harold Mather, Len Martindale, Billy Dougal, (front row) Jackie Chew, Billy Morris, Alf Clarke, Harry Potts, Jack Hays, Tommy Cummings.

Margaret and brother Bert, taken in the late 1920s.

Margaret's mother Doris and father Albert on their silver wedding anniversary

Margaret and the bicycle she was riding when she met Harry Potts
for the second time.

Margaret being presented with the 'Skyline Personality Girl' by W Gibson at the Christmas party of Platers and Stampers Ltd in 1946.

Margaret on the beach at Port Talbot a year later, when she had taken a six months relief post as a hospital sister.

This is the way footballers prepared for FA Cup finals in 1947. Harry, trying hard to keep warm, is second from the right.

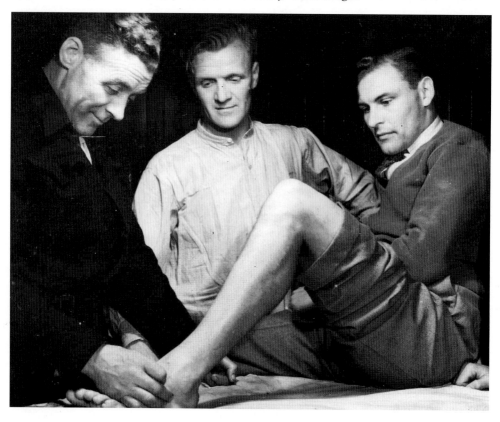

Perhaps it's a metatarsal injury! Billy Dougal checks Harry's foot with Arthur Woodruff looking on.

The Duke of Gloucester shakes hands with Burnley goalkeeper Jim Strong before the FA Cup final, Harry is far right.

Burnley captain Alan Brown congratulates Charlton captain Don Welsh after the defeat at Wembley. Harry is on the extreme left.

c/o. Burnley F.C.
Turf Moor.
Burnley.
6. 5. 47.

Dear Margaret.

I hope the signature of Peter completes your list, and I think if he had been present in the bus, when you were listening to our chants of 'Nursey'; he would have been in the same opinion as the rest of the team, i.e. he would take a chance of recovering if Nurse Hollinrake was in charge of operations!

I caught him just before he went away for a few days rest, and we are hoping he will soon be back to his normal self again.

I was just thinking, you seem to do very well for holidays. However I hope you are having an enjoyable time, if you want a partner or opponent at golf any time just let me know.

Thanks a lot for your good wishes which I conveyed to the rest of the boys.

Yours Sincerely.
Harry Potts.

P.S.
Pulse normal at present.

Harry's first letter to Margaret. It reads: "Dear Margaret,
I hope the signature of Peter completes your list and I think if he had been present in
the bus when you were listening to our chants of 'Nursey' he would have been in the
same opinion as the rest of the team i.e. he would take a chance of recovering if Nurse
Hollinrake was in charge of operations! I caught him just before he went away for a
few days rest, and we are hoping he will soon be back to his normal self again. I was
just thinking you seem to do very well for holidays. However I hope you are having
an enjoyable time, if you want a partner for golf any time just let me know. Thanks a
lot for your good wishes, which I conveyed to the rest of the boys. Yours Sincerely
Harry Potts P.S. Pulse normal at present.

The courting couple in August 1947.

Harry (second left) jumps for the ball with Jack Hayes and Chelsea's Ken Armstrong. Danny Winter looks on.

Harry and teammate Jack Billingham discuss tactics while their landlady Carolyn Livsey looks as if she would rather be somewhere else.

changing rooms, in an area of outstanding natural beauty where training was a pleasure not a chore.

Many of the players Harry Potts took over would contribute to the League Championship title in 1959/60. Angus, Seith, Adamson, McIlroy, Pilkington, Cummings, Miller, Blacklaw, Robson, Pointer, Connelly and White were all on the staff. Potts added just one to the mix, full back Alex Elder, plus there were occasional appearances by reserves such as Harris, Lawson, Marshall and goalkeeper Furnell. One other reserve player, Trevor Meredith, would have a dynamic impact at the season's end by scoring the goal at Maine Road that won the championship.

At the end of the season in which he arrived, Burnley were sixth in Division One. In the following season they were seventh. In 1959/60 they were champions.

You need, however, to do more than just inherit a team, or a youth set-up, or a backroom staff, to win a championship. Potts had a passion and enthusiasm that was infectious; he smiled a lot, made his players fit; he honed, encouraged, and guided his players to even greater levels of achievement. There was no great, mysterious secret to his success. He wore his heart on his sleeve, was uncomplicated, utterly dedicated, honest, fervent, and told his players to entertain, to play with a chuckle in their boots, and to enjoy what they were doing. Pass him in the corridor and he would always have a greeting or a conversation. He had the respect of the older players and was a father figure to the younger players, someone they could always approach. Potts loved the training, the open air, and the contact it gave him with his players. Potts, you might say, was the last piece of the jigsaw.

Dave Thomas, who emerged at Burnley in the late '60s, and went on to play for England, remembers clearly the way as a young lad he was won over by Potts. "You can get an impression of a person the first time you meet: he was just such a gentleman, so fatherly. There was just such warmth and if he sold the club to me it was the way in which he showed he cared, found time for people, he had such a nice manner. You knew this was a man who didn't know how to be devious. He wasn't a bully or a shouter. It's rare in football but he was just such a good man. He was a confidence booster; he could never be sarcastic or arrogant with a player. If you made a mistake in a game he wouldn't give you a bollocking, he'd say something positive about the good things you had done."

Thomas, a member of the 1968 Youth Cup final winning team, has no hesitation years later in saying that he idolised him.

Graham Williams was another young lad at Burnley. He went on to captain West Bromwich Albion when they won the FA Cup in 1968 and win 26 caps for Wales, but he still remembers his time at Burnley. "I was on trial for a few weeks and was in digs with a lad called Ronnie Routledge. We were frightened to death. It was a massive shock because everybody was wearing clogs and the noise on the cobbled streets was deafening. Harry was brilliant with us. Even in those days Burnley were aware of their responsibilities to the younger players, telling them not to do anything stupid and look after themselves the right way. They even sorted out things like bank accounts."

It says much for the attacking nature of the game at that time, that Burnley won the title even though they conceded 61 goals and lost 11 games. Of the teams below them, Wolverhampton Wanderers scored 106 times, and Manchester United 102. Burnley scored 85 and the last two came in the final game of the season at Manchester City, in front of nearly 66,000 people, and they enabled Burnley to win the title by just one point.

Wolves' manager Stan Cullis sat grim-faced in the directors' box and squirmed silently. Nevertheless, although Burnley's victory robbed them of a third consecutive title he was one of the first to congratulate Harry Potts and Bob Lord. It was a championship won in the main by just 12 regular players, with minimal appearances by a small number of reserves, one of whom, Meredith, will be remembered forever because of the goal he scored.

In truth it was an inconsistent season. The team lost unlikely games, and excelled in others, often on mudbath pitches. A key win was the home game against Wolves when Burnley won 4-1 with Jimmy McIlroy playing superbly. Another was a 3-1 victory at Newcastle when captain Jimmy Adamson, of the long legs and silky skills, played his 300th game. Nottingham Forest were annihilated 8-0 at Turf Moor. At Highbury, Burnley won 4-2 with a John Connelly hat-trick after being 2-0 behind. The home game against Spurs in March was critical and resulted in a 2-0 win with stunning goals from Ray Pointer and Connelly. Incredibly, Burnley lost 6-1 at Wolves. It seemed inconceivable that the title could be won after that. Wolves were up for the 'double' and seemed unstoppable. They were so dominant that night that some Burnley players came off the pitch with no idea of the final score. Brian Miller, though, remembers that prior to this game the team had been given various injections in preparation for a forthcoming New York tournament to which Burnley had been invited. Several of them felt dreadfully ill during the game. It was no surprise they lost.

Added to this was the news that one of the foundations of the team, Bobby Seith, was to be sold. He had clashed with Bob Lord. Potts, without panic, simply moved Adamson to fill his place at right half and brought Tommy Cummings back at centre half. The title race was reopened when Spurs unexpectedly beat Wolves. A 1-0 win at Birmingham put Burnley in the driving seat but still not in top spot. There was a disappointing home 0-0 draw against Fulham, while Wolves steamrollered Chelsea 3-1. With Wolves having completed their fixtures, it left just the final game at Maine Road.

I KNOW Burnley fans were arriving in Manchester before lunch and this was for an evening match. They had to close the gates early and lock thousands of supporters out. I heard that the police actually closed some of the roads in the area. We heard stories that some fans had walked there. Two coaches had left Burnley, one with the players, directors and staff and the second with the all the wives and ladies. The stadium was packed, the colours marvellous, the noise deafening, the atmosphere and sense of expectation like nothing I had ever experienced.

"Thank goodness I'm here" was the thought that kept going through my head. I watched with my head in my hands as little Brian Pilkington scored our first goal, but then they equalised. It was more than we could bear in the directors' box. It was more than anyone could stand. What was Bob Lord thinking, I wondered? I looked across at Stan Cullis who I knew from when Harry worked at Wolves. Funnily enough I thought of his abrupt words to me when we were house hunting, "We don't cater for relatives here." His face was like a stone.

When little Trevor Meredith scored the winner we all just went wild. Stan Cullis still didn't move a muscle in his face. We counted down the minutes, sat and fidgeted, watched as Jimmy Mac wasted precious seconds and then minutes holding on to the ball by the corner flag. The referee kept looking at his watch but wouldn't blow the whistle. The whole of the Wolves team were there and more than just a few Wolves fans in their colours to cheer on City. Mac jigged up and down by the flag again. When was the ref going to blow that whistle, we kept asking each other? The tension was enormous, the Burnley fans were whistling and calling and praying. Harry was in his dugout kicking every ball and willing the time away. We looked at our watches time and time again. Our nerves were at breaking point… and then when he blew that superb whistle and we heard that wonderful cheer of acclamation and relief at the end, we just cheered and clapped and felt so elated. It was a feeling I can hardly describe. Claret and blue was everywhere as the pitch disappeared under a sea of spectators as somehow the players got back to the dressing room. There was no champagne; they celebrated with sherry drunk from old tea mugs. I know that for some of them it was days before it really finally sank in.

For a small town and a small club that people from the south thought was in the back of beyond, this was just an incredible achievement. Burnley gained an identity and a pride that night which lifted it out of the doldrums. It was a town of hardship and job losses with its rows and rows of old industrial housing and ancient mills, which had been closing one by one for three decades. It was a place full of neglect, and buildings that were darkened and stained literally by a hundred years of factory smoke and figuratively by low wages.

I was just so proud of Harry seeing him down there at the end. He had done something magical for this tiny place; he had lifted people's morale and spirits and given them hope. The town and club were well and truly on the map and were now known nationally. It was as if our life's journey so far had been worth it. The *Daily Express* of May 3rd 1960, now ragged edged and yellowing, that I still look at to this day has five different pictures of Harry in his dugout during the game. You can see the tension and the strain etched into his face, the staring eyes, the furrowed brow, the clenched fists, and the hunched shoulders. For almost 70 minutes he watched as his team hung on to their 2-1 lead. It must have seemed an eternity.

One image remains and still flickers through my mind and that was of the day he had come home several years previously knowing he had been released by Everton and he had nothing to turn to and no job on the horizon. From that awful period of insecurity and worry to this, this moment of wonderful, magnificent success. If it were actually possible to measure emotion, then the moment of triumph at Maine Road would have been an occasion when it was in fact simply beyond measure. The smiles and jubilation on people's faces around us said it all. I thought, too, of my father, by now not at all well and crippled with arthritis. He would have been listening for the result on the radio and I knew he would have had tears in his eyes that 'his' Harry, 'his' son-in-law had brought such fame to his beloved Burnley.

He, too, could never have thought that the Sunday afternoon all those years ago when the young, fresh-faced Harry Potts had arrived on our doorstep, would lead to all of this, to everlasting fame for Harry and glory and distinction for our little town of cotton and coal.

The journey home was a blur. Just to get into the coaches

outside City's ground the players had to get through the crowds who had gathered outside the dressing room entrance. Then, as we journeyed home, supporters' cars sounding their horns accompanied our coaches. Some passengers were leaning out of windows waving scarves and shouting "champions, champions." It was late at night by the time the coaches approached the Rossendale Valley but people lined the roads and waved and cheered. Each little village and cluster of houses had its gathering of people and reception committee waving noisy wooden rattles and applauding.

A huge crowd, joyous with celebration, had gathered in Rawtenstall centre. The most amazing sights came when the coaches approached Manchester Road into Burnley where a great mass of roaring support lined the route. But the greatest shock came when the coaches reached the Town Hall where an enormous crowd had gathered to give the new champions an unplanned impromptu greeting along with the Mayor, Councillor Miss E Uttley. Somehow the players forced their way through this heaving throng to get to the steps and then into the Mayor's Parlour. From there the Lady Mayor insisted that they go out onto the balcony to face the crowds and make their off the cuff speeches.

The one game that really upset him that season, though, was the cup game against Blackburn. I keep on saying he wasn't a man who came home every night and brought his troubles with him but this was one occasion. I know that Burnley had been winning by some score like 3-0 and everyone was thinking that this could be Burnley's year to win the cup. But Blackburn ended up scoring to make it 3-3.

Harry was so angry that night because the first of the Blackburn goals had been a penalty that Harry said was a terrible decision by the referee. That was a night when he came home and I just kept quiet. Then, of course, Blackburn won the replay and that was that. Harry and referees... he got himself into quite a few scrapes with them but always in defence of his players.

One of the few conversations I had with him about a game afterwards was when he had lost his temper with a referee and I said to him, "Harry, you didn't swear at him, did you?"

"No," he said, "I just told him his decisions had been diabolical." Fined simply for using the word "diabolical". Extradordinary, when you think what players and managers say now.

IN MARGARET'S collection of press cuttings there is a quote from Bob Lord when he first appointed Harry. "Harry Potts was chosen for this job because football today is a young man's game and we believe that with his background, he is the man for us. If Harry Potts and I are still together in eight years, we'll have got somewhere."

Harry and Bob got somewhere with five years to spare.

Tommy Cummings summed up the effect Harry Potts had on Burnley. "This is a happy club and I think that has a great deal to do with it. I think it is fair to say that we all feel pleased because of our manager. Mr Potts is a grand fellow and it is his triumph rather than ours."

"The trouble is," said another Burnley player two hours after the final game, "that we just can't realise we are the champions."

'Two Little Wingers Show The Way' was the headline on Terence Elliott's report in the *Daily Express* the following day and it was only at countless breakfast tables that morning that the triumph finally sank in. The *Daily Express* began its report with the description of Bob Lord standing up at ten past nine, arms outstretched and his face illuminated by a smile. His homespun team, his dream, his pride and joy had cleared the final hurdle. The man he had picked out years earlier to be manager had done the job.

Not surprisingly, the goals were given prominence in the reports. Brian Pilkington was stopped by Ken Branagan but got off his knees and, from the byline, flashed the ball in the general direction of the City goal. To the amazement of the crowd the ball slipped between Bert Trautmann and the post, helped on its way by the groping right hand of the City 'keeper. Within nine minutes Joe Hayes made it 1-1. But then, just after the half hour, came the winner: a foul by Denis Law on Jimmy Robson brought a free kick. Tommy Cummings lofted the ball into the goal area. Branagan sliced his clearance and there was Meredith, standing in for John Connelly, to put it in the net from a few yards out.

In the days that followed, floods of letters and telegrams landed on Harry Potts' desk and it was apt that he paid tribute to his two ever-dependable assistants, Ray Bennion and Billy Dougal. How the latter had kept Jimmy McIlroy on his feet in the latter stages of the season was a credit to his skills as a physiotherapist.

McIlroy remembers those skills, how Dougal would test and squeeze an injured muscle and say, "This is a ten-day job", or "Hmmm, this is a six-day job". Bob Lord gave Potts something far more just a thank you letter, presenting him with a new green Rover car and an inscribed watch. Bob, ever one to save on brass, took Harry's little Morris Minor off him in part exchange.

AT ONE of the celebrations, Bob Lord asked me if I was enjoying the new car. I hadn't even driven it yet so he reminded me it was for both of us. I still remember with amusement the first time I drove the new car. Harry had driven us to the ground to go to an away match and he just got out of the car, gave me a kiss as usual and said: "See you when I get back". I was left in the passenger seat wide-eyed and wondering what to do. I'd only just passed my test and while I was confident in my Morris Minor this was different, a big car with a wide leather front seat. I didn't even know where reverse gear was. I realised the coach would be coming soon for the players so I set off on the long way back to the house to avoid reversing! It was only when I got back that I worked out how to go backwards!

THERE WAS no time to rest or enjoy the championship moment. The next stop was New York to participate in a new tournament in which Burnley had been selected to play several weeks earlier when nobody knew they would be champions. Today, pre-season or end-of-season tournaments are ten a penny and almost meaningless, just money-making ventures for already wealthy clubs. But in those days it was heralded as a huge honour. This was one of the first international tournaments and involved teams from Europe and South America. Even the European Cup was still in its infancy. It was trumpeted as being a grand and prestigious event and Burnley FC looked forward to the great honour of playing in it.

Burnley were guinea pigs. The excitement was immense, visiting the fabled city of New York to pit their skills against the best of the world, and travelling as champions. If they had known what was in store it is likely they would have stayed at home.

IT WAS anything but a success, I do know that. They were away for such a long time and Harry was just relieved and so pleased to be back home when it was all over. You know what they say about things – that the anticipation and the journey are often so much better than the actual event. And that's exactly what happened with the New York trip.

The players and staff left on May 17th. There was no break at all from the football. I hardly saw him, there was so much planning and preparation to do at the club for this enormous undertaking, plus May was when Harry had to tell players if they were staying or leaving and if a young player left he did his best to find him a new club and would be on the phone for hours trying.

To reward the players, Bob Lord had decided they would travel in style by sea on the SS *United States*, which would leave from Southampton. There were no wives; it was strictly men only.

MARGARET POTTS and the rest of the wives gathered at

the club to wave farewell to their loved ones as they left by coach for Manchester at just before 10 am, and then by train for an overnight London stay. It was a scene of almost frantic and chaotic activity as travel agent staff fussed round checking details, loading luggage and completing all the labels. More mayhem took place in one of the changing rooms as some of the players' cases had to be opened and re-packed. The players had been issued with new training boots and some had packed them and some hadn't. So a very flustered Ray Bennion carried out on-the-spot checks to ensure that everyone had a pair packed in their own suitcase. Under his arm Tommy Cummings carried his in a box labelled with large letters TRAINING BOOTS. Ray's worry was obvious, so much so that someone called out "for goodness sake let's get him on the coach". The last-minute checking of several of the cases resulted in half of them refusing to re-fasten because clothes and shoes wouldn't fit back in again. But somehow order was fashioned from all the noisy chaos.

THERE WAS a real holiday air about the place and you could feel the excitement. The players looked smart and elegant in new grey suits and light raincoats. Brian Pilkington, in high spirits, announced that everything he had in his case and on him was new and that the only thing old he had was himself. Jokingly, everyone told each other not to reply to any American with the words "you too". The American U2 spy plane controversy and the trial of Gary Powers, the captured American pilot, was a very sensitive issue.

The anticipation that they were going to play in a wonderful, new, international tournament in the great city of New York filled the air. They loaded up, they clambered aboard and at last the coach pulled away. For them there was the luxury of a five-day relaxing sea voyage. But for us, the wives and girlfriends, there was the prospect of four weeks without our menfolk. Football is not all spotlight and glamour. For those left behind to bring up children and run the homes there is loneliness and worry too. When your husband is 3,000 miles away you are truly alone.

I can't say I know much about what went on out there. I know there were hotel problems, there were reports of rats in the building, and they had to change to a different one; some games they won and some they lost. I know that Bob Lord was far from happy and that it wasn't the marvellous experience they all expected it to be. One thing I remember is the Press commenting on how small some of the players were and calling them 'Potts' Pippins'. Harry's reply was, "If they're good enough they're big enough."

HARRY, AS we know, rarely talked football with Margaret but he did speak about one game in particular against a Scottish side who had been "just brutal", he said, and he did say that the hotel in Brooklyn they were offered as accommodation was just not good enough. In his letters he wrote that Brooklyn itself was a pretty depressing area, that the hotel was badly run down and had few if any facilities.

The one set meal they sampled there was so inadequate that he and the club doctor described it as inedible. They ate in the hotel basement on cracked marble tabletops without even a cloth. How his footballers, who were prime athletes, could exist on this for weeks he didn't know, he announced. He said what they were given wouldn't have fed the chickens in a hen pen.

The press labelled Burnley Football Club as grumblers, troublemakers even, who had stormed out when they asked for a change of hotel to one that could offer the standards they were used to. Bob Lord was livid; only the best was good enough for his beloved club and players. They all felt so badly let down after the promises they had received from the tournament organiser, William Cox.

He had visited Burnley in March and had seen the marvellous game when Burnley beat Tottenham 2-0. He talked long and hard with Lord and Harry Potts about the necessary arrangements and standards expected. According to Potts, Cox had assured them that they would be in first-class hotels, that they were going to a land of plenty and comfort, and that they would enjoy every minute of it.

On their return, Bob Lord and Harry Potts were both deeply upset by the accusations that they had been poor losers and had moaned at just about everything. The American Press had sniped at them continually and the English papers, unaware of the full facts, had joined in, once again pleased to be able to target the outspoken Lord. Even the outward journey aboard the SS *United States*, a thank you gesture to the players, gave ammunition to the Press because Burnley were accused of arrogance and delusions of grandeur in that they had snubbed the tournament charter flight for five days of pampered luxury. The reports neglected to mention that Burnley FC paid for the journey.

Potts made his feelings clear, announcing that the club had been to America to uphold the honour and dignity of the town and their selection as participants. They had not failed, he added. But, he continued, he would not undertake such a tour again without more reliable guarantees about the various arrangements and the standards of accommodation on offer.

They had indeed moved hotels, at their own expense. They did not storm out of the Brooklyn hotel as reported so unfairly, and reports about rows and arguments had not come from the football club. With little fuss and the cooperation of the organisers they found better accommodation in the Governor Clinton Hotel, which was run by a manager who had spent 20 years in Yorkshire. Burnley Football Club met the increase in cost without quibble. It was the organisers who decided to tell the Press that Burnley had made a fuss. There were further reports that mix-ups concerning the flight home had been Burnley's fault but this was certainly not so.

Lord added that the complaints about Burnley were simply a cover for the poor tournament organisation and poor refereeing. Potts had an altercation with the referee after the Kilmarnock game, and complained about the sub-standard pitches. As far as the tournament went, when they were allowed to play their brand of football they had provided good entertainment in front of the largest crowds. But the Kilmarnock game, which they had lost, had been a travesty when for much of the time Burnley players were just hacked to the ground. After the game against Nice, on the other hand, which they won, they had received a standing ovation.

Sadly, the whole thing left a sour taste, much like the first meal they sampled in Brooklyn. Months later the experience was still reverberating round the corridors of the Football League when Lord submitted his report so that other clubs in future tournaments would be better informed.

CHAPTER FOUR

EUROPEAN DREAMS

IT USED to dismay Harry so much that few people outside of Burnley gave them any credit or recognition for winning the championship. There were times when there was a real anger in him and resentment at the idea that if you didn't come from London you almost didn't exist. One report described him as "one of the proudest, angriest, and most mixed up young men in football" and "a man with a chip on his shoulder". What nonsense; he was proud all the time, and maybe angry on occasions, but mixed-up, no. It was an article that described how Harry could be a "chump" sometimes, because of a scene with a referee in New York and because of an incident in Reims in a European game. What an outrageous thing to say.

There was an occasion when I knew they had drawn a game in London 4-4, even though they had been losing 4-0 before the end of the first half, I think. He came back home after that so proud of his team, so on top of the world, yet so angry that people would give no credit to Burnley, which they thought was a place somewhere out in the wilds. Southerners just thought of us as the poor relations of the football world in spite of having such a wonderful team. It was as if people just couldn't understand how such a poor little place could do so well, or even deserved to do well, and even resented it. He used to say if we were a London team they would describe us as the best in Europe and never be away from our door. Sometimes we would wonder if Bob Lord's attitude of "we say what we think up north" backfired and turned people against not just Bob Lord but the club and the team as well. But for sure there was a fire that burned inside Harry and it was that fire that made him leap to his feet from the dugout so often to support his players, to gesticulate in despair at a decision, remonstrate with an official and to kick every ball and feel every tackle.

I've heard it said they won that title a year or two too early, though that sounds a strange thing to say, but in 1962 they came so close to becoming legends when they just failed to win both the league and the cup.

Life seemed more complicated and more demanding at this time. Such a lot was expected of Harry. He had to make himself available to so many people and give so much time to the club, but he never grumbled or complained. "It's the best job in the world," he'd say and loved nothing more than to be out on the training fields at Gawthorpe on a warm afternoon in the sun, "seeing what's what" as he used to put it. It was his idea of heaven. Actually, he loved to be out in any weather and this became a standing joke. Whether it was raining, snowing, blowing a gale or freezing cold on Blackpool sands, or at Lytham on the sand dunes, he'd smile, rub his hands and say, "Great for football today".

He loved to watch the young players coming through and just occasionally he'd mention a name like Willie Morgan or Ralph Coates and that one day they'd be such stars. But I heard him talk too of the abolition of the maximum wage and the first £100 a week paid to a player at Fulham called Johnny Haynes. I know it worried him and at the back of his mind was the thought, could a small club like Burnley keep up with these new high wages? "Where will it end?" I heard him say on the phone one night talking to another manager. I know, too, that he had high hopes that Jimmy Adamson would become a future team coach when Ray Bennion or Billy Dougal decided to finally call it a day.

It wasn't often he would talk to me about football or the club, but when I inevitably overheard the telephone talks he so frequently had, I could always tell when he had anxieties or concerns and nothing concerned him more than when the world outside tried to belittle the achievement of winning the title.

HARRY POTTS was infuriated that his club were labelled unglamorous simply because they came from this scruffy little northern outpost with its national image of dingy back-to-back houses, cobbled streets and permanently smoke-darkened skies. It incensed him that the southern papers should announce it a shame and a pity that Tottenham weren't representing England in the European Cup as they progressed around the country with their flowing skills and lovely football. It annoyed him that nobody could acknowledge that a town with a population of fewer than 90,000 could produce a team just as worthy, which played equally attractive and flowing football. If he had a burning motivation and a passion that so often came to the surface, this is where it came from. Of course, the football world at that time could not know then that never again would such a tiny place achieve the impossible by winning the championship, and then going on to represent the country against the might of Europe.

The 1960/61 season promised so much and ended with so little. There was one moment in March when the club was still fighting in four competitions: the European Cup, the FA Cup, the League Cup and the League. The glory of winning all four trophies beckoned but it was simply too much. In March and April the club faced the monumental task of playing 19 games, plus a 20th on May 2nd when they finally went out of the League Cup in a semi-final replay. In the FA Cup they reached the semi-finals as well, losing controversially to Tottenham. In the European Cup, they reached the quarter-finals and only the width of a post in the game at Hamburg robbed them of a semi-final appearance. In the League they finished fourth.

In April alone, they played nine League games plus two in the League Cup. It was all too much in an age when clubs basically had just the first team and a small number of good reserves. Consolation came when in one of those final games they beat the much-lauded Spurs 4-2. But 'glamorous' Tottenham went on to do the 'double' and it was automatically decided by most people in football that they would do much better in Europe than unfashionable Burnley had managed to do.

In those four competitions, Burnley played a total of 61 games. Just 14 players carried the brunt of that burden with several reserves making just a few appearances each. Today the major clubs carry a squad big enough to field two 'first' teams, and usually all of them are internationals. It puts Burnley's mission-impossible, when players frequently appeared half-fit with patched-up injuries, and often on mudbath pitches, into perspective.

In the League, there were purple patches of consecutive wins followed by surprise defeats; 102 goals were scored but 77 conceded and 13 games lost.

Any one season will inevitably feature games that are significant and stand out for one reason or another. All four European Cup games fell into that category, plus the FA Cup semi-final against Tottenham. There were three semi-final League Cup games against Aston Villa. In the League there were several high-scoring games where Burnley purred like a well-oiled machine but the ones of greatest impact for one reason or another were a 6-2 win at Chelsea, a 4-4 draw at Tottenham and a 4-4 home draw against Chelsea.

MY OWN involvement with the club had increased by now. The children were older and on matchdays my mother was able to look after them. I got on well with all the players' wives, with me taking the big sister role I suppose. I remember well the wives of Brian Miller and Adam Blacklaw who were such good friends. They were affectionately known as the terrible twins.

When I went to watch a game, I could see Harry opposite me in the dugout, which used to be in front of the old Longside across the pitch and opposite the stand where the directors sat. He would be up and down, gesticulating, getting far too worked up defending his players from the dugout. I had a lucky gold charm bracelet I used to hang on to while I used to worry he'd go too far and get himself into trouble.

At functions we'd love to meet people and chat. A function like the championship celebration dinner and dance at the Imperial Hotel, Blackpool, was a simply wonderful affair with absolutely no expense spared. There'd be a stunning menu, grand speeches, presentations, the best wines, dancing, cabaret and then in the early hours there'd even be a bacon and egg breakfast as if you hadn't already eaten enough. On occasions like that you felt glamorous and special. Even the menu and programme was a beautifully produced booklet with photographs of the season. My only problem was that if Harry went to the bar to get himself something, it would be an age before he got back to me because everyone wanted to talk to him. Meanwhile, I wanted to be dancing.

The European nights at the club were special with the electric atmosphere, the sense of expectation, the supporters' passion and noise, the packed ground and, of course, they won each of the home games. The happiness and sense of pride afterwards was enormous. Back in the quiet of our home late in the evening I could sense how proud Harry was that his little Burnley had beaten the best in Europe. I'd put the kettle on and he'd sit with a cup of tea. Yet still he felt that the recognition and praise that came Burnley's way in some of the Press was begrudging and reluctant.

In our private life, though, we very much kept to ourselves. We weren't ones for socialising with the players or other staff. Moments to ourselves were rare and precious and Harry had bought a caravan on the coast that we sometimes escaped to. I would take the children for a weekend if it was an away game. He got a few wry smiles, and comments too, when people noticed we had moved up from our second-hand, faithful, modest Morris Minor to a nice new shiny Rover. I usually drove there in my little Triumph Herald.

I've always been a people person, chatty, sociable, and relaxed in the company of other people, able to laugh and mix with friends and strangers alike. If there were visitors accompanying the opponents' team, journalists, commentators, I was never shy with them. It seemed to me that it was something I should do; to greet them, make them feel welcome, make sure they were being looked after. Perhaps it was to do with the way I was brought up. You didn't just ignore people, you spoke to them.

There were various hospitality rooms and one was a bigger, mixed room for the men and ladies, which is where I preferred to go. While Bob Lord ruled the club, his wife Hilda was in charge of the ladies' rooms. She was an amazing person but it was made quite clear to me on the day, sometime in the '70s, that I went in a trouser suit that it was not acceptable. In the '60s it definitely wasn't done for a lady to wear trousers no matter how smart they were. My relaxed and different attitudes didn't always go down too well. The enclosed world of football was a male domain, and it was the men who should wear the trousers.

Today, the entrance into the biggest stand at Turf Moor is so much grander than the old one we used to get into the old stand along Brunshaw Road as it was called then. Today it's 'Harry Potts Way' and I'm so proud of that. He'll be remembered forever. The entrance we had in those days was small and unpretentious, labelled 'For Players & Officials'. A narrow, dimly lit passageway led to the hospitality rooms. The first was 'Directors Only'. The second was for ladies and the wives of visiting officials. The larger room was for other visitors, journalists and special ticket holders only. Harry would often have someone he had specially invited, maybe someone from the north-east or a relative. They would have been in the stand for the match but would have been given a refreshment ticket. This was when and where I realised it was a good thing to mingle with the visitors and to get to know who owned the voices on the other end of the telephone which I spent so much time answering.

I never felt it was much different from doing my rounds as a Ward Sister tending to people's needs, making sure they were comfortable. I'd been well trained in doing that, especially as there were no male nurses in the war and we had all the men to look after including bathing them. We learned to put them at their ease and that was where I learned not to be coy or shy with men. Looking after pressmen was nothing after that.

Harry Potts – Margaret's Story

I got to know all the well-known national reporters. There was Bill Fryer, Steve Richards, Derek Hodgson, Stuart Hall and a very young David Davies. Then there was Gerry Loftus, Gerald Sinstadt and Kenneth Wolstenholme. The latter was just a face and voice on the box until a cup-tie when the BBC cameras descended on Turf Moor. Harry seemed to be racing round like a scalded cat that day and advised me to get to the ground early because there were so many vans and vehicles there. "All the big guns are coming for this game," I can remember him saying. The car park was crammed and the facilities for press and TV in those days left a lot to be desired.

I know we won, but can't remember who it was against, maybe Bournemouth, but after the game I came out into the badly lit corridor and someone in a huge overcoat came rushing by and just about sent me flying. In the half-light it looked like Harry and just as I was about to give him a good telling-off, a familiar voice said, "Whoa... and who are YOU... we've all been wondering what the inspiration is behind this Burnley team." And there was Kenneth Wolstenholme with his arms around me, trying to stop me from falling over. Well, maybe he was dashing out to get a taxi, or get his train or back to his hotel, or as Harry said, trying to find a phone.

But everything has a consequence, doesn't it? At the next match, as soon as I walked into the Ladies' Only room I was greeted by Mrs Lord with, "And where did you go when you left after the last match?" Someone had been looking for Kenneth Wolstenholme and had been told; "Well, he was last seen in the corridor with his arms around Margaret Potts!"

Years later I met Kenneth Wolstenholme again at the club for a presentation. To my amazement he was telling someone the story. We had such a good laugh about the time I was accused of running off with Kenneth Wolstenholme.

And then, in 1961, Mam Potts and dad came to live in Burnley. Harry's dad had retired and she had always hinted to Harry that it would be nice to live in Burnley and run a little newsagent's shop. Harry didn't talk about the move much, so, almost without me knowing about it, there they were, moving to and living in a house on Montrose Street to be near us. Before the move they stayed with us for a number of weeks at Hillsborough Avenue, another reason being that Harry's dad went into Burnley hospital for an operation.

Harry obviously thought living in Burnley was the answer to our problems. They wouldn't need to be staying with us any more for weeks on end. Instead it meant we spent every Sunday with them, either at their house or ours, with the result that Harry and I had even less private time together at weekends. In no way was Harry a business-minded person and the newsagent's shop never materialised, thank goodness.

Our time together was minimal. He was manager, coach, scout, going to night games here, there and everywhere to watch a team or a player. On top of all that, he was also the manager for the Football League team which played league teams from other countries. On Sunday mornings he'd be in at the club checking up on injuries. He'd drive to Scotland or visit Ireland. He went to schoolboy matches and youth games. If he saw a lad he liked he'd be off to see their parents. I remember one occasion when he set off for the north-east at about 5 o'clock in the morning at the drop of a hat to see a young lad called Dave Thomas and his father.

When he was competing with Don Revie for young players I'd hear him on the phone complaining that Revie would have offered money or something to the parents of these young lads to get them to sign. He didn't like that. If a headmaster rang him to say come and see this young lad, off he would go. He had little black notebooks full of players' names and reports and information about them. He visited the young players and their digs and landladies to check on them; he saw the parents of the new apprentices. He had reports to write, meetings and appointments and interviews galore.

Christmases came and went. Harry loved everything about it, especially the children's parties. Part of him was still a little boy, I suppose. He loved the decorations and the tree, the lights and the streamers, games and surprises. He was so generous with presents and loved the whole rigmarole of wrapping and opening and seeing peoples' faces.

On New Year's Eve there was always a party at Bob and Hilda Lord's house. Of course we were invited, along with friends of the Lords and directors. We went in 1959 and 1960 but the party of December 31st 1961 was the last we went to. My father had died on December 28th and his funeral was to be on New Year's Day. I loved my father deeply and neither Harry nor I wanted to attend the party. Nor did I want to leave my mother on her own.

Harry let them know we would be unable to attend and we were never invited to another. It seemed to be taken the wrong way but how on earth could anyone have expected us to attend a party the night before I buried my father, who meant so much? In truth, the fact that we were never asked again didn't bother Harry. He did not think it was right to socialise with the players or directors because he was the bridge between them. And besides we had our own friends and other invitations, which often included our children. But at Christmas, one party Harry did love to organise was the party for the children of players and staff. He was in his element on such occasions.

THE FIRST of the European games was against Reims on November 16th 1960, but in the month before the Fleet Street reporters noticed that Burnley won four consecutive games, slamming in an incredible twenty goals. The fourth was a 6-2 demolition of Chelsea in London, which gave Potts, and Lord double the pleasure. *The Observer* report by Tony Pawson, summed up beautifully how Burnley were regarded.

> *'There is a quiet efficiency about Burnley which brings them goals and points without fuss or publicity. Year by year they have sneaked unnoticed into the top six and now, when people are saying how unfortunate it is in this season of Tottenham's brilliance that we haven't a more worthy League Champion, Burnley have begun to play with much of Spurs' authority'.*

Potts fumed when he read such stuff.

It was a game in which they gave a near perfect display of possession and attacking football. There were long spells when no Chelsea player could get near the ball. All ten outfield players moved as a seamless unit. Burnley didn't have five forwards; the whole team attacked, moving forward with wonderful precision when even full backs John Angus and Alex Elder were in advanced positions so often it was difficult to work out who were the two wingers.

A Reims director and coach had watched the game at Chelsea and they left the ground with worried and surprised expressions. Potts and Adamson went to watch Reims in Paris. As early as 1960 and still a key player, Adamson was being groomed for his future role at the club, and was very much Potts' protégé. They reported that Reims were a typical continental side, rarely playing a long ball, gaining the ball by interception rather than English-style tackling, and concentrating on possession football. They were impressed and not a little worried by the two star players Raymond Kopa and Just Fontaine. To their relief, Fontaine told Adamson he would not be fit for the first game at Turf Moor. But if Reims had star players then so too did Burnley, not the least of whom was the magical Jimmy McIlroy.

There were 36,000 inside Turf Moor to see Burnley, viewed as the poor relations of English football and only the third English club to take part in the tournament, win 2-0. The Reims players left the field with crestfallen expressions. This was a game they did not expect to lose. In fact, if McIlroy had scored a second instead of hitting the post, the winning margin would have been greater. The game was fast and exciting; the attacking play was relentless. Burnley scored after just one minute; it hit the French like a hammer and stunned them. McIlroy scored the second after 22 minutes. The noise and support from the Burnley fans was incessant. Officials and staff in the Reims dugout were disbelieving.

They had been disbelieving earlier in the day as well when Bob Lord had told them they would not be allowed to take a training session on the Turf Moor pitch prior to the game to test the surface and adjust to the floodlights. They were already gloomy with the news that Fontaine would definitely not be fit after some optimism that he would in fact play. Blunt Bob explained his decision. "This is a big prestige match for us with a lot of money involved, good businessmen do not put all their cards on the table and the training ground at Gawthorpe will give them the chance for a warm-up."

On a lighter note, the suggestion that a mannequin parade in the lounge of the hotel when the Reims players were sitting down to afternoon tea was a deliberate, cunning distraction, was laughed off.

In the *Daily Express,* Terence Elliot wrote that he feared the magnificent football on the night and the two-goal lead might not be enough against a team that had twice been European Cup finalists. He was very nearly correct.

On November 30th, Burnley lost to Reims, 3-2. Two things stood out from that game. John Connelly scored one of those wonder goals which will be talked about forever, which placed him firmly into the 'legends' group. And Harry Potts did something so outrageous that it alone, even if there were no other reasons, would have placed his name into the folklore of Burnley Football Club.

If Adamson and Connelly were adjudged the heroes of the day, Potts was labelled as the villain in the corridors of football power and in Paris itself. The game was fiercely contested. Rockets and fireworks were sent sizzling across the pitch by a fanatical crowd. Thunderflashes roared in the players' ears. The Reims attacks were incessant. The decisions of the Spanish referee were peculiar. Burnley scored first to make the score 3-0 overall. Reims then scored.

During all of this the Reims players had been stealing several yards at each free kick awarded by the referee. Potts was seething at the unfairness of a tolerant referee who either turned his back and didn't see the constant gamesmanship, or saw it and allowed it. Potts decided he had had enough and, marching firmly onto the pitch, picked up the ball and flung it back to where an infringement had been committed. What he did was unparalleled and it incensed the crowd. Gendarmes marched Potts from the field. Reims officials raced on and grabbed him, onlookers tried to punch him, a scuffle involved a dozen people. The gendarmes steered Potts through the angry milling crowd who by now were showering him with rubbish. He was pushed, shoved, jostled and struck more than once.

"The Reims players", he said, "were trying to steal anything up to 25 yards with free kicks – it happened three or four times in front of me and the referee did nothing about it. That's why I ran on to the field."

With Potts away from the touchline the game continued and Reims made the score 2-1 on the night. The tension was unbearable; the crowd were by now even more partisan and fanatical, almost at screaming point and out of control. Then came Connelly's wonderful goal when he raced away from the halfway line on a solo run, cut through the defence and slashed an amazing shot past the goalkeeper. Within two minutes Reims scored again and Burnley now had only the slender one-goal advantage against everything Reims could throw at them. They held on to go through to the next round by the narrowest of margins.

Albert Maddox remembers the scenes vividly. "Harry had become infuriated at the French team's habit of pinching yards at every free kick. When he was taken off the pitch he was escorted up to the stand to where we were sitting and he was still incensed. We all had to move up to make room for him. The stand wasn't very tall and we were still near the front and he continued, still agitated, to shout down at the pitch and the dugout. But afterwards he was jubilant."

Millions in Europe saw the incident on TV. What they didn't see after the game was the sight of several hundred Reims fans waiting by the players' entrance to hurl more abuse at the team. Yet more gendarmes cleared the way. What received little comment, though, was the crowd's generally poor behaviour. A bottle, one of several thrown onto the pitch, just missed John Connelly while he was taking a throw-in. A linesman quickly removed it.

The Spanish referee, Manuel Asensi, disappeared into the night after the game to make his report. Potts would eventually be fined 100 guineas, banned from occupying a seat on the touchline for the rest of the season and warned that any future misconduct would result in suspension.

Brian Miller remembers that after the game Harry was in no way concerned by what he had done on the pitch but was simply cock-a-hoop that they were through to the next round. At the banquet afterwards there was Cremant Binet 1955, Chateau Pichon Longueville 1948 and Champagne Binet Brut 1956. Harry was not a drinking man but he sampled the champagne with relish and washed down his Grilled Turbot Béarnaise and Salade de Saison, followed by Poire Belle Helene and Les Bons Fromages de France. He was, in modern parlance, over the moon, his bruises the last thing on his mind.

At Paris airport Bob Lord told the press that the board would be right behind Harry Potts, adding that he considered him to be enthusiastic and efficient if a little impetuous. "He did what he did for the players, for the board, for the club and for British football because we were being taken for a ride by the French team." Lord grumbled at the crowd, the French players and the referee. He was doubly unhappy that the European Cup Committee representative was also the secretary of the French FA.

Back home he was rather more reserved. "When I talk, I talk straight but this is one time I'm going to keep my mouth shut. Not for all the tea in China or all the coal in Newcastle will I talk."

Margaret Potts did talk to Geoffrey Levy of the *Daily Herald.*

> *"He lives, eats and sleeps football every hour of the day. Don't ask me whether I think his action was right or wrong. But I can tell you this about Harry; his whole life is football, too much so.*
> *"When he left with the team he was happy, after all they were leading 2-0. But I knew the tension was there. I was not really surprised when I saw him run on the field. I was watching the television. I thought, 'Oh Harry, why don't you give it a rest'?'*
> *"This is the reason for it. The tension over the season builds up to such a tremendous pitch that it must find an outlet. Harry was not angry when he ran out*

onto the field and grabbed the ball. He was feeling a tremendous protective instinct for his boys. He did not want to see them cheated. I sometimes feel he has the same feelings for the players as he has for our children.

"But Harry is a wonderful father and husband. It is just one of those things that football has taken over his life and ours too. We can never get away from it. It is not his fault, as sometimes, but only sometimes, he does try.

The telephone rings constantly and it's always football. Shortly before he left for Reims he just sat down, put his head in his hands and said I'll try and take a day off when we come back. But I don't think my husband will find this day. He loves his football but it just dominates his life.

I don't think it was a question of right or wrong him running onto the pitch like he did. It was just his way of protecting his boys. But I am sure that if he had not been so tense he would not have done it. I think if he is asked now to sit in the directors' box he will be very unhappy. He can't feel the game as well up in the stands as when he is sitting down there close to his boys. But when he telephoned me after the game, he didn't mention the incident. He only asked how are the children and what was the latest news at home. Typical Harry."

Harry did not get the day off he so badly craved after that match, a break he had told Margaret he needed. From Reims it was straight on to White Hart Lane for a game against Spurs which turned out to be one of the greatest ever Burnley games.

Having given their all in Paris, both emotionally and physically, it was expected that Burnley would crumble in front of the all-powerful Spurs on Saturday December 3rd 1960. On a mudbath of a pitch, with McIlroy limping after a heavy tackle, and already losing 4-0 with the match not even half over, the Burnley fans in the ground could have been forgiven for assuming that a final score of 8-0 was very likely. But it was not to be.

In the *Burnley Express* Don Smith wrote, "If there were a roll of honour, whereon could be inscribed in golden letters the most meritorious deeds of any club, irrespective of whether they be in the competition embraced by Cup or League, then the performance of Burnley at White Hart Lane would be given the most careful and special recognition."

For a team to fight back for a draw from four goals down was remarkable enough. To accomplish such a feat against the all-conquering Tottenham Hotspur was something that can only be described as superlative. Teamwork, courage, the refusal to acknowledge the word defeat made Burnley the most talked about league side on Saturday night in London.

One could almost have forgiven any team for settling for damage limitation after being 4-0 down before the first half had finished, especially with the home crowd making fun of Harry Potts every time there was a Tottenham free kick. But no: incredibly, one by one Burnley pulled the goals back through Connelly, Pointer, Robson and Connelly again.

The small groups of Burnley fans were delirious as the team covered itself in mud and glory in this classic game. To add to all this, Spurs hit the woodwork twice, but Burnley hit post or crossbar an incredible four times. 58,000 spectators went away exhausted and singing the praises of both teams for providing a football feat in conditions so bad that there were occasions when players could not be identified because they were covered in so much mud.

The next European game was against an unbeaten Hamburg and it took place at Turf Moor on January 18th 1961. Potts had watched them beat Hildeshein 8-2 and saw Uwe Seeler confirm the reports that he was arguably Europe's best centre forward. This time, 47,000 spectators watched the game under the great floodlight pylons on a typical misty winter night. The star of this game was little left-winger Brian Pilkington with two goals in the 3-1 win. The BBC televised the second half live and paid the club the princely sum of just £250.

Burnley shattered two myths on the night: the first being that the Germans, led by the incomparable Seeler, were an unbeatable machine. The second, promoted by the newspapers rather than Burnley, was that Burnley were a moody team full of inconsistencies, on a high one minute and on a low the next when inferior teams could surprisingly beat them. The crucial moment came near the end when the Germans pulled a goal back. In the long run it was to prove decisive.

The worry was that a two-goal lead would not be enough; it dominated every conversation. The Germans, though beaten, were good and had put Burnley on the rack several times during the game. But Bob Lord was ecstatic, describing it as one of the finest football matches ever played at Turf Moor. Again, an audience of millions watched the game via Eurovision and the name and fame of little Burnley spread ever further.

Controversy, never too far away from Bob Lord's Burnley, followed on March 11th. With the away game due to be played in Hamburg on March 15th, Potts and Burnley FC took the step of playing the reserve side for the home League game against Chelsea. The reasons were obvious: the first-team players were drained by the number of games being played, and they were due to play Tottenham in an FA Cup semi-final on March 18th. Potts had submitted his decision to the board on the Thursday before the game. Lord and the board backed him totally.

Had Manchester United not played eight reserves in a game against Burnley, ironically prior to a European game a year or so earlier, he asked? Did that not set a precedent? Had Burnley not played virtually a reserve team against Brentford earlier in the season in the League Cup? Top teams today do this as a matter of course. Then it was considered outrageous and it cut no ice with the Football League.

The rules were simple: "Each club shall play its full strength in all League matches, unless some satisfactory reason is given. In the event of the explanation not being deemed satisfactory the Management Committee shall have power to impose such penalties as they shall think fit". Burnley were fined £1,000.

As for the game itself, the 'reserves' who Potts argued he considered to be first-teamers put on a superb display to draw 4-4 and it was only the genius of Jimmy Greaves who robbed them of a famous victory in the dying seconds. They repeatedly tore holes in the Chelsea side and Harry Potts insisted it had not been a gamble. He regarded these reserves as part of his first-team staff and he argued that they would play much better as a team if he played them all. Andy Lochhead and Gordon Harris stood out, scoring two goals each, but the whole team purred with accurate passing moves, possession football and bewildering switches in attack. Potts was easily vindicated. It was only tiredness, as well as Greaves, that saved the day for Chelsea.

JL Manning of the *Daily Mail,* no fan or friend of Bob Lord, was scathing in his condemnation of Burnley, describing as sentimental twaddle any support written for Potts' team selection and any whitewashing of the situation. The *Daily Mail* sent no reporters to Turf Moor to report on the game. They had already been banned from the Press Box and their reporters stood on the terraces.

"We did the right thing," Potts told the press in Hamburg on the Sunday before the game, having watched them draw 2-2 with St Pauli.

"If the same situation arose I would do the same again. The minds of all our first-team players have been on the match in Hamburg for some time past. The prestige of English football is at stake. We will not make the mistake of trying to pack our goal because it is not our normal way of playing."

More than 70,000 people crammed into the Volspaark Stadium for the return game with Hamburg. Tickets had been sold out two weeks beforehand.

Prior to the match, manager Harry Potts was awarded a new five-year contract. It was thought to be one of the highest, if not the highest, manager's salaries in the country. Potts commented, "I am very appreciative of the gesture. This is a grand club in which we have teamwork from the chairman Mr Bob Lord right down through the playing staff and the rest of the officials." Bob Lord said, "The directors have recognised his abilities, his tremendous work and genuine whole-hearted attitude to the game; it is very much higher than he had before."

Optimism was high even though most of the first-team had played nearly 40 games already that season. Seeler was experiencing a real slump in form. The pitch was in great shape, which Burnley knew would suit their measured football. Could they successfully defend their two-goal lead?

At the end of the game it was the Germans who celebrated as hundreds of fans ran onto the pitch, surrounded the German players, waved their flags and lit mini bonfires on the terraces. Seeler found his form and so did winger Gert Doerful. They destroyed Burnley: the former with lightning brain and flashing feet, the latter with jet plane speed and devastating thrusts. The whole German team played well, but none better than these two. Cruelly, Jimmy McIlroy hit the post with minutes to go which would have levelled the aggregate score. But it was not to be. Burnley, though they were never humiliated, were well beaten. Harry Potts was philosophical. "I am proud of the way we have played. No British team could have done better."

And still this pulsating season was not over.

Only three days after losing to Hamburg, Burnley travelled to Villa Park to face Tottenham in the FA Cup semi-final. The whole country remembered the 4-4 draw in the mud at White Hart Lane. Who would win this one?

Tottenham were apprehensive, as their seemingly unassailable lead at the top of Division One had been cut to four points by Sheffield Wednesday. They had just lost to Cardiff and they were wary of Burnley. Cliff Jones remembered the 4-4 draw at White Hart Lane. Danny Blanchflower tried to unsettle his great friend Jimmy McIlroy with all manner of superstitious comments along the lines of "Oh dear, when we stayed in that hotel, we lost."

It was a game with controversial moments. Burnley had what seemed to be a perfectly good goal by Jimmy Robson disallowed when the Tottenham players were on the way back to the centre circle. To their relief and astonishment the referee gave a free kick. A blatant penalty for handball was not given, which Blanchflower later admitted was a clear decision in his team's favour. Tottenham scored after Burnley had been in complete control when Jimmy Adamson failed to clear a ball that 99 times out of 100 he would have done with elegant ease. But this time it bobbled in front of him. Cliff Jones later revealed that if the referee had allowed the Robson header and the score had become 1-1, Spurs could well have folded, they were so out of sorts and ill at ease. They had already scrambled three Burnley shots off the line. There was an incident when Spurs goalkeeper Bill Brown slipped and appeared to carry the ball over the line. But the luck and the run of the ball continued to go Tottenham's way.

Bobby Smith had been through a poor spell but ironically chose this game to score twice, one goal from another defensive error when a ball was headed straight to him, making the score 3-0 by the end. Such is football. Potts was not best pleased by the decisions which had cost his side the game and a Wembley final, and Spurs went on to complete the 'double'. The newspapers were sympathetic for once. There was some consolation when Burnley beat Tottenham 4-2 at Turf Moor in April. It was another classic game when Spurs went two up early on and Burnley fans and Potts could have been forgiven for thinking that yet again they would lose. But four second-half Burnley goals sent the Londoners packing.

The season ended, however, with yet another anti-climax when, in the League Cup semi-final replay, Burnley's very last game of the season, they lost 2-1 to Aston Villa. The first two home and away games had both been drawn. A paltry 7,953 watched the replay; a sad end to what had been such a wonderful season. They were an exhausted side; the demands had been too much. The disappointment was intense. Football can be a cruel, cruel game.

CHAPTER FIVE

SO CLOSE

WHEN I took a modelling course it helped with my continuing rehabilitation from the lingering remnants of the illness I had experienced in 1958. It gave me confidence again and improved my walk. The Fashion Shows more often than not were just the Mayoress's Charity occasions, and were for worthy causes. Some of the directors' wives came to the functions and were interested in the clothes and where they came from. But others did not and disapproved, thinking that models were slinky women who came from cosmopolitan London, not the Burnley manager's wife.

I opened flower shows and judged beauty queen contests, Lucas factory baby shows and dog shows. Burnley Football Club was high profile and so I was even interviewed about local topics for local newspapers. Harry was quite happy with all of this because he saw that it developed goodwill in the town for the club and us. In fact, it was Harry who often suggested that it would be nice if I was to do these functions when the secretaries of various organisations telephoned or wrote to see if he could attend one of their events.

Jack Butterfield, who later became the football club's commercial manager, was then the Lucas Factory Sports and Gala Day organiser and I was happy to assist him. Jack and Eileen had been one of the first couples Harry had taken me to meet back in 1947 prior to our engagement. They had made me so welcome with Eileen icing buns as quickly as they came out of the oven and Harry, Jack and his three boys devouring them as fast as they were ready. On Gala days, I was asked to be available with my white Triumph Herald in case their special guest needed transport. On one occasion the guest was an up and coming comedian called Jimmy Tarbuck. Shortly after that Gala he was on TV and never looked back. Jack also brought a "singer with a future" to Burnley. His name was Tom Jones.

Mam Potts didn't like any of my involvement with all of this and the bits of publicity I was getting. I just continued to put up with it. I got on fine with the rest of Harry's family and am still in touch with them all. His relatives and cousins would visit us for a day, for a meal, sometimes for a short stay. We had parties for Mam and Dad Potts' birthdays and some great Christmas 'get-togethers' and musical sing-songs.

In the summer of 1961 we managed a proper holiday for the first time in an age, when we had our first holiday abroad in Palma. Harry was supposed to be entitled to three weeks holiday a year but on only one occasion did he take his full allotment. Something always seemed to crop up. There would often be a summer playing tour, then pre-season training and for Harry not much time left in between. There were always young players to settle into their new digs.

The first caravan we had was second-hand, one that we managed to get hold of in the Morecambe area. But it was just a bit too far away; it wasn't the easiest of drives. But the next one was at Cleveleys, near Blackpool, a new one, and that was perfect. It was made in Nelson and I helped design the layout. It was ideal for the children and me when the club went on their New York trip. There were clanking tram rides in one direction into Blackpool or the other way to Fleetwood. We loved the beach and walks. And we'd finish off the weekend with a nice meal. But even at the caravan we would get telephone calls from Bob Lord or the secretary Albert Maddox. The telephone was in the site manager's office and it didn't go down too well with him when he had to come and tell Harry he had a phone call. The phone calls that hounded him even on holiday became one of the reasons why we started going abroad in the summer, just to get away from them.

At weekends I'd collect the children from school on a Friday afternoon and take them to Cleveleys if the first team was away and the reserves were at home. There'd be a picnic tea ready to eat when we got there. We had gas lamps that hissed and sizzled and we had to carry all the water from a tap nearby. I can still hear the sound that rain makes on a caravan roof. If it was a home game Harry would come over in his car when he could and on the Sunday afternoon we often got to the dress rehearsal show for ABC TV's *Blackpool Night Out*. From Cleveleys we could get down onto the beach, go into Blackpool, although we avoided that when it was really busy, or to Fleetwood in the other direction. School holidays meant we could stay all week.

It was the caravan weekends that got me black looks from Mrs Lord again. I can't recall if she actually ever said anything to me but I certainly sensed that it wasn't going down too well, and with Mam Potts as well, that I wasn't showing my face on a Saturday afternoon at the reserve matches. Another occasion for me to wonder what on earth this had got to do with Harry's mother.

"Footballer carrying two pounds of mud on each boot cannot play his best." It sounds like an ancient Chinese proverb but in fact they were the wise words spoken by Mr Choo Seng Quee, the Malaysian national coach who came to Burnley to stay and study the club for a month. My contribution was to make him a typical English meal – sausage and chips. It was typical Harry how it happened. It was a Saturday matchday, Mr Choo had been at Turf Moor and Harry had gone to meet him after the game. Although Harry had intended taking him out for a meal, Mr Choo decided he would like to have his meal with us at home. So Harry rang to say he was bringing him home. With Harry being at the match, the children and I had already had our tea. "Well, he'll have to have sausages and chips then, that's all I've got," I said to Harry. So Mr Choo came wanting to join in a family meal and had traditional English sausages and chips, Ken's favourite meal, and he thoroughly enjoyed them. He loved our roaring coal fire as well. I remember he was a huge, jolly man and Ken was quite young and in all innocence asked Mr Choo why he was so brown and was it because it was very hot and there was a lot of sunshine where he lived? Mr Choo roared with laughter, leaned back on the dining chair that was part of the old post-war utility furniture we still had, and the chair leg promptly broke. He sprawled all over the floor roaring with laughter. He had a great sense of humour and a lovely chuckle. "Why do you play your games on such wet, muddy fields?" he asked Harry. "They look like our paddy fields."

As if Harry didn't ever have enough of football, he was never too tired to play with Ken on the back lawn. By now Ken was seven years old and always desperate for a kickabout in the back garden. He'd be waiting for dad to get back home and we had some little nets and posts. You couldn't just go out and buy them in those days; we had them specially made. If it was dark by the time Harry got back home the house lights would be full on and the curtains drawn back and Harry would drive his car as far as he could to the back garden and leave the headlights on. Ken would then have him out there for as long as he had the energy. It never bothered Harry, who had all the patience in the world with the children. He never said "No, I'm too tired"; he just joined in playing with him for as long as Ken wanted. I'd take Harry a mug of tea outside and he'd have his meal later.

The team were doing well; you couldn't help but feel and pick up the excitement, and it was so infectious. The town was so proud. Every game seemed to be a big game, every one more important than the one before. Jimmy McIlroy was the hero and the town adored him. Ray Pointer was the blond-haired glamour boy. Harry was so disappointed to have lost the semi-final against Tottenham and the games and the rivalry against them were becoming very special. Harry admired the way they were run, he liked the way they played and he especially liked their manager Bill Nicholson. He had first met him in the forces in 1942 and he was somebody who he would talk to on the telephone. Even Bob Lord got on well with the people down at Tottenham.

But somehow they never seemed to have the luck you need to win more things. The team played even better after they won the championship, Harry said, but always something happened to snatch more success away from them. He found that very frustrating and in the season when they nearly won the League again and the cup, 1961/62, he put on a brave face. But it was only a mask and I knew how deeply disappointed he was. I know that with just a few games to go at the end of the season they didn't win many more games and Harry just couldn't fathom what the answer was. "They're just exhausted," he'd say, "just exhausted, it's gone. It's gone." The season they nearly did the double, when they played the best football ever, was the season they should have won the title; in a way they won it two years too soon.

There was so much excitement when we did make it to the cup final in 1962; each game that was won was one step nearer and the nerves among the wives when they got to the semi-final were at fever pitch. It took a replay if I remember rightly, and then when they won there was such jubilation in the town. The phone never stopped ringing: everybody wanted tickets and to talk to Harry. There were endless arrangements and not a meal in peace. Letters and phone calls came asking for tickets, all from people claiming to know us but most from people we had only ever met briefly. It was draining.

The cup final in those days was all about glamour, and for us wives it was about what to wear and where to go shopping in London. I had a nice little dress shop in Nelson that I used to go to. The lady there, Nora Walton, was always delighted to find things for me and for this occasion she didn't just find me something, she actually went to London herself to choose something. "You'll be just as good as anyone else there," she said and she was true to her word, fitting me out with a lovely, blue outfit. It had been Nora who suggested and encouraged me to take the modelling course, telling me it would give me confidence to get out more because there were still just a few, very slight, problems to do with the illness I'd had. There was a lack of feeling sometimes in my left foot.

All the girls looked an absolute picture when they travelled to London. In those days you had to look the part; there were none of these tracksuits, shell suits, casuals or jeans and tank tops. It was hats, gloves, shoes, and what we called matching accessories. Someone had organised little sprays of flowers for them for their lapels in as near to claret and blue as possible. It might have been Bob Lord or Harry. Everybody went down to

London and Burnley seemed to be deserted. On the Thursday before the game we left from Ringway Airport, Manchester, having our lunch there first. From London Airport it was on to the Brent Bridge Hotel.

It was such an adventure, we felt so special, so attractive, everybody's eyes were watching us; there were photographs everywhere, getting off the train, walking round Trafalgar Square, television cameras of course, radio interviews, you felt like you didn't have a minute to yourself and that you were just on public display in a goldfish bowl. Poor dad, crippled by arthritis, didn't make it; he'd died the Christmas before the final. I thought of him several times when I was down there.

Only one thing spoiled it, though only briefly, and that was Mam Potts pushing me out of the way when she saw I was being interviewed in front of our hotel. She just barged in and told the journalist that she was Harry's mother and that it was her wedding anniversary. So the lady journalist went over to a flower-seller who was nearby and bought her a little posy of flowers and gave them to her and said "congratulations" tartly and then continued with the interview with me. I was so upset and turned away to hide my face; I was so close to tears and took pictures of the wives who were on the hotel steps. The journalist was, in fact, quite abrupt with her and then Harry's dad took Mam away.

But other than that, it was a lovely occasion, with everything done for us, the best hotel, marvellous rooms, lovely meals, everything organised. You had nothing to think about except enjoying the occasion, especially being so near to the Queen who was in a claret outfit. Comedian Tommy Trinder, who was very friendly with Bob Lord, kept popping in and out, making us all laugh and signing Linda and Ken's programmes. "You lucky people" was his catchphrase. And then, when the two teams walked out from that long tunnel, I was bursting with emotion. That was my Harry down there, who all those years before had brought me those autographs on the bus back to Burnley when I'd never given him a second thought as he walked back down to his seat. I could never have imagined that I would be part of Burnley Football Club and so many triumphs.

I know we lost, but what a magnificent celebration we had afterwards. From Wembley we were taken to Bailey's Hotel where we were to stay until Monday. From there it was to the Café Royal for the grand evening banquet. There was no visible sense of disappointment and from the moment we had our cocktails in the Empire Room and finally ended our meal in the Napoleon Room it was a wonderful occasion. There's the famous story about Danny Blanchflower calling in at our festivities and being surprised at how happy and jolly we were, even though we'd lost. Even though they had won he told us that their banquet wasn't half as lively as ours.

Then there was another banquet later in the year at the Blackpool Imperial. When we returned to Burnley from London there was a wonderful ride for the team in the coach round the town. Hundreds of fans congregated round the Town Hall just as they had done in 1960. It was just such an amazing time for all of us. It didn't seem to matter to anyone that we had lost. Just the honour of being at Wembley and seeing and hearing the name of Burnley so often in the build-up to the game and on the day itself gave a reason for pride and identity. If the rest of the country had forgotten where Burnley was, they certainly knew now, and people were grateful for that.

SEASON 1961/62 had begun well with a draw and two wins, one of them against Ipswich Town who were managed by an emerging name – Alf Ramsey. Anyone who witnessed the astonishing second game of the season at Turf Moor when Burnley won 4-3 will remember it for a number of things, not the least of which was the strange wing play of a little twig of a man called Jimmy Leadbetter, who to the puzzlement of the home crowd never seemed to progress beyond the halfway line, and the awesome long range shooting power of Ray Crawford and Ted Philips. Goalkeeper Adam Blacklaw's hands that night were bruised black and blue by the time he came off. Burnley were absolutely stunned a week later as down in Suffolk they were blasted 6-2. They could not fathom out the strange playing style Ramsey had developed at Ipswich. It was the style that would win the World Cup in '66. Potts, Lord, the team, the town were shocked. How on earth could the smooth machine that was Burnley lose by such a score? In fact, not just East Lancashire was staggered, it was the whole of the football world.

But then, when demoralisation might have set in, Potts picked up his team, dusted them down and inspired them to a run of seven consecutive wins in which they scored an astonishing 27 goals. His basic mantra of "play passing football, put out the best players and let them get on with it, play with a smile and a chuckle in your boots, and if they score three then you score four" served him and the team well.

Two of those wins were at Birmingham and Leicester when Burnley scored six goals in each game. The display at Leicester was one of those sublime occasions that has gone down into the Burnley history books, and probably Leicester's too. Jimmy McIlroy still remembers it as being a night when the team could do no wrong, when every pass was perfect, when if there is such a thing as football perfection then it was achieved during long spells in that game.

Potts didn't need to sit in his dugout with a clenched, tense, anguished face as he had at Maine Road on title-winning night in May 1960, expressions captured by so many photographs. This time he sat back, smiled, as relaxed as any football manager could ever be, simply wallowing in the display and loving every minute of it. Sometimes in its football life a team achieves heights and puts on a display that will never be repeated.

Real Madrid will never match the display against Eintracht at Hampden Park in that unforgettable European Cup final we were all privileged to watch on grainy black and white TV screens. At Filbert Street on September 20th 1961, Burnley reached that same plateau. Former player Willie Irvine remembers that the Leicester game was shown by Harry Potts to all his players on film in the Burnley boardroom.

The Burnley official handbook described the game:
'The match opened at a furious pace with the familiar pattern of the home side going all out for that vital first goal. Burnley's defence stood firm and then in a spell of just nine minutes, Burnley's every pass and every move clicked to bring them a three-goal lead... nothing could stop Burnley... at half-time the Leicester fans, now apparently resigned to the fact that their team was about to be slaughtered, stood to applaud as the teams left the field... they gasped as Ray Pointer netted a fifth with a shot of such power that, as it came out of the net and was kicked away, the baffled referee at first gave a corner... And as the final whistle came with Burnley still weaving their intricate patterns, and having won 6-2, these fans stayed on to salute the victors with as much enthusiasm as they could have shown had their own team been on top.'

The Burnley team that night was the tried and tested line-up of Blacklaw, Angus, Elder, Adamson, Cummings, Miller, Connelly, McIlroy, Pointer, Robson and Harris. By this time, Brian Pilkington, the Hamburg hero, had been sold to Bolton Wanderers and Potts had replaced him with Gordon Harris.

The *Leicester Mercury* drooled with praise, describing the scintillating technique, their precision and speed, every ball loaded with intention, measured to perfection; no side in the land could have lived with Harry Potts' well-drilled squad. There was scarcely a weakness, there was pace, polish and power on both flanks, the ball coming back like a ping-pong ball on the crest of a hurricane. And all this against the legendary Gordon Banks in the Leicester goal. Jimmy McIlroy remembers that no one, spectators or players, wanted it to end. If there was a football heaven, then this night was it.

At the start of 1962, after 22 games, Burnley were top with 32 points in the days when there were just two points for a win. Spurs were one point behind and Ipswich were not even in the top four. Another championship title was everyone's firm prediction, with no other team being seen as capable of competing with this wonderful football. In the early weeks of 1962 Burnley scored six against Manchester City and a cruel seven against Birmingham.

Ten games later they were still top but, ominously, Ipswich were just two points behind.

In the meantime, progress in the FA Cup went on steadily. In March came the semi-final against Fulham. At Villa Park in early April they battled against not just Fulham but a blinding snowstorm to draw 1-1 somewhat shakily. Goalkeeper Blacklaw was their saviour. The replay at that happy hunting ground of Filbert Street was won 2-1.

The poor semi-final show was, in fact, part of the rot which set in during March. West Ham were trounced 6-0 at Turf Moor but after that it was just a steady slide downhill. Even as late as March 24th, they were still in top place, but after the 2-0 win against Aston Villa that day, there would be only one more league win before the end of the season. It was in a word a disastrous spell. Jimmy McIlroy remembers it as being a time when the adrenalin had stopped flowing, and they were just gone, spent, drained. Points were picked up in scrappy draws, but even they were a struggle. Caution replaced flair. A home defeat by the old enemy Blackburn Rovers merely rubbed salt in the growing wound. The champagne football, the scintillating goals, the teamwork, the passing, the magical individual displays were replaced by leaden legs and uninspired performances. Burnley fans could only despair and shake their heads at these tired efforts. Even with just three games to go it was still in their hands but Chelsea, already doomed to relegation, came to Burnley and drew 1-1. The gloom that was felt after the game was indescribable. A nightmare was coming true.

Should Potts have freshened the team with appearances from a few more of the reserves, such as a newly emerging Andy Lochhead? Was Potts short on answers; could he have done more, been a little more ruthless and rested fading, tiring players? Had falling back in defence and playing safe, instead of surging forward on the attack, backfired? Had they simply forgotten how to do what they did best?

The crowd stood and waited for the announcement of the Ipswich versus Aston Villa game. They sensed what it would be and they were right. Ipswich won and were the champions. The season had been like watching a thoroughbred horse both reaching and then falling away from its peak in the same race. It was heartbreaking.

In truth, an era and a great team had come to the beginning of its natural end and nobody wanted to acknowledge it. In the last ten games there had been just one win, and only six goals scored, and this from the team that in the first two thirds of the season was scoring goals for fun with mammoth scores on an almost regular basis. After 32 games they had scored a staggering 95 times. To this day older Burnley fans wonder just what happened.

Ray Pointer remembers how deflated and disappointed the players were at the way the season ended. He recalls that they really could not believe that they had let it all go so wrong. He thinks, perhaps, it was nerves. The tension had got through to them. Instead of going onto the park ready and expecting to win two more points, without worrying about the opposition, a different mood had settled: one of uncertainty. Defeats came against inferior teams and players returned to the dressing room in silence, wondering how and why. This was a team that weeks earlier had never thought they could lose a game, but now they did. No game had ever worried them, now they did.

The final game of the season was at Sheffield Wednesday. There was no mercy there. At last Harry Potts rested a number of his key players and drafted four reserves into the team. A sad and demoralised Burnley, who had seen their championship chances slowly drain away, were battered 4-0 in the pitiless steel city. It was a silent coach drive back across the Pennines into a deeply unhappy Burnley where more than just a few supporters had shed tears of dejection and disbelief. Harry Potts returned home that day in a far different mood than the occasion he had returned from Sheffield Wednesday as a player to find he was a father for the first time.

The FA Cup Final beckoned just five days later.

I KNEW Harry was deeply unhappy but I also knew that he felt he had to lift those boys somehow and raise their spirits. You could sense the disappointment in him in the way he came into the house and just slumped into his chair looking absolutely worn out. All these years later, some images stick in your mind and this was one. They had lost the very last game of the season badly and it just rubbed salt into the wound. In his heart he knew neither he nor the team could have given more. They were all just tired out. This was just the opposite of how full of life and zest he felt at the beginning of any season when he was bursting with energy and couldn't wait to get back to training and fitness. It was a very rare occasion when he didn't relish the day ahead and with him having been an RAF PT instructor for so long he loved being fit, with all the physical involvement. With Ray and Billy, he did every job imaginable, his finger was in every pie, his influence everywhere.

Every new season began with him out there on the training pitches with them and he always led them on the first run they did when they'd start and finish at the ground. More often than not he led all the way. He was still young, only in his early 40s, but when he came back from that last game of the season he was just bereft of energy and liveliness.

Just sometimes, though, I wonder if something else had an effect on the players at that time and maybe they didn't even realise it. Late in March 1962, there was a terrible disaster at the Hapton Valley Colliery. It was a Thursday morning and there was a gas explosion. Sixteen miners were killed instantly and three more died later from their injuries. The youngest was only 16 years old. You could say that Burnley was still a mining town in the early '60s and the effect on people was dreadful. For the first few days people stood on street corners talking or just at the colliery entrance. The town was in a state of numbed shock for weeks. Everybody knew somebody, or knew somebody who knew somebody, so that not a person in Burnley wasn't touched by the disaster, even if it was only in a small way. The sadness of it drew a whole town together and I'm not the only one who hasn't wondered if the way the season ended at Burnley was in some way connected to the awfulness of that tragedy and the funerals and the mourning that seemed to go on and on for what seemed forever. Maybe the players were affected by it too.

THE NEWSPAPERS feared the worst for Burnley immediately prior to the cup final and urged them to put their weariness behind them and get back to the style of play they knew best: the cultured, measured, elegant passing game with wingers Connelly and Harris using their pace and power to maximum effect, the whole team forever moving forward. Terence Elliot, in the *Daily Express,* urged them to stop back-pedalling into an uncharacteristic nervously defensive posture as they had been doing over the last few weeks. He urged them to forget the fumbling futilities that had lost them the race for the title. Seeing them in their Hendon hotel in good spirits playing a light-hearted game of cricket, he felt sure they had overcome their depression of the previous weekend. He watched them walk out onto the Wembley turf for an inspection of the pitch and to try the run of the ball. For seven of them it was a first trip to the stadium. Then they returned to their hotel for a rest in the hotel deckchairs and a trip to the cinema in the evening. He was sure he had seen enough to convince him that Burnley and Potts had won their off-the-field battle against disappointment and low morale. Jimmy McIlroy, today, might disagree, remembering how flat the whole event seemed to him.

When Elliot met Harry Potts, he was assured that Spurs held no advantage if the game boiled down to pure footballing ability. He was perfectly happy about the mood of his team and that the key players had enjoyed several days without football and would be fit and fresh. Potts told the players it was just another game and to be their normal selves. But Ray Pointer remembers that in some players' minds it had become more than that and there was a degree of apprehension. Potts could see those worries and told them not to be frightened. He told them not to worry but to be themselves. But it was to no avail; half of the team just did not perform on the day, says Pointer.

Elliot's message was simple: go on the attack and curb Jimmy Greaves. But in addition to Greaves, Spurs had Dave Mackay, Danny Blanchflower, John White and Cliff Jones with which to contend.

It was a case of the homespun Burnley, with only McIlroy and Elder having cost tiny fees, less than £10,000 between them, against the superstars of Tottenham. Jimmy Greaves cost £100,000; Cliff Jones £35,000; Danny Blanchflower and Dave Mackay cost £30,000 each; Terry Medwin and Bobby Smith cost £20,000 apiece.

At the Keirby Hotel in Burnley in those days you could have lunch for 13s and 6d (67.5p); rent a TV for the occasion for 10/6d (52.5p) per week; buy a pair of Stanley Matthews continental style football boots for £3 2s 6d (£3.12); a three-piece furniture suite for £48, or a Morris Minor for £416 plus tax. But if you were a frantic last-minute fan in London trying to find tickets, a pair of 50s tickets would cost £75 on the blackmarket. In fact, demand was so great that the touts and spivs were hurriedly trying to buy back tickets they had already sold at an inflated price in order to re-sell them at an even greater price.

The reasons were not hard to find. This had been billed since the semi-finals as the cup final of the century and was the game everyone wanted to see. It was the game everyone hoped would be the final, between two supremely talented footballing sides who on their day were a pleasure to watch. For two seasons their contests had been among the best, their games high scoring, the rivalry intense but full of mutual admiration and respect. It was north against south. It was sophisticated London against working-class small-town Burnley. It was bought against home-made. It was those two wily old birds, Blanchflower against McIlroy. It had every angle you could wish for and was labelled the Chessboard Final.

Bob Lord wore his smile of pride like a badge: from barrow boy hawking meat round the streets of Burnley to becoming the businessman who then became chairman of the club. He made it clear what he wanted – a display of their usual good football which even if they lost they could look back on with pride. He was sure that his team had overcome their slump, their spiritual malaise as one writer called it. "We are ready for the big show," he announced.

But even at the prestigious pre-match luncheon, he could not resist wondering who all these faces were who probably never set foot at a football match between one final and the next. Some of them he commented seemed surprised that it was a round ball that day, and not an oval one. It is part of Wembley folklore that he introduced himself to the Duke of Edinburgh as 'Lord of Burnley'. True to form he made one of his statements that illustrated his forward thinking and his vision. He criticised the dungeon-like, drab, dismal state of Wembley and urged that it should be rebuilt. More than 40 years later it was indeed being rebuilt. Today, if Lord had been in charge, it would probably have been completed on time.

Harry Potts had difficult decisions to make. Young reserve Ian Towers had been appearing on the left-wing for several of the end of season games instead of the muscular, more powerful Gordon Harris. Potts decided on Gordon Harris. Another decision was whether to shuffle the youthful Brian Miller across to centre half instead of old faithful Tommy Cummings and bring in the robust Walter Joyce into Miller's wing half position. He decided on Cummings.

Such decisions always caused him immense anguish for he was a 'people person', always able to put himself in someone else's shoes and empathise with their feelings of hurt or disappointment. He could never be described as cold or ruthless or uncaring. That was not his mould. It is, perhaps, the reason why he did not tinker with the team during the final two months of the season when perhaps he should have done. Other managers might have made several changes in order to stop the decline. He was loyal to the players who served him well; perhaps too loyal, some pressmen commented.

It was a strange final, some of the papers remarked. It had everything you could ever want in a football match, they commented, but it lacked just one thing – real passion, thrills, spills and the nail-biting excitement that comes from 90 minutes of tension and uncertainty. McIlroy's choice of the word "flat" was indeed apt. It was a display of all that was best in measured football from two fine teams but from the third minute it was as if everyone knew who the winner was going to be.

David Prole, in his excellent book *Cup Final Story 1946-1965*, provides a very good analysis as to why this final was so dispassionate.

"The reason lay in the nature of the contestants. English football was by now more or less under the influence of foreign example, and both Tottenham and Burnley were very much of the continental mould. Besides the basic virtues of ball control and accurate passing, they relied to a great extent on positional play by men not in possession, with bodily contact kept to a minimum. It was a radical change from the style of such teams as Newcastle and Wolves in earlier years, and it meant that a meeting of two such similar methods was something akin to animated chess, with appraisal and re-appraisal as much a part of the proceedings as instinct and physical action. Perhaps there was too much similarity and too much skill for it to be a memorable match. Too many players doing too many things without fault can lead to a game without much drama, without the shock of the unexpected..."

Scientific game or not, Burnley knew they had to stop Greaves. They didn't. He scored within three minutes. His goal was stamped with his genius and people still wonder how he swivelled and threaded the ball home with so many Burnley players in front of him and the goal.

But Burnley did not flinch. Instead, they got back into the game, with Adamson picking up his team and building attacks that silenced the Tottenham fans. Five minutes after half-time they equalised through Jimmy Robson at the near post but their joy was to last only a minute. Burly Bobby Smith scored again. Was there a foul? Did he barge into Brian Miller? Nobody argued or protested at the time. The goal stood. Any possible drama vanished. It was back to the chessboard. Potts had no doubts after the game. It was a foul, but he was not angry; this was an occasion where his self-control was greater than the emotions he so often wore on his sleeve. Burnley got back into their stride, but it was to no purpose when Spurs scored the third. But the press were almost unanimous that this third goal should never have been. Up went the linesman's flag for a foul on goalkeeper Adam Blacklaw but referee Jim Finney did not stop the game. "I saw no flag," he said afterwards. The ball bobbled out, Terry Medwin cracked it goalwards and Tommy Cummings handled it on the line. Finney blew for the penalty and Danny Blanchflower scored with ease. Minutes later, when the Burnley trainer went onto the field to attend to an injury, Potts told him to ask the referee if he had seen the foul on Blacklaw.

Credit to Burnley; there were long passages of play where they were at their best but just could not break down the Tottenham man of the match, centre half Maurice Norman. Burnley kept their promise to leave League form behind them and bring honour to the name of Burnley. None did more so than Jimmy Adamson, who at the end of the game walked off the field arm in arm with Spurs manager Bill Nicholson.

Potts was man enough after the game to make no great fuss about the sequence of events that had led to the third goal. It was in the 82nd minute anyway. His post-match reaction was short but dignified: "I thought it was a grand game but we didn't get the breaks. I'm sure everyone enjoyed the game but I didn't agree with the penalty award. Before the ball hit Tommy Cummings the linesman was flagging for Smith's foul on Blacklaw. My players could not have done more for any manager than they have done for me this season."

Would Burnley have equalised again in those remaining eight minutes had Spurs not been awarded the penalty? Of course, no one will ever know. Fate decided that Tottenham would win the trophy for the second consecutive year.

It made no difference to the people of Burnley who lined the streets again to welcome them home. Some 6,000 gathered outside the Town Hall in scenes reminiscent of the championship homecoming. Potts was happy and satisfied that his team had displayed all their talents and had gained even more admirers. Down through the Rossendale Valley they drove again to a rain-soaked town centre. Horns and trumpets sounded, banners waved, spectators hung from windows and even surrounding rooftops.

For Harry and Margaret Potts it was so reminiscent of 1947 as the team drove past the Prestige Factory where Margaret had been on the night shift and watched them from outside the factory. This was where she had watched Harry coming home 25 years earlier.

Harry Potts smiled again, proud but not arrogant, defeated but not downhearted. His team was still intact, a mixture of some players at their peak from whom another season of high levels could be expected, and other younger players who had still to reach theirs. Perhaps only one, Tommy Cummings, would have to be permanently replaced. Their football was still of a supremely high quality; there was every reason to expect that the next season would be a good one. On top of all that there were some great young reserves coming through, the best for a long time. But what Harry Potts did not know was that in a few months time a bombshell would hit with an impact that would shake not just the club to its foundations, but the whole town.

CHAPTER SIX

A HERO DEPARTS

I CAN'T remember if they went away anywhere after the FA Cup final but for a short while life returned to some semblance of normality. We were still living at Hillsborough Avenue. I do remember the one thing that upset the next season was the terrible winter we experienced. It was certainly one of the worst that I can ever remember, not as bad or as long as that of 1947, but it was still awful and in some areas life came to a standstill for a long, long time, including all the football. Roads were blocked, coal in Burnley was running out, farms were marooned, and much of the town was icebound and frozen. We still had to get out and about though.

It meant walking down the hill to the shops to get fresh food. There were no prepacked meals you could put in a microwave. Indeed there were no microwaves! So, in our hilltop position we just dug ourselves out of the snowdrifts and got on with things. And of course we had lots of fun as well, playing in the snow, sledging and building snowmen. At Turf Moor and Gawthorpe there was a change in the training routine. It was mostly digging and shifting the snow.

When Jimmy McIlroy was put on the transfer list towards the end of the season the town was just stunned. At the time I didn't realise just how much of an absolute hero he was. The supporters adored him, and they loved him for his loyalty to the club and the town. All that, plus the fans thought he was so important to the team. But to me, in all honesty, until the great fuss was made when he was put on the transfer list, he was just one of the team.

He was in the cup final team and then put on the transfer

list not much less than a year later. Why was he transferred? I don't know; Harry never talked about what went on in the boardroom or the dressing room but I know it was Harry who got a lot of the blame. There were all kinds of stories and rumours and still are even now. I don't know what you could compare it with today. I know the most famous player at Manchester United was David Beckham and he was transferred and the newspapers were full of it for weeks, it was such a shock.

It was even bigger news in Burnley when Jimmy was sold. Harry was so upset about the whole thing, very quietly and very obviously upset. He took the blame because the press releases Harry made actually said it was Harry who had recommended Jimmy be transferred. One day when I went down town in the car and it was dirty and dusty, I found somebody had written graffiti on it about Harry, words to the effect that it should be Harry going, not Jimmy. And I thought "I don't believe this". It was Harry who only months before got this team to the FA Cup final and nearly won the League as well. It nearly broke my heart. "Part of the manager's job", was one of the very few things Harry ever said to me. "You just have to take these things in your stride."

It was about this time that I met Reg Cook, a Burnley director whom I had known since I was at school, in town and we chatted about the car. "Harry has too many loyalties," he said. "You don't have to tell me that," I replied.

Anyway, I brought the car back home and washed the writing off it but it took a long, long time for things to get back to normal and if I went shopping I could sometimes feel people looking at me as if to say, "Huh, that's Margaret Potts and her husband sold Jimmy McIlroy." It was a difficult time and in a small town like Burnley there was no getting away from it. Even Linda and Ken were the targets of abuse and had a hard time.

Years later people would tell me this or that was the reason he was sold. Everybody had their own idea, but it had been Harry who had to carry the can and make the announcement. If there was ever a reason that it couldn't be made public then Harry and Bob Lord took that reason to the grave with them and they're buried close to each other in Read. In 40 years will people talk about Beckham leaving Manchester United? I doubt it, but I know older people in Burnley more than 40 years later still talk about the day Jimmy Mac left Burnley.

Whenever a player was sold, everyone always knew it was because the club had to sell a player every so often for the finances. So people accepted it, although not necessarily happily, if one of their favourites was sold. But when Jimmy went it was different. He was part of the Burnley furniture; it was totally, totally unexpected.

One thing that helped us was the fact that as Christians and churchgoers, we had great faith, and strength came from that. I attended church regularly; Harry came if he could, if there was nothing to do at the club on a Sunday morning. It had been a year since my father had died and there were times in quiet moments when I still thought of him. I could picture him, a dark, good-looking man, back at home after a day's work, all the shoes laid out in front of him on a newspaper to be cleaned – even the underneath. He wore those shirts with detachable collars and off came the collar as soon as he got in so he could eat his meal in comfort. He had served in the army in World War One but rarely talked about it other than remembering a football match in no-man's-land played against the Germans on Christmas Day when they had a truce.

Dad didn't actually play, the game was in a different area but he remembered it. On a Sunday he would have his day of rest, content to be at home. He'd give us a sixpence to go to the shop to spend 2d on a packet of cigarettes for him, buy mum some chocolate, and for ourselves a halfpenny each on sweets. Dad's favourites were always pear drops. It was nice to be able to tell Linda and Ken as they grew up about my own happy childhood and their grandparents. As children, they loved to go up to my mother's cottage where she was always doing something interesting, jobs or gardening and she always had a dog.

AT THE end of the season when the double had been so tantalisingly close, Jimmy Adamson was named Footballer of the Year. Not only that, but he had also accompanied the England team to the World Cup in Chile as assistant manager to Walter Winterbottom. If his playing career was coming to its end, his coaching career was just about to start. In this respect he was very much Harry Potts' protégé and it was clear that Bob Lord had plans for him when his playing days ended. At the annual general meeting, Bob Lord sang the praises of Harry Potts and then went on to say that Adamson was a jewel. At that time there was a lot of speculation that Adamson, whose coaching and leadership reputation was excellent, would be leaving the club to take up management elsewhere. But to quash these stories, at the club's annual dinner in Blackpool, Lord went on to say that there would be a place for Adamson at Burnley, be he 33 or 63 and that nobody would be taking him away. The scene was set therefore for the Potts/Adamson manager/ coach partnership that was on the horizon. But years later, though the dark days to come were a long way away, it would not end happily for either of them. Potts would one day be moved into a hazy general manager role, so that Adamson could take over as team manager. And then, several years after that, Adamson himself would be sacked when Harry Potts at Blackpool masterminded an FA Cup win over his old club Burnley.

In season 1962/63, however, Burnley were still a force to be reckoned with, even though Adamson played only 18 of the League games and Jimmy McIlroy just 22. Potts had plenty of young, emerging reserves almost queuing up to take Adamson's place and the magnificent Brian O'Neil would eventually clinch it. There was nobody, however, to fill McIlroy's shoes quite so quickly.

Though there was the eventual success of third place and some notable victories, it was a season not without problems, controversy and difficult moments. The consolations came from the emergence of a whole new group of exciting young players, and the continuing development of reserves who had already made their first appearances. The Gawthorpe assembly machine was in full, productive swing and Harry Potts still loved nothing more than to be out on the training pitches with younger and senior players alike.

The magical Willie Morgan made his debut towards the end of the season. He had arrived at Turf Moor in 1959 as a 15-year-old from a village where there were neither telephones nor televisions. At first he had no intention of staying. He was wanted by Manchester United, Arsenal, Chelsea and several others and says he had never heard of Burnley. His plan was to look at all of them and then go back to Scotland and sign for Celtic but at Burnley he broke a toe, was in plaster for several weeks and as the club and Harry Potts were so good to him, he decided to stay.

"Harry Potts was the manager and he was an absolute diamond, a gentleman in every respect," Morgan said. "Another nice man was Tom Thornber who worked in the office and reminded me of my dad."

Margaret Potts, too, remembers Tom Thornber and the way he always gave her children Ken and Linda tins of sweets at Christmas.

Willie Morgan's tribute to Harry Potts does a lot to explain the secret of the man and the way in which young players could respond to him and respect him. They felt comfortable with him, he exuded a fatherly relationship, from him stemmed the family atmosphere. Then, of course, when the 'different' Harry emerged on a Saturday, they knew he was on their side and would back them to the hilt.

Legendary centre forward Andy Lochhead had already made several appearances but in 1962/63 made the position his own. At the end of the season a young Irishman, who would go on in a future season to smash the post-war scoring record, would make his debut; his name – Willie Irvine. Together Lochhead and Irvine would eventually become the most feared strike partnership in the division.

These were the good things and it was by no means a disastrous season. This was still the small-town club up there with the big boys and Burnley lost only ten League games in the season. Only Everton and the old enemy Tottenham were above them by the end. The latter scored a mammoth 111 goals but couldn't beat Burnley in three games. But the labels of being unfashionable and unglamorous, forever attached to Burnley FC, were impossible to shake off.

It was a season when an horrendous winter played havoc with the fixtures; one of the Tottenham games was so brutally ugly that it left Harry Potts enraged; there was a major incident to handle between two players in training, and to the shock and amazement of the whole of East Lancashire, Harry Potts and Bob Lord put the incomparable Jimmy McIlroy on the transfer list.

Nobody could understand how the same Tottenham who played such delightful football in the cup final could then kick Burnley off the field in a vicious and ugly cup game in the third round at White Hart Lane in January 1963. Potts was incensed and made his feelings known. On a difficult, snowbound pitch he left the choice of footwear to his players. It was a critical decision for his players chose a short-studded boot as opposed to the flatter plimsoll type boots that the Spurs players wore. Burnley kept both their feet and their heads. Tottenham kept neither. In a game of bad tackles, raised tempers, fistfights and mass confrontations, mostly provoked by Tottenham, Burnley won 3-0. It was sweet revenge for the Wembley defeat.

The next round was against Liverpool but the dreadful winter played havoc with the fixture. At one stage a foot of snow covered the pitch and blizzards nearly buried the queues of people lining up for tickets on one of the days they were on sale. It says much for the supporters that in spite of the atrocious snowfall 16,000 tickets were sold that day. When the tie at Turf Moor did take place on January 26th it ended in a 1-1 draw with Burnley hanging on at the end for grim life after John Connelly had equalised a first-half Liverpool goal. It was a game where one newspaper noted the minimal contribution of Jimmy McIlroy.

The replay did not take place until February 20th. The week before that Bill Shankly had verbally blasted Harry Potts for what he deemed to be interference during a pitch inspection after which the referee had declared the pitch unplayable. Earlier in the day a local referee had given it the OK and as a result fans streamed to the ground by train, coach and car, sure that it was going to be played. But George McCabe decided otherwise and Shankly was furious at the presence of Potts during the inspection. He accused him of interfering and making it clear he did not want the game to go ahead. Shankly added that he very much resented his presence there. This was the same Bill Shankly who once used to ring Potts at all hours of the day and night for help and advice. Shankly was livid but Potts was diplomatic, saying he had no comment to make other than he wanted to see the pitch to decide on his line-up and on what boots the players should wear. Years later Shankly would pay affectionate tribute to Burnley's achievements, calling them "that village team". He thought it quite remarkable that a small-town club could achieve so much for so long.

It wasn't a particularly good week for Potts, for just a few days later he was severely criticised by the press for not releasing three players for an England practice. His answer was simple: in view of the fact they hadn't played for two or three weeks because of the bad weather he wanted his team together for training for the forthcoming cup tie – whenever it might be played. This was an era when the FA and the Football League could act in a high and mighty manner. Today it is the Premiership clubs who pull the strings. Dennis Follows, the FA secretary, commented, "The actions of Mr Potts have not gone unnoticed." But Potts stuck to his guns, adding that Burnley hadn't played a game since the end of January and the Liverpool game could be any time.

When it did take place it was decided by a bizarre sequence of events, which then led to another sequence of events back in Burnley. It is not untrue to say the latter had enormous impact nationally and caused both fury and bafflement locally.

In extra time, Harry Potts could only look in amazement and horror as Adam Blacklaw as good as gifted the game to Liverpool. Blacklaw was a tremendous goalkeeper, one of Burnley's best ever. But even the greatest make mistakes and this one sadly was in a high profile game in the FA Cup. With the score at 1-1 was it a mistake though, or just a huge slice of bad luck? Maybe it was a mixture of both as he elected to kick a back pass from Alex Elder straight back up the field from the edge of the area. Instead of reaching one of the Burnley forwards in the Liverpool half, the ball simply thudded into Ian St John the Liverpool striker who was just yards away.

St John was after it in a flash and would have put it in the back of the net had he not been brought down by Blacklaw. The penalty was put away by full back Ronnie Moran and Blacklaw was close to tears afterwards. It had been the goalkeeper, in fact, who had kept Burnley in both ties with strings of great saves and interceptions until those fateful last few moments of extra time when the game was only seconds away from another replay.

Again, Jimmy McIlroy came in for criticism. It was said he was rarely seen in an attacking role, that he spent far too much time in no-man's-land and was ineffective. That he meandered and never lived up to his reputation. It would be his last game for Burnley Football Club. An era was over.

Newspapers pointed to the defensive style of Burnley on the night, how they had packed their defence and abandoned their normal sweet-moving attacking style. They had rarely put Liverpool under any pressure. If these defensive tactics had been deliberate, they had backfired with a vengeance.

On the following Sunday, Bob Lord called a directors' meeting at his Lowerhouse factory.

On the Monday it was Harry Potts who made the announcement that the club had decided to place Jimmy McIlroy on the open to transfer list. Potts refused to make any other comment save for saying that it was a club matter. When the newspapers hit the streets there wasn't a supporter who was not shocked, speechless or baffled by the news. There is no official record of any meeting of Bob Lord or Harry Potts in between the Liverpool defeat and the Sunday morning directors' meeting but Lord insisted that it had been Potts' recommendation that McIlroy be transfer listed. The *Daily Mirror* referred to it as a "ruthless and mysterious decision" and McIlroy himself has never accepted that it was Potts' choice to take this action.

McIlroy was called into the manager's office and told the news. Little elaboration came from Potts himself and it was McIlroy who gave the gist of the conversation between himself and Potts to the papers.

"I went into Harry Potts' office and he told me straight out that the board of directors at a special meeting had decided on his recommendation to place me on the transfer list. I asked him why and he said he was not satisfied with my playing efforts. In fact, he said he was disappointed in me and that there was nothing more to it."

McIlroy added that it had then been explained to him that it was purely to do with the playing side of things, nothing to do with finance, and that there was no friction between himself, Potts, any of the directors or Bob Lord. In short, he was baffled. Surely, he reasoned, if he was playing badly the normal thing was to place him in the reserve team for a spell.

When the subject of the Liverpool game was brought up by reporters, McIlroy explained that he had merely being playing to Potts' instructions: to drop deep, to take a defensive role.

After the interview Potts suggested to McIlroy that he miss training and go home. This he did and gave the news to his equally shocked wife Barbara.

Within 24 hours supporters were starting petitions, holding meetings, bombarding the press, demanding answers, threatening never to set foot in Turf Moor again, and daubing graffiti around the town.

It seemed that everyone who possessed pen and paper put down their views, including Tom Finney and Danny Blanchflower. "Burnley must speak up," wrote Finney, who added that McIlroy had commented about being caught up in club politics. Perhaps this was in connection with the buying and selling of Burnley Football Club shares and that this involved McIlroy's father-in-law, a simple enough matter, but probably not as far as Bob Lord was concerned. Perhaps it involved his friendship with one particular director and his family (Jimmy Adamson had warned him to be careful about this). It was in the car of the son of that director, not the team coach, that McIlroy left Anfield after the game.

Blanchflower's lengthy piece in the *Sunday Express* hinted at financial reasons, that other players were resentful of his star status, the back slaps he received, his higher salary; thereby implying that the balance of the club was tottering and that McIlroy's sacrifice was the way to restore it and was necessary to avoid higher wage demands by other players. Blanchflower alleged that he had spoken at length to his international colleague, and dwelt in his column on the way McIlroy would now feel until his transfer was resolved, the vacuum that would exist around him, the isolation, the uneasiness displayed by others in the dressing room.

"It must be finance," wrote Blanchflower.

"When they beat Tottenham, Bob Lord and his merry men probably thought they would win the cup. But Liverpool had other ideas. Another cup run to Wembley would have put thousands of pounds into the Burnley kitty. Maybe they were counting on that. And on the added support that a good cup run would bring to their League matches. It's been a hard winter. Funds are low all round. McIlroy is getting more money than the others. Perhaps the others are starting to ask for the same. Simple solution: sell McIlroy, get some cash, cut the feet from under the others with regards to asking for more. That's better for the club in the long run or at least it would seem to be."

McIlroy, too, alluded in a *Daily Express* piece to the possible discontent felt by other players that he was on a far higher salary. He questioned the legendary family spirit of the club and suggested that, in fact, ripples of dissension were beginning to show as a result of the new differences in wages. In the same piece he quite clearly suggests that on the playing field itself other players were not exactly in tune with him, that they had actually had enough of the sound of his voice, and that some of them in no uncertain terms were telling him to shut up. It made him feel like a "general without a baton".

Were these then the reasons behind the decision? Particularly Lord's needing to avoid other players demanding more money to match McIlroy's and his plans to build a giant new stand. Was it that he could sell McIlroy while he was still valuable?

On the other hand, is there still some other reason that none of us will ever know, now that Lord and Potts have taken the answer to the grave with them?

'Potts Ends His Silence' was the *Burnley Express* headline on March 6th after Burnley and Stoke City had sealed the deal to take McIlroy to the Potteries. Potts spoke at last.

"When I first told Jimmy McIlroy last Monday that Burnley had decided to put him on the transfer list, it was agreed between us that there should be no public slanging match. I have seen that this has not occurred and because of it I have been unable to say to the Press until now any more than that this was a club matter. Now I can tell you our side of the story. Jimmy McIlroy has left Burnley and the only person responsible for this is Jimmy himself."

Potts explained that McIlroy had not been giving 100%. Jimmy on his own admission had become complacent and no club could afford the luxury of a player not giving every effort. McIlroy could have remained at Turf Moor for the rest of his playing days with a third benefit and testimonial game to be arranged, Harry explained, but his lack of effort was the reason behind the decision to sell him.

Lord stayed silent and it was left to Potts to make the statements. As a result it was Potts, as much as if not more than Lord, who was subjected to abuse and criticism from Burnley people. It was a most difficult time and undoubtedly the most traumatic event Potts ever had to deal with in his managerial career. The insults on his car, and the abuse on the walls around Burnley, hurt him and Margaret deeply.

More than forty years later, McIlroy says he is still baffled by the whole thing. "On the morning I saw Harry he looked in pain and uncomfortable. He looked in a worse state than me. When I asked him why I was being transfer listed, he replied that I hadn't been doing it on the field, so I asked, well, why not drop me? Well, he replied, you don't drop players like you. Since then I have always thought then why did he sell me?"

Of all the theories and explanations put forward over the years perhaps it really was just the simplest one; the one that people can't quite accept, that even the incomparable legend, Jimmy Mac, had at last reached his sell-by date. Perhaps Blanchflower was indeed correct in his analysis.

Or, perhaps there was some other very private reason that was covered up, the club closed ranks; and it remains unspoken to this day, known only to an ever-dwindling handful of people, and something that few, if any, other people will ever know.

Jimmy McIlroy, himself, can have the last word. "As far as I'm concerned, only two people know why I was placed on the transfer list and that secret will remain with them. By coincidence they lie close by each other in the graveyard at Read Church."

The punch-up between Jimmy Adamson and Gordon Harris during an indoor training game was not nearly as difficult for Harry Potts to deal with. At the time of the incident the players were ordered by Potts to remain silent. It was, after all, the 'Footballer of the Year' and assistant manager to Walter Winterbottom in the 1962 World Cup, who had been laid out. It was described as a scuffle but was deemed serious enough to warrant a meeting of the directors. Somehow it appeared in the papers and Adam Blacklaw could only suggest that one of the players must have leaked the story. Potts denied he had seen it, saying there was no incident while he was there. What he did, though, was take Harris to Adamson's house where for thirty minutes they discussed the matter. When they came out, Harris was angry only that the matter had become public. Potts insisted to a *Daily Mail* reporter that there was no longer a problem.

"There has been a lot of fuss about nothing. I was told there had been a fight between Gordon and Jimmy. I had been with the players all morning and hadn't seen anything myself. But nevertheless I decided to investigate. Gordon came to see me and together we came to sort this business out. Nothing at all took place as far as I can gather. Gordon and Jimmy are the best of pals and deny there was any argument or fight."

The *Daily Express* reported that Jimmy Adamson wouldn't see anyone afterwards.

Willie Irvine, who would make his debut not long after the incident, remembers it well.

"What happened is still crystal clear in my mind. For a start the two of them weren't getting on very well and in the game which ended that particular day's training, and in which some of us ground staff lads were playing, matters came to a head. Adamson body-checked Harris. They had words. Jimmy Adamson laughed. Adamson body-checked him again and brought him down. Nobody could say that Jimmy wasn't brave but Gordon was not pleased and you could see he wanted retribution.

"He kicked the ball hard against the gym wall and in the same movement kicked Adamson up into the air. As he came down Gordon caught him with a solid punch and it was at my feet that Jimmy landed with the blood running from his nose into his mouth. I stood wide-eyed at him lying at my feet with the blood making funny little gargling noises in his mouth. Gordon turned and walked straight out of the gym without a word. The newspapers said that Harry took Gordon to Jimmy's house so he could apologise but to my knowledge Gordon never did actually apologise. Gordon was a very accomplished player with one international cap and his eventual partnership with Brian O'Neil became the bedrock of the mid-1960s team that did so well. But his temper was well known and his altercations with referees were frequent. You didn't mess with Gordon 'Bomber' Harris. If you did, basically you got walloped for your trouble."

Jimmy McIlroy tells another story of Harris's powerful punch when Alex Elder appeared one day with a large black eye courtesy of the Bomber.

Training ground and gymnasium confrontations between players are not uncommon at any club. But at Turf Moor, famed for its family atmosphere, team spirit and 'togetherness', the 'Adamson punch' made huge headlines at the time and coming on top of the McIlroy transfer had Burnley people wondering what was going on at the club. Potts, always able to make a disciplinary decision when one was called for, dropped Harris for the next game. Into the side came the next diamond from the Gawthorpe/Potts production line – the incomparable Willie Morgan. Every dark cloud has its silver lining.

Replacing Jimmy McIlroy had been less easy. Jimmy Robson was given the first attempt, and then reserve Peter Simpson briefly took on the role. Eventually another reserve, Arthur Bellamy, was handed the unenviable task, and in a fine debut game scored one of the goals in a 5-2 win at Manchester City. A rebuilding process was under way. Adamson was now frequently absent through injury, a new generation of players was emerging and a new team taking shape. One of the new generation, Willie Irvine, was given a full Northern Ireland cap before he had even made his first-team debut. Centre forward Andy Lochhead was developing the skills and prowess that would make him one of Division One's most powerful players, feared by just about every centre half in the land. The championship side was well and truly a thing of the past. A transition period was under way. Potts and Lord asked supporters for patience.

Because of the backlog of games to be played as a result of the appalling winter, the season dragged on until May 14th. Nine games were played in April. Post-McIlroy, 19 games were played with nine wins and just five defeats. This was hardly disastrous and Burnley finished a very creditable third. A 7-2 mauling at Wolves was the only

*Mr and Mrs Harry Potts. Married on Wednesday March 31st 1948 at
St John's Church, Read.*

Burnley captain, and later manager, Alan Brown, congratulates the happy couple.

Three of Burnley's finest: Harry Potts, Ray Harrison and Peter Kippax.

Time for relaxation between coaching sessions at Filey.

Four generations in 1949. Mam Potts (back) looks on as Harry holds daughter Linda with his grandmother Mrs Purvis next to him.

Harry signs for Everton. Standing is their manager, the former Burnley boss Cliff Britton.

Linda is not sure that moving to Everton is a good idea.

Harry Potts' Everton new teammates.

EVERTON FOOTBALL CLUB CO. LTD

SECRETARY W. DICKINSON

Telephone
AINTREE 5263

Telegrams
FOOTBALL LIVERPOOL

GROUND & REGISTERED OFFICE:
GOODISON PARK
LIVERPOOL · 4

OUR REF

YOUR REF

DATE

25th April 1956

H. Potts, Esq.,

Dear Harry,

      In accordance with the Regulations of the Football League, I have to inform you that my Board do not intend to retain your registration for next season, 1956-57.

      You have been granted a free transfer.

      Yours sincerely,

      Everton Football Club
        Co. Ltd.,

The perfunctory letter which told Harry Potts he was no longer needed at Everton.

Mr Harry Potts,
     1 Earls Close,
          Liverpool 23.

Dear Harry,

          I am aware that you are severing your connection with
Everton and I would be glad to know if you are desirous of
continuing in football either as a player or Coach.

          I shall be glad to learn of your intentions in which
case please let me know as early as possible and if you decide to
telephone ring 76037 Leeds, reverse charge, and I am available
any morning from 10 to 12 noon.

                              Yours faithfully,

*Everton may not have needed him but Raich Carter, then manager of Leeds United,
was quick with an offer. He was even prepared to allow him to reverse the charges.*

*But after a brief spell as coach at Wolves, Harry was appointed manager of
Shrewsbury Town. He and chairman C Lewis Edwards welcome Johnny Sphuler
the man Harry recommended to replace him.*

Harry signs for Burnley as manager with Bob Lord making sure he misses nothing.

Retail, Wholesale & Contracting Butchers

Contract Work
a Speciality

F. Lord & Son, Ltd

Directors: R.W.Lord, H.Lord

Telephones:
Head Office: Padiham 620
(5 LINES) PRIVATE BRANCH EXCHANGE

Branch Shops
93, COAL CLOUGH LANE · 360, COG LANE
9, YORKSHIRE STREET · 14, PLUMBE STREET
5, CHANCERY STREET · 18, HOWE STREET
7, CURZON STREET · 2, GARDEN STREET
150, COLNE ROAD - 291, PADIHAM ROAD - 214, COLNE ROAD
BURNLEY
AND   79, BURNLEY ROAD, PADIHAM
17, RAILWAY STREET, BRIERFIELD

WAREHOUSE PREPARATION DEPT. AND MANUFACTORY
AT GREENBROOK WORKS
LOWER HOUSE LANE, BURNLEY

Greenbrook Works
Lower House Lane

P.O. BOX No 36

Burnley, Lancs.

SPECIALIST SUPPLIERS TO SCHOOL MEAL KITCHENS, HOSPITALS, INSTITUTIONS, RESTAURANTS, HOTELS, CAFES, WORKS CANTEENS & HOLIDAY CAMPS

March 1/58

Dear Margaret.

Many thanks for your letter received this morning, I knew you will feel proud, as I do, that Harry is back at last. Now we can all look forward to getting some where, some time, some how. Team spirit is the whole secret, and I am sure Harry can stand in the middle on that score.

Hilda joins me in wishing you well, and looking forward to seeing you. Have remember all of us to the children.

Sincerely Yours.
Auntie Hilda & Bob.

Bob and Hilda Lord's welcoming letter to Margaret.

A manager's job involves signing players. Here he greets Alex Elder, the one addition Harry made to Alan Brown's team. Ray Bennion looks on.

The manager's wife had her duties too. Here Margaret models a kitchen she designed herself for the Burnley Express women's pages.

The first goal from Brian Pilkington (out of picture) in the final match at Manchester City which Burnley won 2-1 to clinch the title.

The Burnley team which won the championship. Back row, right to left: Alex Elder, Tommy Cummings, Adam Blacklaw, Brian Miller, John Angus. Front row: Trevor Meredith, Jimmy McIlroy, Jimmy Adamson, Ray Pointer, Jimmy Robson, Brian Pilkington. inset: John Connelly who missed the deciding match at Maine Road through injury.

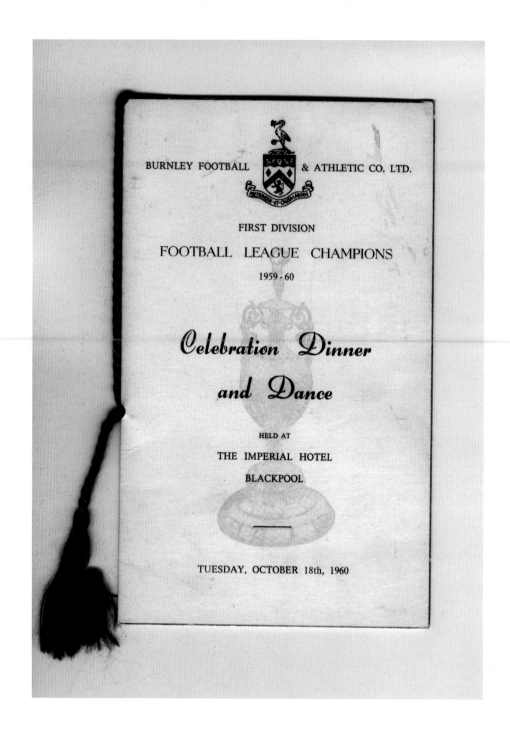

Burnley celebrated the title with a grand dinner and dance at Blackpool. Margaret recalls it was a: "a simply wonderful affair with absolutely no expense spared".

Leading Burnley out at Wembley for the 1962 FA Cup final against Tottenham. Bill Nicholson is at the head of the London team.

One of the best places to watch a match is as a mascot. Harry's son Ken proudly wearing his replica shirt.

real blemish and even that was seen as a fluke. Both the team and travelling supporters came away scratching their heads as they watched Burnley outplay Wolves yet lose in one of those strange games when the opposition seem to score every time they move upfield.

But in a later game against West Brom, Potts unearthed the newest gem in Brian O'Neil, who, in his first contribution, feinted, beat a man and delivered an inch-perfect pass. In the same game, Gordon Harris demonstrated to reporters that he was at that moment the best left winger in the country and another win was chalked up. Bill Fryer, that canny reporter, commented on the prodigious talent of the Burnley youngsters with an average age of only 22. But Burnley fans demonstrated their fickleness, chanting slogans against the team and showing their displeasure at the lack of goals. Fryer was disgusted. The memory of Jimmy Mac refused to go away.

In the final two games of the season the next discovery was unveiled as Willie Irvine made his debut with a goal in an away win against Arsenal and then scored a hat-trick in the final game of the season at home to Birmingham. 'Potts Pulls Out A Winner' was the headline above Norman Dixon's report in the *Daily Express*. Willie Irvine has a vague recollection of the team talk before the game and it was typical Harry Potts. It went along the lines of: "It's been an age since you last won an away game and the way things are going it will be another age. So please go out there and do something about it." Irvine, no mean header of a football, remembers, too, how Potts, to improve their jumping skills, would have players put chalk on their hands and then compete with each other to see how far they could leap up and leave a handprint high up on the wall.

Who could argue that, in spite of the McIlroy affair, things were not still rosy under the Potts umbrella at Turf Moor? The season had seen the first appearances of three stars in Willie Morgan, Willie Irvine and Brian O'Neil. Gordon Harris was dazzling on the left wing. Andy Lochhead, scorer of 20 goals, was terrifying at centre forward. The two full backs, John Angus and Alex Elder, were still young and awesome. In goal, Adam Blacklaw was outstanding. In the Central League, the reserves had won the championship in front of an average crowd of more than 6,000. If Potts had a problem, suggested the *Burnley Express*, it was not so much who to select for the first game of the next season but who to leave out, such was an embarrassment of riches among the forwards to choose from.

Twenty-five officials and players left for a two-week Mediterranean cruise on the liner *Iberia* and if supporters, a very hard lot to please in Burnley, were still disgruntled with things in general, Harry Potts and Bob Lord were not, as they steamed off into warmer climes.

CHAPTER SEVEN

BE PATIENT

I DIDN'T mind that he disappeared for those two weeks on the cruise. I just accepted it as part of the job and if there was a consolation it was that I knew he would at least be able to unwind and rest. The postcards would come thick and fast and I still have them all today. Bob Lord bought himself a cine camera but it ended up in Harry's hands most of the time and he put it to good use. I still have the films. There'd be Bob, Harry, Albert Maddox and most of the directors. It always struck me that no matter how hot the sun or how blue the sky Bob would usually be in a suit of some sort. How well he treated the players and staff.

During the season, Harry would often come home drained and exhausted, working all hours with just a very small staff to support him. Bob Lord thought the world of him and the local newspaper reported how he had praised him for his hard work and his exceptional success. The father-son relationship was still there.

With the run of the ball, both Harry and Bob thought that more success would come their way. They continued to see each other often, not just at the club but Harry would spend some evenings at Bob's home which was now in Read. I remember he always used to ring him to say he was coming because Bob had two large dogs and Harry was frightened of them. Once, as a young lad at Hetton, he'd been out on his bike when a dog had attacked him. Since then he'd never been a great dog lover. There was a story, too, that Bob kept an Alsatian at the factory. Bob was frightened of nobody but he was very wary of that dog.

Ray Bennion, Billy Dougal, who would retire in 1965, and George Bray were still at Turf Moor, plus Joe Brown, who had joined the coaching staff in 1961. But with more than 50 players of varying ages at the club there was no end to the work and the worries. And as the next season arrived it was a worrying time with a lot of injuries at the club and people in Burnley still smarting from the sale of Jimmy McIlroy. We were particularly friendly with Billy and Jeannie Dougal, who every Christmas gave us one of her hand-made pieces of pottery which I still proudly display.

But one thing he didn't have to worry about was buying players. It was something Burnley didn't do, though the day that they would was not too far away. What continued to hurt him most, though, were those awful days when he had to tell a young player he would not make the grade and the club would be releasing him, or when he had to tell an older player who had perhaps done well in the reserves and might have had just a few first-team games, that he was being sold. Such a player was a loyal young lad called Billy Marshall who captained the reserves to great success but just wasn't quite good enough to be a first-team regular. To the very end of his career as a manager he found it just as difficult as ever. He was just very sensitive I suppose to the feelings of others.

The middle 1960s, and we were still in the house at Hillsborough Avenue, Brierfield, with his mother and father not far away at Montrose Street. His father enjoyed a drink at the local club and a game of snooker but he and Harry did very little together on account of Harry being so busy. His mother used to comment how Harry had the house at the top of the hill and they had to have one down below.

Harry's father, though, was quite a handyman and one job he did was helping me to build the paths around the garden. And he loved to chop the firewood we used.

Hillsborough, a stonebuilt semi-detached house, wasn't a large place by any means. There was no grand detached house for the manager of Burnley Football Club. But it was surrounded by market gardens when we were there and the golf course was a little higher up. We had the feeling of being in the countryside with our own privacy. It wasn't actually in Burnley but Brierfield nearby.

But still the phone never stopped ringing; there was no escape from answering calls. The garden was my sanctuary but the phone had to be answered and in I dashed. I felt like an extension of the Burnley Football Club secretary's office and an unpaid receptionist. But in the garden I could forget the tensions that went with Harry's job.

Private though it may have been in that house and garden, I still rarely saw him truly relaxed or able to unwind. The job followed him constantly. He had no interests other than football. "I don't have the time," he would say with a resigned smile. But the children: yes, he always had time for them. And then there were his cups of tea. Harry saw a good cup of tea as the answer to any problem. Bonfire night, though, was a night when I could see him visibly unwind, relax and enjoy himself. I can see it now in the photographs I have. He loved to saw up the wood and help build the fire, then in his warm sweater and with a scarf wrapped round his neck he'd laugh with delight when the time came to throw the Guy onto the roaring flames.

For me, it was a busy, full life as the 1960s went by and the things I became involved in increased in number as the years rolled on. There was charity work and church events; I was a member of St Luke's' Young Wives Group and the Young Wives Keep Fit Group. There were the children's interests with Brownies and Cubs to take them to and our house was always full of their friends who came to play. There was the constant shopping; and I mean the everyday shopping you did for foodstuffs. Because there were no freezers in those days you bought fresh food on an almost daily basis from the local shops and every street seemed to have a shop on the corner. There was endless cooking, baking and preparation. You couldn't dash along to a supermarket to buy ready prepared vegetables and instant meals like you do today. Harry had a grand appetite and we always sat down together as a family, like you did in those days, for our meals, including a proper breakfast. He loved cereals, toast, bacon and eggs, or a bacon sandwich.

There was so much housework to do; I had one of those typical 1960s Hoovers – huge, noisy and very heavy, almost too heavy to push. Then there was an old-fashioned Eubank to just sweep up the crumbs, one of those things you pushed up and down the carpet by hand on a long handle. You didn't need to go to an expensive gym or a leisure club to keep fit, not that there were any; just doing housework kept you fit. I still have the Eubank I used to use at the caravan.

And then there was the 'donkey-stoning' which today is a lost art. Many years ago doorsteps, windowsills and even stone kitchen floors were 'donkey-stoned' by house-proud women after they had mopped the backs and fronts of their homes. A donkey-stone was simply a hard block of compressed stone you used to rub your front steps with, to provide a non-slippery surface and also just to make them look smart. They were first used in the mills to stop the flights of stairs from becoming greasy. They were made of soft stone crushed to a fine powder, mixed with water to a paste, poured into a mould and then dried out. They were sold at every corner shop, or rag-and-bone men gave them in exchange for old clothes. And I can still well remember the rag-and-bone men who used to come round, always with a horse and cart, calling out "rag 'n' bones... rag 'n' bones" and the slow plod of their horse pulling the cart laden with old rags and clothes they collected for sorting and re-use. In a place like Burnley, with the long rows of little terraced workers' houses, 'donkey-stoning' was a definite ritual that enabled neighbours to catch up on gossip as they did their steps.

There were no dishwashers then so there were endless piles of washing-up. There was all the washing and ironing and a lot of that had to be 'starched'. Harry liked a clean shirt every day and if there was a meeting to go to in an evening, or a match, he always changed. And all of them had to be starched. You starched the tablecloths, the handkerchiefs, napkins and pillowcases. Starching was a real job. You did the washing and then afterwards dipped it all into hot water and soaked it in a tub or the sink into which was mixed the starch and a dolly blue. The dolly blue, made from a mixture of china clay, caustic soda, sulphur, pitch and other substances and baked into a brick, brought out the whiteness, and the starch that you bought in a cardboard box stiffened everything. And when men wore a starched collar many years ago it was separate from the shirt and fastened to it with collar studs. It's always been a mystery to me today how people find the time to be bored.

The children were in their teens, growing rapidly now with a pony each. Harry would still play football on the lawn with Ken. I remember when Ken was only four he and his friend Howard went missing. We looked all over for them before they turned up tired out. Howard had been telling Ken that his father was a car salesmen so they had all these new cars. Ken had said his father worked at football. Howard didn't believe him so they walked to Turf Moor. They were just four years old but they managed the two miles there and back, crossing busy roads. When they got there they marched into the reception and Ken asked if he could see Mr Potts. Not surprisingly the receptionist refused to get Harry, who was furious that he hadn't been found, until I explained that anyone could walk in and ask to see him and that the receptionist couldn't be blamed for not recognising Ken.

For Harry, with the job, his mother and father, functions, meetings, scouting, there was little time left over. He tried to visit his mother and father every day and then we spent every Sunday with them. I tried to visit my own mother whenever I could. But living next door to my mother was her sister and husband so I knew that she was not alone.

I tried to make the home almost a refuge for Harry, although, in truth, I hardly saw him. I didn't mind that he just relaxed and put his feet up whenever he had the chance, though that was rare. Handyman jobs were not his speciality and this became a family joke. The garden was my responsibility, and I loved that.

An evening home together was a rarity; being together meant being at a dinner or a function. An evening together, such as we used to have at the theatre or the cinema, was now no more. With all of that and his mother continuing to interfere in our lives and being unpleasant to me, never in front of Harry by the way, I thought I would just carry on and develop my own private and social life. Linda, Ken and I attended the premiere of *Whistle Down The Wind* at the Odeon in Burnley because the film had been made up on the hills around Burnley and at Downham in the Ribble Valley. Harry had been given the tickets but he was away.

There was one occasion when Harry had bought a tape recorder for Linda, and Mam came up to the house. She was in another of her 'humours' over something, so I went to switch on the tape recorder, warning her I would let Harry hear everything she said. Even letting Mam Potts use our caravan caused friction. She and Dad Potts had the use of it on a few occasions. They took their relatives and friends two or three times as well but visitors always had to pay a nominal ten shillings for the use of the washrooms and facilities. The proprietor used to keep an eye out for any visitors and would go round and knock on the caravan door and ask for the money. Ever after it gave her the chance to say that I made her pay for using the caravan. That was after I'd driven them there and given her some spending money. Of course, Harry, wrapped up in his football, remained oblivious to all this.

I immersed myself in cancer relief work as well. One of our events was a sherry morning on a Sunday and the committee had to help on the various stalls. I went to it. And then at the next home game at Burnley comments were made that I should have been at home looking after my family. On one occasion near Christmas I sold raffle tickets at the club in the hospitality room. When it got to Bob Lord's attention I received the message via Harry from Bob that I should not do it again.

Harry was happiest when we were on holiday on the beach and in the sea. Only then could he relax and let his hair down. He could be a normal person for a short while, not the well-known manager of a top football club. We never told anyone who we were, although there was usually one person who would recognise him, but by and large we were left alone. He loved the swimming and the boating and always grabbed the nearest pedalo. And nobody tanned like Harry. A holiday abroad would usually be two weeks, although we did once manage the three weeks that he was entitled to.

Be Patient

Only once on holiday was there a situation that did slightly annoy me; 1965 it would be. We had no idea that in our hotel we'd find Ray Pointer and family plus Jimmy Adamson and his wife. Jimmy knew he was going to be appointed as coach to assist Harry and Harry had told me about it; that was one of the rare occasions he told me anything about what was going on. One day we were all gathered round the pool with a German doctor and his wife whom they had befriended. Jimmy was giving the impression that he was in charge at Burnley and the doctor's wife asked me if Jimmy was the boss. I thought I would nip it in the bud, remarking that it was bad luck that the boss had unexpectedly turned up to spoil his players' holiday! I explained to her that Jimmy was helping Harry and was going to be first-team coach.

Bob Lord and Jimmy were both Masons but Harry wasn't. It wasn't long before one or two people were telling me to watch out; Jimmy one day would want Harry's job. That was the holiday when Ken had his eleventh birthday and Harry did a typical Harry 'thing' when he went out to order a lovely Majorcan birthday cake that we had at a beach party.

IN 1963/64 Burnley's programme began at Ipswich and Harry Potts was in a positive mood. "Last season we finished third in the First Division and the reserves won the Central League Championship. I can see no good reason why we should not do as well this time. The injuries to Elder and Pointer are both big blows but these things happen in football and it is a challenge to us to get over them. We will give a good account of ourselves. My guess is that we will win more matches than we will lose."

He rejected any suggestion by discontented supporters that the club needed to break their policy and sign a big name to capture the local people's imagination. "You can take it from me that we will continue our youth policy. It has been successful so far, why should it fail us now?"

Meanwhile, Jimmy Adamson announced he would like to continue playing for another two or three seasons, but by now recurring back problems bedevilled him. He and other senior players believed another top six position was achievable but they were aware that big city clubs with big money incomes were beginning to dominate the game and that small-town Burnley would find it increasingly difficult to maintain their success.

"But," said Bob Lord, "we have the finest potential within the club that it has ever had. We have experience, there is no better defence in the country, and the number of forwards the manager has to choose from is an embarrassment. If some formation can click, there is no reason why we should not be successful."

Maybe Bob Lord's words "if some formation can click" summed up the season by the time it ended. Potts had already warned supporters that this would be a season of transition. The transition was not helped by seemingly endless injuries, both short and long-term, and resultant team shuffles. Finding that formation was difficult. The same line-up for more than two consecutive games was a rarity. Frustrating was the word used to describe it by Harry Potts. "A grand harvest of mediocrity" was the summing-up by the local press after it ended.

It was a sensational end, in fact, when, in the final week, Connelly, a stalwart of the great championship side, was sold to Manchester United and in the final game Tottenham were thumped 7-2. But attendances had continued their steady decline, averaging only just over 20,000 from the previous season's 25,000. Bob Lord might have been publicly as bombastic and confident as ever, but in private he was worried.

At least the final win gave Potts something to be cheerful about.

"Naturally I was delighted about Tuesday's win. But quite honestly it did not surprise me. I have said all along that our team is as good as any other if things are equal. We knew this season would be a period of transition and that's how it worked out. What we didn't know was that we would have such a tremendous number of injuries. More than anything else they have caused us to finish lower down the league than usual. We have had to be patient for a time and have taken a few brickbats here and there. That's part of the game and we have to take the rough with the smooth."

The rough might have included a 3-2 cup defeat at West Ham when Bob Lord described the third Hammers goal as being one that should have been disallowed for an obvious foul. "Robbed," he announced, "we got robbed of a semi-final trip." It was that kind of season. The only consolation was possibly the knocking out of West Ham player John Bond by Gordon Harris in an incident that set off Bomber Harris's definitely short fuse. Bond was out cold. But Harris got away with it. Just a few days later Burnley won the league fixture 3-1. In this game, Harris, for an encore, gave Bobby Moore a good kicking and again got away with it with just a booking. Such incidents could be seen as an indictment of lenient refereeing in a decade when players such as Andy Lochhead would say it was a game where no quarter was given and none asked.

Potts paid particular tribute to the younger players who had taken part in the season and the way all players had rallied against the injury jinx. Without that spirit, he added, Burnley would have been in relegation trouble as a direct result of all the injuries. John Connelly was added to the early season list when he had an appendix operation. Jimmy Adamson played only ten games in the season. By the end of the season Burnley did not have a single fit full back.

An occasional game stood out. They went away to Everton and beat them 4-3. It was Everton's first home defeat in 44 games. The star of the game was inside forward Arthur Bellamy, who had made his debut in March earlier in the year, and at Everton scored a superb hat-trick. Bellamy, now the groundsman at Gawthorpe, remembers Harry Potts with great affection.

He was a young lad who came down from the north-east to join the groundstaff as a 15-year-old from school. His first real concrete memory of Harry was being told as a 20-year-old that he'd be making his first-team debut. Before that he'd been working his way steadily upwards through each team. But he always knew that Harry had his eye on him. It was the morning of the match when Potts told him he was playing, and told him if he'd said anything before that he'd have been too nervous about it.

Bellamy recalls: "He wasn't a shouter or a bully; he loved the training and the playing. He'd take part in everything. Because he was a fitness fanatic he could outrun and outlast a lot of us in spite of being 20 years or more older. He just loved the outdoors and the training and that rubbed off on everyone. He'd be out in his tracksuit, full of life, cheerfulness and enthusiasm. It was just infectious. He'd come jogging out and announce that it was just a 'grand day for a football match'. He'd look at Pendle Hill if it had a bit of snow on and say 'just like Switzerland this'. 'Better than being down the pit', was another one. He loved the involvement and could always take a joke. Brian O'Neil used to call him Skidsby as he began to lose his hair because in a five-a-side game he'd head the ball and it would skid off his head. His input was his participation, not his standing there watching or just giving instructions.

"He was such a decent man that players wanted to play for him, but he was a real Jekyll and Hyde. In the week he was the nicest man you could wish to meet. On a Saturday he just changed into a different person. He could get so worked up; so angry, so furious with rage he could sometimes go purple. On a Saturday he'd get so agitated. All trace of niceness vanished and from the touchline he could shout at players as loud as anyone and I can always remember the way he'd shout at Les Latcham. There was a time when Les's name was always first on the teamsheet but all the way through a game it would be Latch this and Latch that, Latch do this, Latch do that. He never let up."

Bellamy also remembers that Harry Potts did his best to protect and defend his players. In an early game at Tottenham, Dave Mackay kicked Bellamy dreadfully. At half-time in the tunnel Harry absolutely flew at Mackay, demanding to know why he was doing that to a young lad just starting in the game. Mackay was a hard man but Harry just went for him. Bellamy knew he'd done it and it made him feel so good that his manager would stick up for him.

"They say nice men can't be winners but Harry showed that you could be. That's not to say he couldn't tear a strip off a player when the time was right. On one occasion, Dougie Collins was on the receiving end of a half-time rage from Harry when he just about went purple because he thought Dougie wasn't bothering listening to him. Then there was another game at Manchester City in the late '60s and Burnley were absolutely slaughtered 7-0. At the end of the game in the dressing room when Harry was fuming, Steve Kindon went up to him to ask could he go straight home to Warrington. Steve found out that's not the best time to ask a manager something like that when Harry went absolutely mad with him.

"Harry belonged to a certain era and his era as a player was a lot simpler than mine. In his day a manager had his best eleven players and put them out week after week and so it was in his early time as a manager. The championship side was basically his best eleven players and unless they couldn't walk, they played. Jimmy Mac played half the season unfit.

"That changed as the '60s went on and when Jimmy Adamson became coach things changed a bit. Harry was never a great tactician but Jimmy introduced new routines, moves and free kicks. Harry's championship side had one way of playing and that was to go forward and attack and the number of goals they scored shows that. They had great players, two of them at their peak, who didn't really need telling how to play. But as the '60s went on, the next game was planned more carefully.

"The way Burnley played could depend on who they were playing and team selections began to be made on the basis of who would be the best man for a particular role. Jimmy Adamson was perhaps one of the first of the new tacticians, the first of the modern-day coaches and talkers. Harry was a great man and a great manager, players wanted to play for him, but he was not a great coach in my opinion. He was a smoother of troubles and he gave players confidence. While Jimmy Adamson taught me to do things I didn't know I could do like playing sweeper,

Harry Potts followed it up by giving me the confidence to do it.

"Gradually Jimmy became more and more responsible for the training. It seemed like they worked well together, complementing each other, but things became more technical and planned under Jimmy. The man from the next era was slowly replacing the man of the old era.

"There was definitely a Harry Potts way. He taught players right and wrong and to look after themselves. I respected him so much. He was thoughtful and sensitive. When I eventually moved to Chesterfield Harry was not even at Burnley any more. He was at Blackpool when he learned I was leaving and he wrote to wish me well. He was the only person who did that – and that was Harry. It was a typical Harry gesture."

Bellamy was a pall-bearer at Harry Potts' funeral and felt that it was an honour and a privilege because he taught him so much. "If it was a great life being a footballer, it was Harry who had made it so."

Four goals went past Fulham in the next game. Old enemy Blackburn were beaten 3-0. There was an amazing 6-1 win at home to Manchester United at Christmas, in front of 35,766 spectators, when Andy Lochhead scored four times. Willie Morgan was unplayable, United were run dizzy and towards the end Paddy Crerand was sent off for thumping Ian Towers. Twenty-four hours later, they lost 5-1 at Old Trafford in the return game when George Best exploded on to the scene, and in his second appearance ran John Angus ragged.

The game everyone was waiting for took place on November 6th. It was Burnley versus Jimmy McIlroy at Stoke. It was an astonishing game that had all pundits reaching for superlatives. It had everything from drama to tension, to a stunning climax. When Stoke City went off the field at half-time leading 3-0, McIlroy gave a wry smile to the directors' box. With only ten minutes remaining, Stoke led 4-2 but with just two minutes to go Gordon Harris got Burnley's third with a rocket free kick from 20 yards. It was Harris who scored the equaliser in the 88th minute. McIlroy was outstanding in the first half but almost invisible in the second. "This was no Supermac by any means" reported Burnley's local reporter Keith McNee. When Stoke came to Burnley for the return game, McIlroy was hardly in the game, said the local report.

It was in November, too, that Harry Potts was widely quoted when he announced that it was time that soccer was sorted out. Burnley had lost 3-2 at Tottenham but two of the goals were controversial, resulting from fouls on Burnley players that went unpunished.

"Our players obey the rules which forbids protests to the referee and that is why they did not say anything to him, although they no doubt felt like doing so. This perhaps puts us at a disadvantage."

If there was always one thing guaranteed to incense Harry Potts it was unfair decisions but this was one occasion when he kept away from the referee – "What good would it have done?" he said. But he did add, "It makes you wonder just what is going on in the game. There was no rough stuff at Tottenham or crowd incidents, but if it's not one thing, it's another."

On the same day all 22 players had been called together at Elland Road, the home of the emerging Leeds United, and told to cut out the rough stuff. "Are all managers doing all they can to stop rough play?" asked Potts with Revie certainly in mind. Potts, whose philosophy was based on fairness and entertainment, would come to detest Revie and the gamesmanship that he stood for.

If Potts controlled his anger at Tottenham, he had less success at Birmingham City at the beginning of '64. The fixture list and results for that season record a stark 0-0 draw but Potts was infuriated by the disallowing of four Burnley goals. There was a classic Harry Potts verbal clash after the game as they walked off the pitch. It was Birmingham captain Trevor Smith who described the after-match arguments between Potts and referee Aldous. Not for the first time Potts was reported to the FA and the Football League.

The last game of the season, in which Burnley stunned Tottenham 7-2, showed there was reason to be cheerful. The young breed, O'Neil, Morgan and Irvine were outstanding as were Lochhead and Harris who had been team members for a little longer. A rampant Burnley producing brilliant attacking football were fantastic with another Gawthorpe production line youngster, 18-year-old Sammy Todd, making his debut and being seen as Burnley's man of the match. Yet again, Potts demonstrated his knack of pulling a rabbit out of a hat and being unafraid to use these young players, when the occasion needed it.

But during the season 1963/64, speculation had already started about Jimmy Adamson's future and the role he would play at Turf Moor. There were rumours in one newspaper that someone would move over and make room for Adamson. Bob Lord immediately denied such stories. Now he was saying that, regarding the matter of what would happen, he already had something in mind, but it just hadn't come about yet. One day, he added, Potts and Adamson might well form a team at the head of the dressing room.

"I don't stab anyone in the back," he said. "I am not impressed by the rumours. He goes with the wallpaper at Turf Moor."

If there was one incident that Harry Potts would certainly not have got away with today, it was after the away game at Nottingham Forest when the coach was stoned and windows were smashed. Potts jumped off the coach, grabbed two of the culprits and held them in the coach until the police arrived. In today's upside down world of political correctness and individual rights, it would be Potts who would be charged with assault and kidnap. Willie Irvine was still combing glass out of his hair several days later.

One player above all others had certainly come to the fore during the season and that was Willie Morgan. He had a Beatle haircut but hated being called Ringo. Once upon a time, supporters would say they were not attending if Jimmy Mac wasn't playing; now they said the same of Morgan. He was called a tramp at away grounds because he wore long baggy shorts as opposed to the short ones that were the vogue. He found them far more comfortable. "The Johnny Staccato of dribbling" was one description of him. His most disappointing moment was when Harry Potts gave him a stand ticket at West Ham instead of playing him. "I had a transfer request written out after that – but I never posted it." It hurt him when one director said he fiddled about too much. Then he cheered up when he learned the same director had said the same thing about Jimmy McIlroy. Morgan was a self-confessed individualist but Potts gave him room to breathe and a licence to be himself. With John Connelly sold to Manchester United at the end of the season, Morgan's place in the side was secure. There was the usual bout of supporter indignation at the Connelly sale but the proceeds compensated for the decline in gates.

It could be said that Connelly was the first of the players to be sold when still at the height of their powers. Until then players sold had either been on the fringe of the first team or past their best. A new precedent was set. "Who will be next?" asked supporters. It also confirmed that the once great side of the early '60s, with some players gone, other players like Adamson injury prone, and other players off form, had well and truly retreated into the shadows. Potts had hoped that with just one or two gradual changes it could have gone on and had continued success. It was not to be. The drawing board beckoned. The "formation that would click" was still elusive. For the first time in many years, there was neither a summer tour nor a luxury cruise.

"Give over daydreaming, Burnley," a loud voice bellowed down from the Turf Moor terraces during the opening game of the season in 1964/65. It would be the ninth game of the season before they did stop and win their first game. Maybe it was during this time, and shortly afterwards, following a 5-1 clattering at Sheffield Wednesday, that Bob Lord began to feel that Jimmy Adamson, the ex-England assistant, should have more of a say in team matters and that new ideas were needed. Speculation ended when it was announced that he would become player-coach and it came just a week after Sunderland were refused permission to approach him about their vacant manager's job. Even Keith McNee, the *Burnley Express* man, who knew just about everything there was to know, described the new appointment as "coming out of the blue".

Potts, too, was the subject of an alleged approach from Sunderland and Bob Lord expressed his outrage and fury, threatening to report the north-eastern club to the Football League for what he considered a flagrant breach of regulations. Little that was concrete emerged although Potts wrote about the affair in his programme notes.

"Over the past week, gossip and rumour has had my name linked with the vacant Sunderland Football Club managership. How or why this came about I do not know, but the true facts, so far as I am concerned, are as I now take the opportunity to explain. On Tuesday of last week, to my surprise, I was informed by our two local Press representatives, Keith McNee (*Burnley Express*) and Granville Shackleton (*Lancashire Evening Telegraph*), that they had received information from the Sunderland area regarding myself and football managership. That was the first intimation reaching me on the matter. Still later in the day, Steve Richards of the *Daily Herald* arrived at my home concerning the same report and he also told me that he had had it from a Sunderland official. To each of these enquiries I replied that I knew nothing about it and that I had certainly not applied for the job, nor had I been approached by anyone about it. I am very happy in my present position... and regard it as unhealthy and unfortunate for the game of football that false rumours of this kind are so often put out through soccer's grapevines."

Bob Lord was angry that Sunderland did nothing to quell the rumours and told them that next time they came to Turf Moor they should bring just their eleven players and their trainer. Lord did all the talking while Potts remained silent other than in his programme notes. Sunderland responded by saying they were astonished that Lord had not disclosed their approach for Adamson. It gave Lord another opportunity to state his intentions regarding Adamson. "We haven't finished with him yet and if I have anything to do with it we won't have finished with him for a very long time." In that statement lay Lord's intention that one day Adamson would replace Potts as manager.

But, at the time of the Adamson coaching appointment,

Potts made all the right noises. "It's a great pleasure for me to welcome Jimmy as senior coach. We have worked together well as manager and captain for so long. Jimmy has been a credit to himself, the club and the game and with his qualifications and experience, he should be a great asset to the club."

In the third game of the season opinions were expressed that this was the worst Burnley side of the last ten years. They were criticised by Derek Hodgson in the *Daily Express* for being "destructive", desperately in need of a schemer. Several games were described as "battlefields". The local papers cried out for a forward who could score. The Blackburn game was "the battle of Turf Moor". The club abandoned plans to build a giant 17,000-seater stand; the abolition of the maximum wage had seen to that. There was a reported £60,000 bid by Liverpool for an unsettled Alex Elder. The Chelsea game was described as a "disgraceful shambles".

"Football has deteriorated with the bonus system," said Potts. "There's too much win-at-all-costs play and too little football."

But, bit-by-bit, Burnley and Potts clawed their way back into the season. A third of the way through the campaign, relegation had been a stark possibility and a topic of many supporters' conversations. But, after just two wins from the first fifteen games, results took a turn for the better. By the end of the season there were just two defeats in the last twelve games and seven of those games were won so that Burnley ended in twelfth position.

In mid-season, one game perhaps summed up the growing divide which now existed between the city clubs and small-town Burnley. A scoreline of Burnley 1 Liverpool 5 was symbolic of the power of one and the weakness of the other. Thick fog and gloom before and during the game would have done a kindness had it been bad enough to warrant postponing the game. Humiliation was an understatement. "Heart-breaking, shattering, disastrous, sickening and relegation" were the words used as Burnley reached their lowest post-war ebb. "What happens now" was the recurring question? Could Adamson put his playing boots back on? Would the same players be endlessly permutated, or would the club buy?

Following this result, the team was subjected to several changes and there was a run of four consecutive wins. Something was indeed beginning to click. Relegation form was replaced by buoyancy and convincing victories in twelve games in the second half of the season. Of the next 21 games, only six were lost. Players hit form. There were demands that Gordon Harris be selected for England. The twin strike force of Willie Irvine and Andy Lochhead was becoming awesome. They ended the season with 43 league goals between them.

Potts, meanwhile, ignored the FA's new 'code of conduct' advising managers to sit in the stands. "I wasn't trying to be awkward. I have always sat in the trainer's box because I can concentrate better on the game from there."

It was during this season that another new name emerged, that of Ralph Coates. Another gem had been unearthed. Coates was one of those north-east lads who made their way to Burnley via the superb scouting system. The Gawthorpe production line and coach Joe Brown then made this barrel-chested, short, stocky, unlikely looking footballer into an absolute pedigree player. Before long he would have the Burnley staff purring in admiration. He would end up joining Tottenham for a record transfer fee and playing for England. Nobody will forget the local derby against Blackburn when he was just 18, and he stopped the game dead by pausing to sit on the ball. He came from Hetton-le-Hole just like Potts and tells the story that when he was just 16, "me mum didn't want me to leave home and if Harry Potts hadn't been the manager and she didn't know his parents, she wouldn't have let me come." He played just three games in 1964/65 but a new star had been found.

"Looked at from any angle," reported the *Burnley Express*, "this had been an ordinary, average season for Burnley FC."

Generally speaking, results hit a middle course, being neither very good nor very poor. In the final statistics this stands out like a beacon. What could be more indicative of an average season than Burnley winning 42 points from 42 games, scoring 70 goals and letting in 70? They won 16 games and lost 16 games, finishing halfway up the table. Of the great team of earlier years, McIlroy and Connelly had already been sold, Adamson had hung up his boots, Pointer was plagued by injuries, Cummings was gone, and now Robson was sold to Blackpool for £10,000.

If there had been one blot in the second half of the season it was the 5-1 defeat at Leeds United. The result flattered Leeds but it was a game when referee Jack Taylor called all 22 players together at one stage to tell them to cut out the rough stuff. It would be the first of several games between the two sides to be rated as X-certificate.

But yet again optimism reigned. Bill Fryer purred after watching Burnley beat Sheffield Wednesday 4-1, saying that if selling a player a season could compensate for gates as low as 12,362 then they were on course to win a championship again with the remarkable forwards that were coming through. There were indeed good young players on the production line and in the final game of the season again there was another demolition of a London glamour team. Chelsea were hammered 6-2 when in the running for the title, although their cause was not helped by the infamous escapade when manager Tommy Docherty sent home eight players because they defied his midnight curfew and sneaked out of their bedrooms to carouse the night away in Blackpool where they were staying overnight. Docherty sat up half the night to wait for their return and then handed them all a Saturday morning train ticket back to London.

There were 15,213 spectators to see Andy Lochhead score five of those goals. Again, it was a game of physical challenges and flare-ups in a season when Burnley were no shrinking violets and could dish out the rough stuff as and when required, as opposed to the near gentlemanly play of the great championship side. A game between Burnley and Liverpool just a week earlier had been just as bad.

But after the Chelsea game and the ending of the season with two victories there was a definite feel-good factor. Staff and players dispersed full of optimism.

CHAPTER EIGHT

SO CLOSE AGAIN

ALL THESE years later I think it was a miracle that Harry and Bob Lord kept the club so close to the top in a town of just 80,000 people. I know a lot of support came from outlying districts, some of it from Rochdale and Halifax, but the fact remains that this tiny town, against all the odds, still managed to produce a team that could take on the likes of Liverpool, Manchester United, Tottenham, Arsenal and all the other teams with their bigger crowds and bank accounts. They could constantly buy; Harry had to constantly sell.

I could sense in his moods that he was more optimistic than ever about the coming season. There was a spring in his step. He just knew he had good players and they were young players, one by one as good as any belonging to any other club, and he was still managing to get very good young lads from all over the country to join from school. He just loved to work with them in training at Gawthorpe and many times he'd say to me "You'll have to come down and see Gawthorpe, it's so beautiful." But somehow I never managed to get to see it until just recently when a good friend took me down to meet up again with Arthur Bellamy who showed me round all the places Harry had been for so many years. Arthur and his wife Maureen had visited Harry in his final months at Dove Court. Harry said Gawthorpe was such a green and tranquil place and it still is. No wonder Harry could never wait to get there. I could so easily picture him as I wandered round, taking the path leading over the bridge that goes to the training areas. The old, huge, ancient stone barn that was once the changing rooms still stands but is no longer in use.

So Close Again

The biggest change was the introduction of Jimmy Adamson to the management staff. Until now it had been a partnership between Harry and Bob. Now it was Harry, Bob and Jimmy and I remembered speeches that Bob had made at dinners and functions where he said Jimmy's future was at Burnley. Just sometimes I felt uneasy about it, I had this sense that one day it would be the end for Harry; that he might just be edged out even though he got a new, long contract in 1965. Maybe it was my imagination, or just some sixth sense, but it was almost as if Bob's relationship with Jimmy was becoming similar to the one he had had with Harry all those years ago.

We were great friends with the Reverend Alan Reid who became the vicar at Brierfield in 1963. Alan, a Burnley lad, had watched and supported Burnley since he was a boy and could remember Harry playing for Burnley when he came back from India. Alan remembers him coming back as brown as a native, as he put it. Harry, Alan says, had a reputation for always trying to get in the area and then fall over to get the penalty. Anyway, Alan was delighted to see Harry and me in the congregation at his Brierfield induction in 1963 and made a beeline for us with the result that he and Harry struck up a great friendship which lasted until Harry's death. Alan thought up until then that football managers didn't go to church and that you couldn't manage by being nice, but Harry disproved that.

Alan still laughs when he remembers saying that Harry would never make a footballer, because when he saw him play his first three or four games after the war he was too slow. But that didn't stop Harry many years later giving Alan tickets for the directors' box when he was able to watch a game. Alan and Harry talked a lot, often on car journeys when Harry wanted some company while he was driving somewhere to do some scouting.

He forecast to Alan that the abolition of the maximum wage would open the floodgates and that football would end up with just a few clubs being at the top with all the best players. How right he was. Bob Lord did his best for so many years to pay his players well enough to compete with the top clubs. But it was just a vicious circle. He paid the players well, but to afford to pay them handsomely, he had to sell them as well.

There were quite a few funny stories Harry told Alan which Alan still remembers. There was the one that many years ago before the war, long before Harry ever got to Turf Moor, there was a little bit of intrigue when the Burnley chairman, Tom Clegg, handed the Burnley captain a brown envelope to give to the captain of the team they were playing in London because if they didn't get at least a draw they might not stay in Division Two. Now whether it's true I don't know, but apparently years later the captain of whatever team it was, it might have been Tottenham or Charlton, said he never got the envelope. What happened was that when the Burnley players got on the train on the Friday they opened the envelope and found there was enough for £10 each. So they all looked at each other and had a bit of a think, kept the money themselves and still got the draw they needed.

Another lovely story Alan tells is the one about the cup final ticket in the butcher's shop window in 1947. Everybody wanted tickets, of course, and they soon sold out. But there was a butcher's shop at the top of Towneley Street and the owner put a ticket in the window with a note to say the highest bidder could have it. It was all very neatly written. The ticket was there for a few days but that didn't go down too well with all the people who walked by. They weren't pleased at all that this chap should try and profit from it. Now, this was a lock-up shop, which meant nobody lived on the premises, so one morning the owner came back to find a big hole in the window, the ticket was gone and whoever had taken it had left the exact money. "Serves him right, the stingy beggar" was everyone's reaction when they went by the window that day. "Serves him right."

Then Harry would tell Alan the story of how Burnley players Harold Mather and Reg Atwell bought a greyhound and kept it under the stand at the cricket field end of the ground. That's where this poor dog lived because they couldn't keep it in their digs. When it was wet, the players used to train under this stand so all the players became quite fond of it and lots of them backed it when it raced but it never won. Anyway, when it died, Harold Mather looked at it and said, "Well that's t'first time ah've seen that bugger ever finish owt."

Harry used to tell another story to Alan about Bill Shankly when he was at Preston. He was coming to the end of his career and one summer he went to negotiate his next year's wages and they offered him £15 for playing during the season and £10 for the summer. Then Bill found out they had offered the much younger Tom Finney £20 for playing and £15 in the summer. So Bill went back to the chairman and asked for an explanation. "Well he's a better player than you, Mr Shankly," said the chairman. "Not in the summer he isn't," replied Shankly.

Alan has been part of our lives for so many years and even when Harry became manager at Blackpool he was there again because he had taken a parish in nearby Lytham. Following that, he moved to the village where we are now, Read, so that even today when he lives in Whalley just a few miles from me he is still such a good friend. Alan jokes that wherever we go, he is sure to follow.

Tommy Cummings, already at the club when Harry arrived as manager, always tells a lovely story about Harry. Every year in the summer there was a cricket match between the club and the local cricket club at Read. Harry was a keen cricketer; in fact he was a good one as well and his mother always used to say she wanted him to be a cricketer rather than a footballer because he looked so smart and handsome in his whites. It was one thing that Mam Potts and I agreed on, and watching Harry play cricket was something I always enjoyed. Anyway, one year there was a game and it was so very hot and as we all know, football players do like a drink… or two. But Harry, of course, was not a drinking man at all. Well, the players knew they would be parched and didn't want Harry to see them in the clubhouse drinking, so they gathered several crates of beer round the back of the clubhouse out of sight and the minute Harry went out to bat they all dashed round to consume a few bottles each. Harry was never any the wiser.

"IT LOOKS as if Burnley could do very well this season," said Chelsea manager Tommy Docherty after the first game of the season. Docherty held the Burnley youth system in high regard and before long his teenage son Michael would join the club. Ron 'Chopper' Harris had his first experience of opposing the elusive Ralph Coates during the game. He would later say Coates was the player he least liked to play against.

"The most mature and settled football since the McIlroy era," said Derek Hodgson in the *Express* after Burnley outplayed Blackpool and won 3-1 in the second game.

Don Hardisty in the *Daily Mail* wrote that after the line-up that had been torn apart and rebuilt since the last championship, this was now the one that could break the monopoly of the First Division's big five. The dapper, elusive, creative Arthur Bellamy was now seen as the spark.

Fleet Street and provincial press were all agreed: the good times were back. It was just as well; supporters were tired of transitional seasons. The heights of 1960, '61 and '62 were badly missed; there was no longer a wish for a top six place, it was a demand. Surely, thought Harry Potts, the club were due a break from the ceaseless injuries of the last two seasons, of which he thought, supporters seemed to take little account.

In September of 1965 Potts was given a new five-year contract at a salary of £5,500 a year. It was indeed a very good salary. A young teacher just starting out in the profession earned about £600 a year. Lord clearly still had full confidence in Potts and had no immediate plans to hand over the manager's post to Adamson but it is very reasonable to surmise that it was in his mind to make the change in five years' time.

Nobody had made a bigger contribution to the early games than Brian O'Neil. If England had a better right half than this stocky powerhouse then he had not seen him, wrote Keith McNee in the *Burnley Express*. Like two players in one, he said, a destroyer of other teams' attacks and a perpetual motion force of his own. The more other teams tried to kick him, the better he played. In the mud he was incomparable. Margaret Potts remembers how fond Harry was of Brian and how Harry would show her the bruises O'Neil had inflicted on him in the five-a-sides. Harry would come home, have his bath, come downstairs and then roll up his dressing gown to reveal his legs covered in bruises. "Here's a bit more of Brian O'Neil to show you," he would tell her, grinning.

In September, the minnows beat the giants when Burnley defeated Manchester United 3-0 at Turf Moor in front of 30,137 people. It was absolutely clear that here was a team that could take on the champions, Crerand, Best, Law, Charlton, Connelly, Stiles and all, and win convincingly. United had spent £400,000 on this team and been beaten by players who were home-grown and home-made.

But at Newcastle events showed that controversy and Burnley were never far away. Burnley lost 3-2 but this was in a game described by both Potts and Lord as a disgrace. It was a game in which every Burnley player received an injury of one sort or another and afterwards more than one player had to be helped to the coach. Willie Irvine had his nose broken and an eye blackened. The referee called all the players together on the pitch to lecture them about their conduct. And Gordon Harris was so bruised, cut and marked that Potts had a photographer take pictures of the dreadful state he was in so that they could be shown publicly.

"Harris has a diabolical injury," fumed Potts, "which is dreadful to look at. He is black and blue with stud marks from his legs to his shoulder and his thigh is an absolutely terrible mess with the bruises."

Chairman Lord announced that next time they went to Newcastle they would take elephants, not players, and that Newcastle should be playing in a menagerie.

"I am no softy," said Potts, who had been up and down out of the trainer's box in fury several times, "but these are the things we all want to stamp out. The pictures prove our complaint better than words. The injuries are the worst I have seen in 20 years. I don't mind hard tackling, we all expect it, but when it comes to vicious kicking it is time to draw the line."

There is no doubt that the game was played in a period when a player could take the field and have no confidence that he would not come off with a broken leg. There was some play that was quite brutal. Attempts to take a player out of a game were commonplace and skilled players were targeted. The press were certainly aware of it and voiced their concern. They pointed too to the fact that many managers were aware of it but would not complain officially, only privately. Players who played in that era remember it well but will simply say that it was just the way the game was played.

Lord used the Newcastle game as a chance to vent his spleen at the new four up and four down proposals. It would create divisions where poor teams tried to clog their way into survival. Manager Joe Harvey at Newcastle had got away with it, he grumbled; if the manager had been Harry Potts he would have been reprimanded.

It was immediately prior to the next game at Leeds that Potts showed that he could be ruthless and punitive when necessary. He was not always 'Mr Nice Guy'. All that was revealed in the papers was that Andy Lochhead had been dropped for a "breach of training." It was no small matter to drop one half of the most lethal strike partnership in Division One before a game at Elland Road against a team that was taking roughness and gamesmanship to new heights, but Potts did it.

The "breach of training" was, in fact, high spirits in the hotel at Blackpool where the players had been taken for some relaxation as well as preparation work on the beach. The second night they were there, the players, not unnaturally, headed out for a drink or two, and several came back in the early hours somewhat the worse for wear. Andy Lochhead tells the story that after various schoolboy pranks up and down the corridors, he ended up locked out of his room wearing not a stitch.

Some hotel guests were understandably upset and made complaints. The following morning the players were assembled and Potts asked who the culprit was. Lochhead commendably stepped forward, and was immediately fined £100 and dropped for the Leeds game. Potts, a man of principle, was certainly no softie. In effect, he sacrificed a point, for Burnley drew a game in which Lochhead might have made a difference. It was a game that was so good that even the referee applauded the two teams.

By the end of September, Potts had taken Burnley to the top place in Division One. Some of their football was outstanding. Their play was fast, frenetic, constantly moving. They mixed football with power and had players who as well as being able to play could also mix it with any team who chose to do so. 'Set To Go Places' was Frank Clough's prediction in *The Sun*.

In early November they regained the top position, Irvine and Lochhead having claimed 23 out of the 36 goals scored. Then came the climax of the season, a 4-0 win at Sunderland that had every reporter reaching for the superlatives. The performance they put on ranks up there with any of the great Burnley displays on a day when they were just untouchable. It was a game that Ralph Coates can still remember and talk about. After the game he was taken to meet the Sunderland chairman who demanded to know, "Why didn't we sign this player?"

The experts predicted that the championship would come back to Turf Moor as brilliant man-to-man passing and superb football had Sunderland bewitched, bothered and bewildered. The greatest compliment was simply the observation that this was a better side than the McIlroy–Adamson team. The team at Sunderland cost just £110 in signing-on fees and was described as a team without weakness. There was continual press coverage as Burnley hit the limelight.

"What's the secret?" Harry Potts was asked.

"There isn't one," he answered. "We have players of outstanding ability, they have come through together, they know what is wanted of them and they give it. They are young but already experienced. Alex Elder is only 23; others have played for their countries. Next season should see them mature to their full effectiveness. If I was asked what quality I like best about them I would answer – their wonderful will to win."

Alex Elder pointed to changes in style brought about by changes in the game generally. There was a new emphasis on not conceding goals.

The wins piled up but it was not to last. A run of six games without a win beginning in January was their downfall and the big teams pulled ahead. Heads drooped, questions were asked and by the time the revival began, eight wins from the final eleven games, it was too late and there was too much ground to catch up even though there was a notable win against eventual champions Liverpool. Potts, though, would not throw in the towel.

"I know it looks as if Liverpool are running away with the League, but it is not over yet. Just think back to 1962. We were in an even stronger position then, than Liverpool are today and we seemed certainties for the title. But we picked up only one point in a terrible spell at the back end of the season. Perhaps this time it will work our way." But it didn't.

Three things cost them dear: that run of six poor games; a defeat at Liverpool when Burnley had a weakened side; and then the disgraceful game at Turf Moor against Leeds United at the end of the season, a 1-0 defeat in which every one of Potts' opinions about Revie was confirmed. Several games during the season had been described as a "war" but the Leeds game sank to new depths.

At this time Leeds had a simple strategy – to win at any cost. They took bullying, intimidation, gamesmanship and physical play to new depths of dreadfulness. Pitch that against a team like Burnley who had the likes of Angus, O'Neil, Harris, Blacklaw and Lochhead, who could be as physical as the next team when necessary, and it was a recipe for disaster. Add to the mix the need for both sides to take both points and it was yet another game where all the players were brought to the centre of the field for a dressing down.

Field Marshal Viscount Montgomery of El Alamein, the club's special guest for the day, watched it. He must have

148

thought he was back in the middle of a World War Two battle. The word "brutal" was inadequate. Leeds won with the most bizarre of own goals when an Elder back pass cum clearance – nobody will ever be sure what it was – sailed over Blacklaw's head from somewhere near the corner flag. It sort of summed up Burnley's season, a mixture of the very good and occasionally brilliant, to the bad and the downright ugly as in the case of this cruel, terrible, 90-minute brawl.

In the FA Cup, Bob Lord once again went on the rampage when he threatened to burn the BBC cameras unless they were removed from the ground and announced he would sue the BBC for loss of gate revenue when the press announced their tie with Bournemouth would be highlighted on TV later in the evening.

The cup game came in the spell when nothing was going right for Burnley. Potts had already said when things were going well for the club that success still depended on that elusive factor called run-of-the-ball. With it you could win championships. Without it you lost games like the 4-3 cup defeat at White Hart Lane where they had taken an early 2-0 lead. Team and staff were heartbroken when Spurs scored the winner two minutes from the end.

So honours eluded Burnley, although there were consolations. They finished third, just six points behind Liverpool, and missed second place from Leeds only on goal difference. Their position earned them a place in the next season's Inter-Cities Fairs Cup, no mean feat for small-town Burnley. The fact that Burnley was not a city almost cost them their place. And if there was another consolation it was the scoring record of Willie Irvine, who set a new post-war record with 29 league goals. In total, he scored 37 and he, along with the likes of Coates, Morgan, O'Neil, Lochhead and Harris formed the basis of all the optimism for the next season.

Add to this the defensive backbone of Blacklaw, Angus, Elder and Miller, still there from the great 1960 championship side, and this was some team. Blacklaw won his third Scottish cap and Harris had his first England call-up. Formations were fluid: mostly 4-2-4, sometimes 4-3-3. Adamson's coaching had made an impact. In Ralph Coates they had made the discovery of the season.

The overall feeling was that the youth policy could indeed match big-city spending, but if there was a fault, an Achilles heel perhaps, maybe it boiled down to one inescapable fact: they were still a small-town team, and maybe it was the residual small-town mentality that would always hold them back. A Liverpool team, Tottenham or a Manchester United could always swagger, a Burnley couldn't. Maybe they did not feel they could compete with these teams on an equal footing, and that resulted in an inferiority complex no matter how hard they denied it or fought it. Maybe some Burnley players felt just a small tinge of envy. Whatever the reasons, the next season full of promise, and off to the expected great start, would end sadly. The lean years were not far away.

There were three straight wins to start 1966/67, with only one defeat in the first twelve games. The spotlight remained on Burnley, as the football writers, in raptures over their performances, descended on Turf Moor to analyse the secret of their success and the magic of the Gawthorpe production line. The firm forecast was of at least a top six position, with their proven ability, power and organisation. As the season progressed, it was Adamson taking the spotlight more and more in the papers; he was described as the man grooming this collection of players. In the American magazine *Life,* one of the outstanding picture magazines of the era with a worldwide circulation, there was a lengthy feature on Burnley covering several pages. It was a measure of the interest that this tiny club from this tiny town could generate. Just how do they do it, was the theme of the feature. It was Adamson who received the greater coverage and Potts, who was hardly mentioned, was briefly likened to a producer, portly and short-fused.

In September, there was another fracas of a game with Leeds United at Turf Moor. 'Soccer shame' was the description of this brutal game when players' legs rather than the ball were the targets. By all accounts it was even worse than the one the previous season.

"Why must it always happen when we play Leeds?" Potts asked and challenged Revie to meet him in a television debate about the game. "They should put their own house in order first," answered Revie. "I can't think of anything more useless."

"We can't be blamed," said Potts, "we try to play the game constructively, and we have a reputation as a footballing side." Revie retaliated, telling Potts he had a team of "fairies", not quite the best thing to say about men like Angus, Lochhead, Harris and O'Neil. Potts repeated his assertion that the problem lay with Leeds' gamesmanship.

After seven games Burnley were undefeated, and although a 4-1 defeat by Manchester United followed, it was a prelude to another three straight wins, putting Burnley into second place just one point behind the top team, Stoke City.

But slowly it went wrong and inconsistency crept in. A game at Sunderland summed up how erratic they could be. Winning safely 3-1, the game was thrown away and Sunderland won 4-3. Potts was not at the game; he was in Zurich for the Inter-Cities Fairs Cup draw. In his programme notes following the game he did something very rare for him and publicly criticised the display. "Instead of building up our lead we proceeded to put the brake on our commanding enterprise… in the light of what we had done earlier, and could so easily have continued, the result from our point of view was ridiculous… it was a punishing reminder of our folly… the remedy is in our own hands and must not be ignored in future".

In these words lay his simple philosophy; if you have scored three, then go on and score four; don't settle for what you have and sit back. There are some who think it was as much a criticism of Adamson as the team.

After 21 games they were still in the top six but Stoke City did the double over them in December and although there was a 5-1 win over West Bromwich Albion on the last day of the year, that was it and decline set in. In the 18 remaining League games until the end of the season there were only five wins. In the same period the previously free-scoring Burnley managed only 15 goals and one of those was an own goal by the opposition. The penultimate game of the season was a 7-0 drubbing at Sheffield Wednesday. Only 11,634 spectators watched the tame anti-climactic final 1-1 draw with Everton at Turf Moor.

The Inter-Cities Fairs Cup provided the gloss on the season. The first game, a 1-1 draw at Stuttgart, had Potts in a storm again as he described two refereeing decisions as "diabolical", one of which involved the sending off of Brian O'Neil and the other an unwarranted penalty. The second leg game at Turf Moor was won comfortably. The two games against Lausanne of Switzerland were won easily enough but the away leg demonstrated the growing influence of Jimmy Adamson. Willie Irvine was dropped, replaced by Arthur Bellamy, who played as a sweeper. Irvine was far from pleased but it was in a later game against Naples when his anger at being left out really surfaced.

By the time of the Naples game in late January, Jimmy Adamson had decided that Irvine was the reason behind Burnley's faltering performances against Leeds and Newcastle, or so it seemed to the player. But maybe there was another reason. The squad spent some preparation time in Southport and after the coach journey home Irvine slipped into a local club and had a shandy. He did enjoy a drink but to this day he says it was one shandy and nothing more. Jack Butterfield, the club's commercial manager, was also there and he reported that Irvine had been drinking. He was discarded for the Naples game and he fumed silently as he watched the game from the stand. It was Harry Potts who gave Irvine the news that he wasn't playing but told him the decision was nothing to do with him. But he was the bloody manager, Irvine thought, what did he mean it was nothing to do with him? Who was picking the team now, him or Adamson?

The two games against Naples are well established in Burnley mythology. The first, which Burnley won 3-0, was worse than any game against Leeds United and one Italian player was sent off for kicking Andy Lochhead's head. The Italians swore revenge and retaliation in Naples. Former Burnley secretary Albert Maddox had a foretaste of what was to come when he visited The Woodman Inn with George Bray for a drink one night. "We used to know an Italian in there. He was an ex-prisoner of war and had settled in Burnley. He knew Naples well. After we won that first game in Burnley he told us we wouldn't get out of Naples alive after the return game. He was very nearly right."

On February 8th the Naples stadium was a seething mass of hate, vitriol and rubbish hurled onto the pitch at the Burnley players. Somehow, against all the odds, Burnley held on to gain a 0-0 draw and progress to the next round. The Italian players and fans fumed and the place was a tinderbox. Lochhead recalls that it was Harry Potts himself who sparked many of the after-match scenes. "Naples had this winger called Sivori and all through the game he'd been giving Les Latcham, our full back, a hard time. Les had a head wound that needed bandaging but he managed to carry on. Anyway, the trainer's bench was very close to the touchline and there was Harry with the trainers and coaches and reserves. Sivori must have fouled Latcham once too often because, right at the very end of the game, as Sivori is running down by the bench I see Harry is fed up of all this and sticks out a foot and trips Sivori up. Well, that was when all hell broke loose."

At the end of the game even the English journalists feared for their safety in the press box as furious fans spoiling for trouble penned them in. The police ushered them out to safety to waiting taxis. The story is told that Harry Potts had no idea they were safe. So, concerned for their well-being and realising that they had not reached the coach, he set off alone to the far side of the pitch to find them and lead them to where they were supposed to be. He hadn't received the message from one of the journalists that they were being led out by the police. What Potts did was an act of genuine, selfless bravery bearing in mind the scenes that he had already witnessed.

Ralph Coates remembers him in the dressing room afterwards. "Near the final whistle Willie Morgan and I were near the tunnel and both made sure we could get off as fast as possible. Once off the pitch we ran as fast as we could down the long corridor and went to the dressing room. What I remember clearly is Harry and the first thing he said was, 'Are all the players in,' and he began to count us all to make sure we were back."

I REMEMBER those games we played against Naples. The town was so excited that we should be playing such a fabulous Italian team. There was this image of our tiny little town up against this glamorous international team of stars. It really was a sort of David against Goliath. After the first game at Turf Moor Harry came home and sat down with such a huge smile on his face. And then after the second game I was just so amazed to see in the papers how rough it had been and how army vehicles and soldiers escorted them away from the ground because they were worried that the team's coach would be attacked.

I have recollections of hearing about the game on the news afterwards and wondering what was going on and would Harry and the players be safe. And then somehow a reporter from the *Daily Herald* turned up on the doorstep, knocked on the door and asked did I know anything about what had gone on. Somehow he had found out where we lived. His appearance and questions made me worry all the more.

WHEN BURNLEY drew the first leg of the quarter-final away game 1-1 against Eintracht Frankfurt there was great confidence that the job had been done and the semi-finals beckoned. It was not to be. The Germans came to Turf Moor and gave Burnley a football lesson. The 2-1 scoreline did their superiority scant credit. Keith McNee, the local reporter, did not mince his words, and his indictment of the performance could well have applied to any one of many games at the end of the season. He described the fans as being disgruntled and shattered seeing their hopes raised and then dashed with this confused ragbag offering of baffling team selection, irritating tactics and rank bad performances. Adamson said it was the absence of John Angus. Potts said it was the absence of Andy Lochhead. Fans said it was an absence of everything. The season was over.

If one tries to look for reasons for the change of fortunes at Burnley Football Club when there had been so much promise and potential, then maybe it was that because of constant injuries there was rarely a settled side in the second half of the season. Maybe it was an increasingly suspect defence, maybe it was because Adamson tinkered with formations; when it worked he was praised but it didn't always, as in a 5-1 thrashing at Leicester. On top of all this, two key players, Irvine and Bellamy, suffered broken legs. Plagued by other routine injuries, a settled team became a rarity. The team that played the final games bore little resemblance to that of the first half of the season. Only O'Neil and Harris were the ever-presents. Maybe the eight games played in the Inter-Cities Fairs Cup were a diversion and took concentration away from the League.

But one thing is for sure: the goals dried up, and they did so with a vengeance after the 5-1 thrashing of West Brom. Following that came Willie Irvine's broken leg at Everton on January 31st in the FA Cup replay. There was a dreadful scene in the medical room after the game when the Everton manager Harry Catterick, a former playing colleague of Harry Potts, came in to see Irvine as he lay on the medical table. "Well, you got what you asked for," Irvine recalls is what Catterick said to him. Potts, who was checking Irvine's condition, flew at Catterick in an absolute rage and the latter was pulled away from the scene by the Everton trainer.

Meanwhile in the Everton boardroom, Lord had one of his rages and was told to leave. He did so and swore never to set foot in the place again. Potts, too, continued his fury in the private directors' lounge after the game, so much so that Everton made an official complaint afterwards. Their complaint was discussed at a later Burnley board meeting.

"Consideration was given to a letter from Everton Football Club complaining of the behaviour of the manager in the private directors' lounge after the cup replay at Goodison Park on 31st January. It was resolved that the directors should send a letter to the Everton club stating that the directors were appalled by the bad manners of their Chief Director, Mr J Moores in ordering the Chairman from what he called my room."

It is rare that the absence of one player can make such a difference, but in this case it did. Irvine hadn't had a particularly prolific season and had been dropped for important games but he was nevertheless one half of the best strike pair in the Division and there was no adequate replacement. Not only that, but Andy Lochhead's goals dried up. He played in only three of the final ten League games. By December 31st he had scored 18 goals. After that there were none.

The statistics are cruel but they tell the stark story. After December 31st the Lochhead/Irvine partnership scored not one League goal that season. From once having an embarrassment of goalscorers, the cupboard was now bare.

The 7-0 defeat at Sheffield Wednesday in the penultimate game of the season was the final straw and served the purpose of underlining once and for all that the great years had truly ended. Potts selected a young Stan Ternent, who years later would himself become Burnley manager and achieve promotion to Division One. The week before, they had lost 4-1 at home to Arsenal, and the now toothless, aimless team received the slow handclap. "What's going on at Turf Moor?" was the question so frequently asked. Potts had no answers and made no comment. And then came the Sheffield massacre. Not only did Wednesday score seven, they missed a penalty and hit a post and Burnley keeper Harry Thomson made stunning saves on a number of occasions. A side that six months earlier was being lauded to the skies was now in tatters; "cut to pieces like dog meat and then flung aside contemptuously", said one report.

Players who six months earlier had been described as outstanding were now simply drifting. Burnley were described as a disgrace to their long traditions. Keith McNee described the result as like the death of an ailing relative finally put to rest after all lingering hope that the patient might recover had gone. It was clear that the people who paid at the turnstiles did not accept Harry Potts' regular references to injuries and bad luck. After the game he refused to be among the critics and said that goals change games and that the score would have been different had Burnley taken their chances. Supporters were not impressed; it was not the rallying call they wanted and calls that Burnley should buy increased.

There were few consolations. One was the debut of future star Dave Thomas. Years later, Dave says quite openly that he idolised Harry Potts and still does. He loved his fatherly manner, the way he looked after his parents, his openness and honesty. "What you saw was what you got. If you had a problem you could take it to him. If he passed you he always had a greeting and a smile, an enquiry about how you were, how things were going. If you were injured he genuinely wanted to know about it because he cared for you as a person. Because of that you wanted to play for him and win."

Coach Joe Brown also remembers how Potts was a man of his word and if he said he would do something, he did not forget. Harry Potts had contacted Brown and invited him to be a coach while Brown was still a Bournemouth player. Brown would have jumped at the chance but had agreed to go to Aldershot as a player. "Go to Aldershot and I'll telephone you again in a few months' time," said Potts.

"That's the end of that, I'll not hear again," thought Brown as Potts said his polite goodbyes. But to his amazement, Potts did ring him again to offer him a post as coach. To this day Brown has not forgotten that phone call.

Another consolation had been the progress in the Inter-Cities Fairs Cup and the excellent displays in all but the final game, the only one of eight they lost. But, in truth, these were scant rewards in a very disappointing season when supporters felt thoroughly let down. Not only had they seen top three hopes evaporate, and Inter-Cities Fairs Cup dreams dashed, they had also watched many games where the description "ill-tempered" underplayed the state of the game at that time. Andy Lochhead must have lost count of the times he was laid out unconscious during the season, there were the two broken legs in first-team games, five in all at the club during the season, several games described as brawls; and Burnley, in spite of Harry Potts' claims that they played by the rules, could be as rough as anyone. Everton supporters, for example, considered Burnley were so rough in the FA Cup replay at Goodison they chanted that they must be Leeds in disguise.

Though Angus, Elder, Harris, O'Neil, Coates, Lochhead and Morgan were still there, many of the new reserves and stand-ins were just not good enough. Even the infectious Harry Potts found morale hard to boost.

Genuine championship aspirations had turned to disappointing, dismal dross. It was time to buy.

And on top of all that, as the decade moved into the late 1960s, it was becoming increasingly clear that the partnership between Potts and Adamson was not working. Jimmy Adamson increasingly wanted sole control, which was in no way an unnatural ambition. He had his own theories, tactics and ambitions. It meant, however, that there was growing confusion about who was in charge and whose instructions should be followed. If there is one thing that footballers want, it is clarity and this, at Burnley Football Club, was becoming blurred, whilst loyalties were becoming split.

CHAPTER NINE
HANGING ON

HARRY DIDN'T make a big fuss when he finished his tenth year as manager in 1968 but I know it was quite an achievement. There were no special celebrations or anything done by the club to mark the event. A shame, I thought, he's done so much for them. But today I can look back and whenever I pick up a souvenir that Harry brought back from a tour, a gold charm bracelet I have, even the old watch he was given for winning the Championship, I can relive those years we had. The watch is broken but I still keep it. I showed it to a friend one day who closed his eyes, held it tightly in his hand, and he was sure he could feel Harry beside him.

Clement Freud, who at that time was a newspaper and TV celebrity, wrote about him in one of the daily newspapers. He described how safe Harry's job was and what a wonderful relationship there was between Harry and Bob Lord. But was there? Was Bob Lord already thinking about making Jimmy manager? Did I already not sense that Jimmy would one day want Harry's job?

I was so proud of Harry and what he had done for the town and so were Linda and Ken. People knew where Burnley was because of the football, the team and Harry. When you think that in his time he'd brought such triumphs and taken them to Wembley. Then he'd travelled to New York and European places such as Stuttgart, Lausanne, Frankfurt, Paris and Naples of course. I hadn't heard a single person in all that time say a bad word about him. Everyone respected him and he himself had the greatest respect for people like Bill Nicholson and

Matt Busby and they, too, had been at their clubs for many years.

For me, being the wife of a football manager for ten years was special. I'd had such a wonderful time, especially as the children grew older and I could spend more time at the club on a Saturday. Of course, I'd seen the atmosphere change bit by bit as from the great years of the early '60s things became just a little more uncertain and not quite so successful as the '60s went by. I know by the end of the '60s they were struggling to keep up. But only rarely would I see any worry in Harry's face. I just continued to think that it was nothing short of a miracle that this town could keep a club in the top division for so long. Did the people of Burnley think that, though? Burnley Football Club was almost the last outpost of a time when clubs could compete on level ground and small-towns could support a team in the top division. But then when you realised they had people who worked as hard as Harry, Ray Bennion and Billy Dougal and all the other coaching staff with all the young boys who came to train, you knew why. And I know why they all looked up to Harry so much.

One example of his care for them was the time a very young Steve Kindon had some kind of row with his landlady while he was in digs and she more or less turfed him out on the spot. Even as a boy Stephen had a mind of his own. Every parent had our phone number and it was his parents who phoned Harry to say what had happened. Harry just went round straight away to find Steve, collected him and brought him back to stay overnight with us till new digs could be sorted out. Knowing Harry he would have given the landlady a flea in her ear as well. I put Ken on a camp bed and Steve had Ken's bed. Steve was such a big lad even then, and his feet were hanging over the end of the bed. Nothing was too much trouble for Harry as far as the care of his players went, be they young or old. I know that even today Steve Kindon has never forgotten that gesture of Harry's.

The dinners and banquets were such marvellous occasions and I loved to dress up for them. There was one long, white, glamorous dress I had with a halter neck. I had bought it for a Greek holiday, it was backless and Harry, bless him, didn't approve of it. He made me alter it and I never wore it in Burnley. Perhaps it was a bit too daring for Burnley in the '60s and Harry was very conventional in dress matters, as was Bob Lord. But nothing could ever have bettered the weekend at Wembley and the wonderful time we had there. These were the times when Bob Lord was in his element and you just had to admire how this self-made businessman, from such humble beginnings and background, had built up the club to what it was – it was almost an institution respected throughout the land by every other football manager who wondered just how it was done. As far as I could tell it was based simply on paying the players well and looking after them as well as possible. Of course, I knew from the papers that Bob got himself into trouble sometimes with the remarks he made and his blunt speaking but as far as Burnley Football Club was concerned nothing but the best was good enough and he was never going to let anyone get away with criticising it. And then when you saw him hosting the banquets and functions or sitting at the top table in his dinner suit and with his centre parting, he radiated such pride and sense of accomplishment. Bob liked Hilda to wear velvet and she often had a velvet choker necklace. She looked so elegant at these functions.

The changes for us in that ten years, I suppose, were minimal in the sense that Harry worked all hours in his first year as manager and still worked all hours ten years later. In addition to all that he was also manager of Football League representative sides. His coaching staff had increased but it didn't lessen any burden on his shoulders and he certainly was never in any position to relax more or find just a little extra leisure time. He never worked any less or spent any more time at home, so my time with him continued to be fleeting to say the least. I just carried on with the family, the home and the garden and my own interests. I learned to treasure our summer holidays where we had two weeks abroad in the warm sun and sea.

He was so proud and delighted when Linda got married and he loved the whole occasion. It was definitely a claret and blue wedding with our great friend Alan Reid there to officiate as well. Bob Lord and Hilda were there and several of the staff from the club. Linda had gone into nursing just as I had done and she married Philip on July 26th 1969. While she was nursing I do know there was at least one occasion when if patients found out who she was and things weren't going well at the club she would be grumbled at and be very upset. But that just shows how there is no such thing as a private life when your father is the manager of the local club. And if during the ten years so far that he had been manager there was one unpleasant thing for all of us, that was the time that Jimmy McIlroy was sold and Harry took so much of the criticism.

Anyway, I can remember Bob Lord at the wedding, beaming and telling Ken he had done his duties so well that he named him man of the match. Jack Butterfield was MC. As much as possible was in claret and blue: the decorations, the bridesmaids' dresses and even the flowers as near as we could get them. It was a real Burnley Football Club family night.

Towards the end of the '60s, we moved house from Brierfield right across to the other side of Burnley. Harry's mother was not best pleased. We just thought it was right for a move and as Ken and Linda had ponies we thought moving nearer the stables was a good idea. So we moved to Simonstone.

HARRY POTTS and his staff were down-to-earth people. The 1960s in a place like Burnley was still a time when the footballer was very much the chap next door. Few, if any, had airs or graces. Lord paid them well but never enough to have grand detached mansions like footballers do today. Most of them were from ordinary working-class backgrounds, or humble beginnings, so they had their feet on the ground. In fact, almost into the late 1950s, some of them had to serve their time working for the NCB instead of doing National Service.

None of them had underground jobs but several of them worked as joiners or electricians. Adam Blacklaw was a bricklayer and John Connelly was a joiner. Brian Miller can recall working there in the daytime and training in the evenings after he had finished. If there was a Tuesday evening game he got an afternoon off. They had stopped doing that by the time they won the Championship but certainly in the very late 1950s when Potts first started at the club as manager many of them had daytime jobs.

Burnley the town was slowly changing as the '60s ended. There was still much poverty and acres of poor terraced housing; the cotton mills and coal mining had all but vanished but a number of new industries came in to give some employment. They called those years the swinging '60s but in truth there wasn't much evidence of that in Burnley. London might have been swinging, but fashion, prosperity and good times came to Burnley rather slowly. There was the story about Ralph Coates, one of Harry's favourite players, transferred to Tottenham in the early '70s so the bills could be paid. When he got to London, the players asked him why all his clothes were so out of fashion, telling him that at Tottenham you weren't allowed to wear the same shirt twice. And when Willie Morgan opened his fashion boutique in the town it was not long before it closed. Burnley wasn't quite ready for people dressing up in Sergeant Pepper outfits and the fact that Morgan's boutique was next to a butcher's shop, with a window full of carcasses and strings of sausages, did not help.

Bob Lord, meanwhile, was desperate to modernise the ground and a new stand, complete with warm air heating, was built behind one of the goals. For years Lord had worried that the old stand along Brunshaw Road was dangerously unstable and then years later he was criticised for replacing it, raising the money by selling Martin Dobson. The truth is, it was a disaster waiting to happen. In addition, he wanted to build a huge leisure and entertainment centre, convinced that it could be a great social asset for the town as a whole and not just the club, but it never happened. Today most big clubs have these centres with hotels and shops attached and Lord, given the money, would have built one thirty years ago. He even went as far as having plans drawn up but that was as far as it got. Bob Lord, for all his faults, was a marvellous visionary. In the predictions he made and his unfulfilled plans for the ground, he was years ahead of his time.

It was in September of 1968 that Harry Potts reached his tenth anniversary as Burnley manager. But the new season had begun as the old had ended, with yet more injuries and illnesses. Potts again asked the detractors to "keep things in perspective", adding that "we are convinced our staff when fit is as good as any… as good as any in the First Division bar none".

It had been noted that Joe Brown had watched Frank Casper, a young forward, at Rotherham. Casper's skills had already been seen against Burnley in an FA Cup tie in a previous season. There was no question that Potts was ready to buy. Casper was, indeed, the target and was bought for £27,000. It is fair to say that the soccer world was stunned. Since when did Burnley buy players? With five goals in the first five games he was a successful purchase and went on to serve Burnley wonderfully well for several seasons until a serious injury ended his career.

The tenth anniversary of Potts' management period was marked by a superb 5-1 win over a Tottenham side unbeaten in their last 33 games. It was a fitting result with which to celebrate his past achievements; a title, a runners' up spot, a cup final, great performances in Europe, the continuation of the Gawthorpe youth system, the production of so many great players, and all done without the need for bullying and unpleasantness and shouting at his own players. He was living proof that managers can be 'nice' people. It is a word used by so many of his ex-players and colleagues when they talk of him.

His achievements by then were outstanding, his record spoke for itself, but with the benefit of hindsight it seems reasonable to ask just a few questions. Could it have been even better? Should he have freshened the side in 1962 during that tame end to the season when from a position of dominance and superiority in Division One, the championship slid from his grasp as the team's legs, strength and adrenalin ran out? Should he have identified those players who were desperately jaded and needed a rest and brought in some badly needed enthusiasm and fresh energy from reserve players? Was his sense of loyalty to his regular first-team players his Achilles heel? Burnley fans of that era still ask how their team could win only one of their last ten games and throw away another title when prior to that they had been such a goal machine?

In the cup final were they beaten before they even set foot on the field? Spurs were judged to be the more modern of the two teams, and outplayed Burnley. It was as if the team that had embraced the new era beat the team from the old. In that game did Harry Potts again show too great a loyalty to what had been a great team, but one which had an outdated style and belonged to an era Spurs showed was obsolete? Did he motivate them enough? Was being at Wembley, in itself, the pinnacle? Looking at it coldly, Burnley could not match the Spurs forwards' ability to swap positions, and to break fast from defence in the 'new' modern style.

In 1965/66 and 1966/67 it had looked as if Potts had found a new great team but that, too, went wrong and its rich, enormous promise was not fulfilled. In fact, it all went so badly wrong, for whatever reasons, that at last Burnley was forced into becoming a buying club.

But none of this should detract from the outstanding achievements during his decade in office. He kept a small-town club up there competing with the best when others such as Preston, Blackpool and Bolton had fallen by the wayside, unable to compete with the city clubs. He continued to persuade, with his own fatherly and gentlemanly personality, some of the best youngsters in the country to join the club. It is a testament to him that the outstanding Dave Thomas chose Harry Potts the man, in preference to the financial temptations Don Revie placed on the carpet in front of him and his father in the Thomas living room in West Auckland.

Any other manager might have sent Steve Kindon packing with a flea in his ear when, as a young raw teenager, Kindon unwittingly let Harry Potts have a piece of his mind when he was pulled out of a trial game. He had no idea it was Harry Potts he was speaking to so rudely. Harry let it pass; he had seen enough and had already made up his mind that

Kindon, who showed his power and pace in the trial, should be offered a place at Burnley. Kindon still remembers it. This then was Potts' great skill.

Steve Kindon speaks warmly about Harry Potts. Like Margaret, he still remembers being given shelter in the Potts' home. "The landlady I had was pretty neurotic and we'd had an argument over something silly. I think it was over how good Manchester United were – she was a United fan. Anyway she threw me out. So, there I was with my suitcase out in the street in the dark – it was quite late. I phoned home, tearful like and my dad got onto Harry. Within fifteen minutes Harry arrived in his Jaguar and took me home with him, having said some straight things to the landlady. He made me feel totally at home. You don't forget that."

Steve Kindon became a member of the Burnley first team at a very early age and he tells another story about Harry Potts.

"As a player I had various strengths. I had speed, I was big and I was brave. My game was simple; I just used those strengths until one day I began to watch players like Dave Thomas and Ralph Coates who had real skill. So I thought, 'OK, I'll do some of that fancy dribbling and beat a man with cleverness'. It maybe worked once in every four attempts. The other three I fell on my arse. Harry Potts said nothing.

"But it was 1968 and the European Cup final was between Manchester United and Benfica and the man of the match wasn't Best or Charlton or anyone like them, it was a little John Aston. Now, John Aston played the game of his life that night. He just ran at players, beat them through sheer pace and caused havoc. Man of the Match. It was then that Harry called me into his office.

"Stephen."

"Yes boss."

"Did you watch the match last night?"

"Yes boss."

"And who was man of the match?"

"Aston boss."

(Slight pause).

"Stephen, are you faster than John Aston?"

"Yes boss."

"Are you bigger than John Aston?"

"Yes boss."

"Are you better than John Aston?"

"Yes boss."

"Well then, Stephen, no more of this fancy dribbling, just play to your strengths."

The penny dropped; that was the genius of Harry Potts and he hadn't raised his voice once.

Ralph Coates is another player who has never forgotten the kindnesses shown to him. His mother was very ill in Hetton and news came that she had died. It was Harry who drove him all the way up to the north-east.

"Harry knew how close I was to my mother and when she died one of the family rang the club to tell Harry. They must have asked him to tell me because the next morning there was a knock at my landlady Mrs Cooney's door and it was Harry standing there. He didn't actually tell me there and then but asked me to pack a bag and he would take me home because she was very ill. When I came down with my bag I could see Mrs Cooney crying, so in hindsight it was obvious that he had told her what his intentions were, to take me home, and tell me when we got nearer to Hetton. She would be all right, I kept telling him on the drive, she was tough. Very near to Durham, Harry made as if to pull in to a lay-by. In that instant I knew she had died. Something told me and I said to Harry 'Don't stop boss, drive on, I know she's died, there's no need to pull in'. That was a huge thing he did for me and he himself must have been in a terrible state, knowing that before we got to Hetton he was going to have to tell me.

"Then there was the time he visited me in hospital. For some reason one weekend there was no game and we were all given time off to spend as we pleased. I decided to drive home but when I got there I felt so ill I just went straight to bed. The next thing I know is that my half-sister has called for an ambulance and I'm being rushed in with acute appendicitis which they operate on immediately just before it is about to burst. Three days later who should walk in to the ward unannounced but Harry with a basket of fruit. He'd driven all the way up to Sunderland to see me and at a time when it was not an easy drive on a lot of poor roads. What other manager would have done that?"

When Burnley beat Tottenham 5-1 it was another false dawn. It was described as one of the best Burnley performances ever, ruthless, powerful and efficient. Not many weeks later they would go to West Brom and lose 8-1.

In this game there was another buy on display – the young Colin Waldron was bought from Chelsea after Potts and Jimmy Adamson had watched him play in a reserve game. The club that had home grown a procession of strikers had bought Casper and now the club that had produced a procession of centre halves had to buy one. Bob Lord had joked that he hadn't slept for ten days after he bought Casper; now he said it would take him three weeks to sleep after buying a second player. Waldron must have wondered what he had joined as he played his third game in the 8-1 debacle. It was a defeat that stunned Potts, although his public face expressed the view that they had been playing well and it was a surprise to lose like this. As ever there were no histrionics, no broken teacups, his instructions were simple – go out and win the next game. They did, beating Newcastle 2-0.

Waldron, however, became one of a rare breed – a player who came to dislike Harry Potts. At a later date Waldron wanted to open a restaurant with Manchester City footballer Colin Bell and asked Lord for his approval. Potts didn't want him to, fearing that it would distract him from football and would have him burning the candle at both ends. Potts was a fitness fanatic and the 'Harry Potts Way' was early to bed, focus and concentrate on football. Potts thought it reasonable and proper to veto the idea along with Bob Lord. Colin Waldron, by then Burnley's captain, has always thought it was Bob Lord's decision and that Potts then implemented it. Waldron went ahead anyway and opened the restaurant. There were inevitable confrontations. Potts stripped him of the captaincy and dropped him. Potts then "shredded" him (Waldron's word) when he parked his car in the wrong place one day, making him train with the youths and on some days train alone. There is no question that Potts, on occasions, could certainly drop the 'nice' man image. It was not a happy time for either of them. Not until Potts was moved upstairs and Adamson became manager did Waldron regain his place.

With Adamson there was always a weekly meeting in his role as captain to which he had been restored. They would discuss team matters, the game, tactics, and sometimes player replacements. Waldron remembers that when he was captain under Potts, prior to the restaurant request, there was no such contact, and he never felt that there was any rapport with him. "I can't even remember him ever asking me a question, although that's not a criticism, it's just the way he was." Nor does Waldron think that Adamson deliberately manoeuvred Potts out of the job. "All of us were totally surprised by the announcement that Adamson would be the new manager. So it couldn't have been something that we had all suspected."

A 2-2 draw at Manchester United summed up the whole Burnley problem. They went into a two-goal lead as a result of two superb Lochhead headers; he was playing so well the press were demanding he be picked for Scotland. But then in the last five minutes United equalised. It epitomised the season – full of promise but coming to nothing.

Letters in the papers blamed Adamson's tactics and formations for the ordinary season. One in the *Burnley Express* demanded that the team went back to the 'Harry Potts Way': attack and be damned; if the opposition score two, then we score three. Nostalgia grew for the good years, which hadn't been all that long ago.

But, in the meantime, player sales took off with a vengeance. Potts had to accept them, he had no choice, and he knew as well as Bob Lord that selling was the basis of survival. Players were paid well, so was Potts, and gates did not cover all the expenses of running the club.

In July 1967, Adam Blacklaw went to Blackburn Rovers,

in August 1967 Alex Elder went to Stoke City, in March 1968 Willie Irvine went to Preston and in the late summer of that year Willie Morgan went to Manchester United. Before the year was out Gordon Harris had gone to Sunderland and Andy Lochhead to Leicester. In fractionally over 12 months half a team was sold. These were not reserves or has-beens, these were established first-teamers still at their peak with much still to offer. But even so, this little-town club hung on against all the odds to their position in Division One right on into the 1970s. It was a staggering achievement.

One major reason was the crop of youngsters who emerged at the end of the 1967/68 season and won the FA Youth Cup. There still seemed no end to the Gawthorpe home-grown production line.

The scouts sent them down, the fatherly Harry Potts welcomed them, soothed and calmed their concerned parents, and the coaching staff honed and trained them. A classic example of the way parents chose Burnley to send their boys and still saw it as the best place to learn came in the form of Michael Docherty. His father was Tommy Docherty and the young Docherty had been at Chelsea with his father. But then it was decided that Burnley was the best place to send him. Docherty's comments lauded Burnley from top to bottom and Potts was delighted to be praised so highly.

"Turf Moor is without doubt the finest finishing school of them all for a player. This is a superbly organised club and in coming here to learn the arts and crafts of the game so young, my lad gets off the right way." Mick Docherty would be one of the group of players that formed the last harvest of talent before Potts was replaced.

If there were other reasons for Potts' stubborn clinging on to that prized Division One place they included the retention of Ralph Coates and the emergence of the elegant Martin Dobson. Dobson was a Bolton discard, but Potts, with his eye for talent, had seen his potential. Dobson's father had telephoned Harry Potts and asked him to give his son another opportunity and to see if he had any chance in football. Potts went to see them both and took him on. At Turf Moor he saw his obvious promise and Dobson blossomed, becoming one of Burnley's finest servants.

Such was football in the '60s when you could telephone direct the manager of a First Division football club and get through. Hardly likely you could do this today with a Mourinho or a Ferguson. Dobson realised it was his last opportunity and took it with both feet. He remembers that joining the Burnley coaching set-up was like opening the pages of a book with every detail attended to and players knowing exactly what was expected. Swearing was banned: do so and you did five press-ups. With Dobson, Potts showed his understanding of psychology. Dobson made the first team but went through a dip in form. "I was inconsistent, form dipped, I didn't feel on top of my game, lost some confidence. So Harry didn't put me in the reserves, he put me in the 'A' team. It gave me a jolt. They wanted a reaction from me and they got one. I was annoyed. 'I'll show you', I thought. It had the right effect and wound me up. I learned a lesson, scored twice and was never in the 'A' team again. Within months of that I came on as sub against Manchester United and scored the winner, my first goal for the club."

Burnley finished 14th in 1967/68 for the second successive season (they were to finish in the same place in the next two seasons as well). It was a season when more games were lost than won. The 14 victories, some of them excellent, such as the home win over Spurs, were mixed with embarrassing debacles. They scored 64 goals, two more than Chelsea who finished sixth. But a team which concedes 71 goals will not finish in the top half. One player who did come back from injury was Willie Irvine, but he was never to be the same force. His transfer to Preston ended his career at Turf Moor.

It was a season in which, again after a game against Everton, Harry Potts showed his disgust at the seamier side of football. He publicly berated Everton following an incident when a Burnley player was laid out by a punch to the stomach. It led directly to an Everton goal.

"Burnley have made an effort to stamp out this kind of behaviour," he stormed in the *Burnley Express,* "and it is surely time that others in the game followed suit."

Burnley had indeed set an example after alleged 'thuggery' on the field during a game. It was never publicly made clear exactly what he had done, but Gordon Harris was transfer listed and sold. "If he doesn't like it, he can lump it," said ever blunt Bob Lord. In the *Burnley Express,* Harris's wife lambasted Lord and the club for making her husband a scapegoat.

A win against the old enemy Manchester United, a superb home record, occasional flashes of genius from Willie Morgan, and progress to the quarter-finals of the League Cup, kept interest alive but the icing on the cake came at the end of the season. Other than a final unexpected success at the season's end, it had been a "grand season of mediocrity", according to Keith McNee, with supporters becoming restless and dissatisfied by some of the dross they had seen. The signs were evident that city clubs held all the high cards and though it was generally recognised that Burnley FC was run on sound business lines it was struggling more and more to compete. Worryingly, attendances had fallen, income was down and the incomparable Willie Morgan, having turned down a new contract, would be sold to Manchester United at the beginning of the new season. Andy Lochhead would be the next star player to be sold to pay the bills.

It was also becoming clear that tactics were changing as Jimmy Adamson's influence increased and he became the dominant figure. Gone were the days when it was assumed that Burnley's fabled attack would win the day and there was no thought of playing defensively. There were two opposing philosophies at work on the training ground and on the field of play, one being the freestyle approach of Harry Potts and the second the far more technical and tactical approach of Jimmy Adamson. Criticisms were made that the players were now having defensive tactics stamped on them. As ever, it was the manager who carried the can and was left to field the criticisms. It was left to Potts to defend the season's results.

"We have ability," he told the *Burnley Express,* "but we have not shown consistency and it was a season of contrasts and I have to admit that while we have done well at home our away results have been mostly bad."

The loss of Brian Miller, the ever dependable and excellent defender whose career was now over because of injury, was crucial. There was no adequate replacement. Indeed Andy Lochhead was moved to centre half for several games in an attempt to solve the problem. While he was there the attack was woeful. When he was then returned to the front, it was the defence that was wretched. Ironically, John Talbut, a solid and dependable centre half previously sold by the club, was due to appear for West Brom in the FA Cup final.

For the first time, Potts made comments about future problems in a harshly competitive league. He pointed out that they had been close to another Wembley appearance in the League Cup but had let it slip against Arsenal. "The margin between success and failure is very narrow," he added, the classic comment of a frustrated manager. In private he was worried.

But, with little fuss or limelight, the club's youth team was quietly making its way to the Youth Cup final. It was a remarkable achievement. This little, homely club, set in a town with its fading industries, growing unemployment and general gloom, still seemed able to pull rabbits out of the hat and attract some of the best young players in the country to the club. The best of Harry Potts' managerial career was over certainly but there was still another trophy to come in this prestigious tournament. It brought pride again and another sense of achievement to the town and club and was thoroughly merited. It was achieved in an era when clubs nurtured their own homegrown players as opposed to the youth teams of Premiership clubs today that are filled with foreign teenagers and other young players bought from smaller clubs.

Already the glamour clubs pulled in the best of the young schoolboy talent but Harry Potts saw his young boys beat Manchester City, Manchester United and Everton along the way to the final against Coventry City. Potts offered no bribes or inducements to parents of these young schoolboys unlike other unscrupulous rivals, the most notable being Don Revie. But still they came because it was recognised that the Burnley coaching set-up was exceptional and remained one of the best in the country.

On a rain-soaked night and a mudbath of a pitch the Burnley Youths won 2-0 to overcome a 2-1 deficit. One of the abiding images from that night of glory is the memory of the boy-mountain Steve Kindon ploughing unstoppably through the mud and spray. David Hartley scored both goals but then faded into football obscurity as so many youth team players do. Supporters and players, staff and management were all ecstatic. It was a superb achievement by a group who had been given special coaching by Jimmy Adamson.

Of the eleven players who took the field, five of them went on to make regular first-team appearances – West, Thomas, Probert, Docherty and Kindon. Of those five, four had outstanding careers: West, Docherty, Kindon and Thomas, and the latter played eight times for the full England team, although by the time that happened he had been transferred to Queens Park Rangers. The wastage from winning FA Youth Cup teams is frequently high, but this crop of Burnley youngsters was exceptional in that it provided a bumper crop of players who had lengthy careers. It is perhaps unfair to single any of them out, but of that particular team Kindon, Docherty and Thomas were the cream. Eric Probert, who never really fulfilled his early potential, sadly died in 2004.

Success in the FA Youth Cup went some way towards consoling supporters who were disappointed at the preceding events of the season. Without it there might perhaps have been rather more angry letters to the local paper than indeed there were.

When Clement Freud wrote his piece about Harry Potts in *The Sun* neither he nor nor the manager could have known that the piece was as good as out of date before it had even been read. Football was changing, but Harry Potts was not. Clement lauded the relationship between Potts and Lord and how safe Potts' post was. "Come wind or water on the field of play, his chairman gives him a weekly smile of reassurance and says; never mind lad, at least your job is safe. Go home and have a good night's sleep."

Potts told Freud he was probably the safest manager in football. Freud ended his article by saying that Potts left the coaching to Adamson while he himself concentrated on policy and plans. Potts at this point still had two years left on his contract but there is conjecture that his day was already over in Bob Lord's mind. The 8-1 defeat at West Brom must have left a deep wound on Lord. Football tactics had changed.

England's win in the 1966 World Cup had changed forever football tactics in this country. And Adamson was one of the new breed of coaches changing the way the game was played. While Bill Nicholson at Spurs had been able to adjust and adapt, Harry Potts had not, and Bob Lord was astute enough, and knew enough about football, to see this. Jimmy Adamson was knocking on the managerial door; he wanted the job himself. That was natural enough; he could coach but had not got full control. It had reached the stage where, according to one eminent player, Adamson demanded of Bob Lord that he keep Harry away from him and the players. It left Lord in a quandary. He wanted to keep Adamson and had made that clear some years earlier. But it would be two years before he was finally persuaded to give the job to Adamson and move Harry out of the way.

The following season, 1968/69, began with more proclamations that Burnley were now working at a huge disadvantage and that miracles had been worked to stay in Division One since 1947. Clubs like Blackpool, Preston, Bolton and Blackburn had all dropped into Division Two. Bob Lord commented that city clubs were throwing cash round like confetti, but that Burnley were countering this with their plans to build two new stands and an entertainment centre with the finance coming from a development association and the commercial manager. At the level of Bob Lord and Harry Potts, the talk was a mixture of defiance and optimism. At supporter level, it was of another grim season of fighting for survival. It was the supporters who were the more accurate.

Two things brightened up what would otherwise have been another gloomy season. The first was a run of eight consecutive victories in October and November. The second was the team's progress to the semi-finals of the League Cup. But as usual, a suspect defence leaked goals like a sieve and there were the, by now, almost routine hammerings by large scores. Twice they conceded four goals and, worse, suffered defeats by five, six and seven goals. Even the most partisan supporter realised it was simply a matter of time before relegation was certain. Attendances continued to dwindle and, to add to it all, Brian O'Neil, still only 24, was very unsettled, unhappy with tactics and the atmosphere at the club, although it was never made clear exactly what he meant by that. One might surmise that it was the lack of clarity in exactly who was in charge of the first team, Potts or Adamson, a situation that could only produce confusion. Throughout the League there was a clear trend; the goals for and goals against columns, season by season, were shrinking. An exception was Burnley. The goals for column shrank; the goals against column increased.

In the early stages of the Potts/Adamson partnership, Adamson was clearly the subordinate. Ralph Coates tells the story of when he was about to play his second game.

"It was away at Leicester City, made one and scored one. I must have played well because afterwards Jimmy Adamson came up to me and said if I played well I'd keep the place. The next game was at home to Sunderland so I sort of just assumed I would keep the place because of what Jimmy had said. The Sunderland Supporters Club from Hetton Working Men's Club had organised a coach to bring them all down and my mother was coming on the coach as well. Anyway, Friday came and I bump into Jimmy Adamson in one of the corridors and he says that the boss wants to see me and that he has nearly lost his job. So I see Harry and he tells me I am not playing, Gordon Harris is back in the side but he tells me my chance will come. It was pretty clear that Harry had told Jimmy that he had no business telling me I would keep the place but there was no sign of any row or anything. But it did show that at that point Harry was firmly in control still."

Although Ralph Coates saw no signs of the alleged unrest at the club towards the end of the '60s, he did wonder, along with several other players, just who was in charge of the team. The players would ask each other who was picking the side. No one seemed to know and perplexed players do not play well.

The sale of a player of the calibre of Willie Morgan for a reported £117,000 to Old Trafford raised barely an eyebrow on the terraces; the supporters were well resigned to it; it was seen simply as an inevitable consequence of the increasingly difficult struggle to keep a small-town team surviving in Division One. Long gone were the days when the target was a place in the top three. Now it was to stay out of the bottom two. Leeds United wanted Morgan as well. Lord disliked both clubs but money was needed.

It would, however, not be season 1968/69 when relegation finally happened and that was very much due to the run of eight wins. Six of these came in the League and the twelve points they garnered were the foundation of safety that season. Take away those twelve points and Burnley would have been relegated.

Two stark September statistics painted a gloomy picture. Tottenham put seven goals past a humbled defence in one game and three days later just 5,928 fans turned up to watch Burnley play Grimsby in the League Cup.

Yet in the next League game there was a 1-0 win against Manchester United, Morgan, Charlton, Law and Best et al. O'Neil's blistering 25-yard strike in the dying minutes settled the issue. Andy Lochhead showed he was still a force to be reckoned with, giving Bill Foulkes a torrid time when a copy of the Queensberry rules would not have gone amiss.

But this did not solve the problem and once again Harry Potts had to dip into the transfer market to sign two players: Doug Collins, a forward from Grimsby for £30,000, and defender Jim Thomson from Chelsea for £40,000. It is worth noting that the four players signed by Potts thus far, Collins, Thomson, Waldron and Casper, became the bedrock of the great side that Jimmy Adamson created in 1972/73 which took Burnley back into Division One. With money at a premium, Potts bought well, and his eye for a player was unquestioned.

But it was the homegrown 'Burnley Babes' who took the headlines just days after a 4-0 thumping at home by Liverpool at the beginning of October. Even today, more than thirty years later, the explosion of talent unfurled is still talked about. With seven members of the first team unavailable for one reason or another, Potts had no alternative but to name what was an almost brand new team full of youngsters. Having just suffered that defeat by Liverpool there was little confidence on the terraces that more humiliation would not be inflicted by West Ham. But the youngsters did Potts proud with a 3-1 win.

By the time the team travelled to QPR in November for their eighth game they were sixth and they consolidated their position by winning 2-0. The newspapers were ecstatic, and the fans disbelieving. In fact, one *Daily Express* reporter enthused that this team could go on to dominate English soccer for the next three or four years. A club that had rarely won an away game for two seasons was now frequently winning away from home. If one result made people take notice it was the 5-1 win over top of the table Leeds United at Turf Moor. The world of football, and certainly Don Revie, was stunned. Leeds were simply torn apart. A Leeds defence that had conceded only five goals in the previous seven matches now let in five in one game. The performance of Dave Thomas, in particular, prompted Don Revie to say the lad could go on to become the finest player in Europe.

"Burnley's capacity for producing the goods just when they seem about to join the other Lancashire teams in the Second Division is enough to send rich clubs flocking to see what the Turf Moor boffins do in their mysterious laboratories", it said in the *Daily Telegraph*. Football writers from the daily newspapers and the monthly soccer magazines flocked to Gawthorpe to interview Harry Potts in attempts to learn the secret. "The finest finishing school of all," said Bob Russell in the *Daily Mirror*. With characteristic modesty, Potts pointed to his backroom staff and Bob Lord's willingness to leave him alone to manage without interference on the playing side. With this new crop of talent now available it was decided to sell Andy Lochhead.

But it couldn't last. Wolves drew at Turf Moor to break the spell and then there were three consecutive defeats, including a 7-0 mauling at Manchester City. That match produced one of the rare occasions when Potts blew his top with a player. At Sunderland, it was ex-Burnley Gordon Harris who set Sunderland on the way to victory with a thunderous free kick... sod's law.

The dream of Wembley and a League Cup final was shattered when the semi-final replay was lost heart-breakingly to Swindon in extra time as Burnley more or less gifted them two goals. The 'Burnley Babes' phenomenon faded. One by one the old guard returned to the team as it was decided that the 'boys' could no longer do a man's job. Leeds gained ample revenge for the Turf Moor beating by winning the return game 6-1 in a wonderful display that Adamson described as setting the yardstick to which Burnley must now aspire. The comment was a bitter pill for Harry Potts who detested Revie. Not too many years earlier other teams had aspired to be like Burnley.

There were occasional wins but the season petered out tamely. Only a few more than 10,000 people watched the final game of the season at home to Sunderland. Burnley lost. Letter after letter was printed in the local *Burnley Express*. Perhaps this one sums things up.

As a visitor to St James' Park (Burnley had lost 1-0) I had the misfortune to witness another apathetic performance conceived by the Turf Moor nerve centre. When is the gentleman in charge going to realise that today's game cannot be played at the same easy going pace to which he and his famous contemporaries were accustomed? Watching Burnley move out of defence at Newcastle was like seeing my grandfather getting out of the bath. The slow motion, sideways, backwards, style of play enabled the opposition defence to regroup and snuff out any Burnley player who had the courage to cross the half way line. When

*are we going to see a return to the fast, direct style,
which brought such great results before Christmas?*

Twenty-seven players were used during season 1969/70.
There were allegations of an unhappy camp. There were
several transfer requests, and grumbles at tactics such as
the sideways passing. There were continued complaints
about what players considered the over-emphasis on
tactical planning which seemed to leave players frequently
bewildered on the field. Local reporters Granville Shackleton
and Keith McNee pointed to players such as Dave Thomas,
Brian O'Neil and Steve Kindon, players with immense natural
talents, having the brakes put on them, being subjected
to the rule of the blackboard rather than whatever came
spontaneously.

In Kindon's case it meant he was unable to use his natural
battering ram pace and power. The old Potts philosophy of
put out the best eleven players, play to their strengths, and
let them get on with it, had been replaced by Adamson's
more complex tactics. If Potts' game was all about the talent
of the individual being given licence to express itself, then
Adamson's was the new ethic of teamwork and 'the team
player'. A selection of newspaper report headlines painted
a grim picture:

Clarets face hard winter unless they improve.
Mountainous task lies ahead.
Clarets huff and puff but get nowhere.
Pretty as a butterfly and just as much sting.
Clarets get a lesson.
Headaches face Clarets.

But after a dozen games with just one win, Harry Potts
continued to put on a brave face. As manager, it was he
who faced the press.

"I felt more downhearted than anything else (Burnley
had just lost at home to Ipswich). Once again it was a case of
playing well but not scoring goals and losing a match that
we should really have won. I have heard people mention
the word 'crisis' but let's keep things in perspective. We
are not in a good league position but the First Division is

a marathon not a sprint and these are early days. We need some luck and more than anything we need a good win. I have every confidence in my playing staff and the players themselves have not lost confidence. Things could be better but the remedy is in our own hands."

The barrage continued in the papers:

Boos and whistles hit Clarets.

Burnley hit the bottom.

It's time to make some changes.

"I'm still thinking," said Harry Potts, when pressed for his answers. "There are a number of alternatives." And at last the second win of the season was recorded plus two more in immediate succession, taking Burnley away from bottom place.

In fits and starts, Burnley continued to plod their way through the season. There was another run of three consecutive wins which started in January and at the end of the season there was just one defeat in the final eight games, which included four draws and three wins. Bearing in mind that after just twelve games Burnley were bottom of the division, to finish in 14th place might just be seen as a creditable achievement. But the nagging questions remained: where were the strikers of the calibre of Lochhead and Irvine? Why was natural skill and spirit being stifled? Was coach Adamson swamping his players with theory? What was Bob Lord doing about it all? What he did was totally unexpected. Jimmy Adamson got his wish.

It was in February, during season 1969/70, that the town was rocked by the news that Jimmy Adamson would replace Harry Potts as manager and that Potts would move into a new role designated as general manager.

CHAPTER TEN
DEPARTURE

IT WAS totally unexpected and when he came home he was devastated. "Jimmy... Bob," he kept saying over and over again. Jimmy Adamson and Bob Lord were Masons and sometimes I think they played snooker together on a Saturday night after a game. I certainly know one person who said to Harry that he needed to watch out for what was going on there. I had seen Harry very emotional at Linda's wedding and we'd laughed at that, saying that it wasn't dad taking Linda up the aisle, it was Linda taking her dad. But this was worse; it was different. I knew as soon as he came in that something was wrong; never before had I ever seen him so inconsolable as he was that day. I'd heard rumours that something like this was going to happen. I'd had phone calls, heard whispers and even, would you believe, a visit to the door by someone to warn me. Burnley is a small-town and people talk. Someone always knows somebody, sees something, puts two and two together, and stories begin to circulate. "There's always rumours," Harry said and shrugged it off.

But once he knew for certain, all I could say to him to try and console him was that as one door closes another one opens and as far as being general manager went we'd just have to see how it went. This was before the public announcement came in the local paper so by that time he'd had a chance to come round and gather his thoughts. He was just so dignified in his responses and answers to journalists. I have the old newspaper somewhere. 'Adamson Is Clarets New Manager' it said in great high letters and there was a picture alongside it with Harry shaking hands with Jimmy and Bob Lord and

Stepping out for the FA Cup final. Left to right (front) Margaret, May Adamson, Sandra Connelly; (middle) Florence Angus; (back) Sheila Blacklaw, Mary Miller, Brenda Robson (half hidden).

Footballers' Wives circa 1962, complete with handbags and matching gloves. Margaret takes a photograph of (front row) Florence Angus, May Adamson, Sheila Blacklaw, Sandra Connelly, Joy Cummings, Barbara McIlroy. (back) Rhona Elder, Joan Harris, Brenda Robson, Marilyn Pointer. Ken looks on.

Burnley lose at Wembley and Harry consoles his players. (left to right)
Adam Blacklaw, Tommy Cummings, Gordon Harris (backs to camera), Ray
Pointer and Alex Elder.

But Burnley still loved them. Harry Potts, Bob Lord, Margaret, the Mayor,
Cllr Sandy, Joy Adamson and Jimmy Adamson examine his losers' medal.

Back home. Margaret, Linda and Ken welcome Harry back from the six-week summer tour in 1960.

Bob Lord and Harry Potts. "A father, or big brother, relationship," says Margaret.

A rare chance to be a family when football did not intervene.

Relaxing in Palma in 1961, their first holiday abroad.

Margaret shows Ken and Harry that she can play football too.

Getting ready for the Inter-Cities Fairs Cup. Burnley prepare to fly to Europe.

See Naples and die. Harry Potts points out the Burnley fans to Dr Iven and Bob Lord.

Some saw Naples and nearly died. Adam Blacklaw is thrown down concrete steps.

Harry Potts was a good enough cricketer to play at the highest level had football not come first.

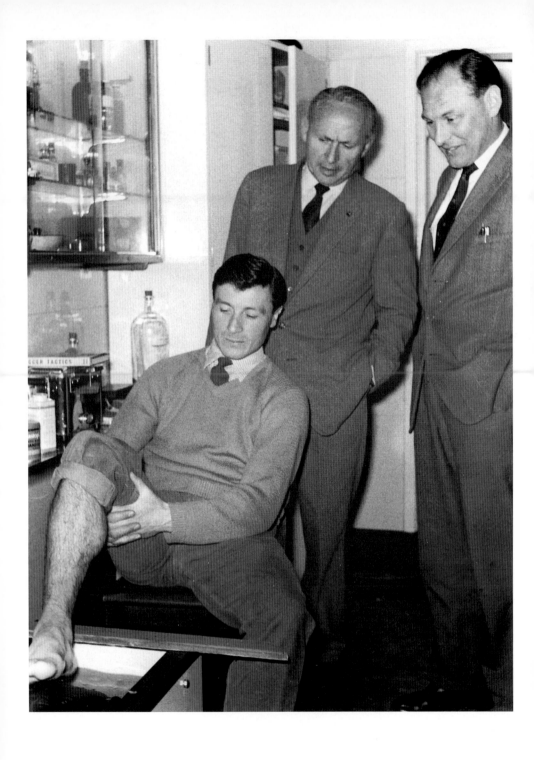

Harry and Dr Iven check on Burnley's star player, the legendary Jimmy McIlroy.

Preparing for the future. Harry signs soon-to-be England winger Dave Thomas.

Burnley's nursery was so highly regarded that even other managers sent their sons to it. Michael Docherty signs, watched by Harry and father Tommy.

The next generation. Harry with (left to right) Colin Waldron, Colin Blant, John Murray, Martin Dobson, Steve Kindon and Dave Thomas.

Linda gets married and the family have a saying: "it wasn't dad taking Linda up the aisle it was Linda taking her dad".

Harry doing what he liked best, wearing a tracksuit in the fresh air and leading training.

Sometimes it was talking tactics with Billy Dougal and Ray Bennion…

… sometimes it was partying with Reg Cook, comedian Tommy Trinder, Bob Lord and Cliff Britton.

captain Dave Merrington looking on. It hurt him enormously to look at it, but nobody but me saw the hurt, although maybe Bob Lord did when he told him of his plans. I can't imagine that Harry would have looked anything other than shocked unless he had already seen the writing on the wall. But Harry was so innocent in many ways, there wasn't a devious bone in his body, and it made him vulnerable and unsuspecting.

Anyway, I know what I thought, and after it had been announced in February, the club had one of their usual dinners at Mitton Hall. It was a 'do' that I was determined to go to even though I had been in hospital again for a major operation in December and had been steadily getting better since then. This was one of the dinners for staff and management and directors and wives and they were always lovely occasions: long dresses for the ladies and dinner jackets for the menfolk. Bob always put on a really good meal and there were always gifts for the ladies. There had been so many of these dinners over the years and I always enjoyed them. But this one: I expected to be treated as we had always been treated, for Harry if not for myself, and we had always been on the top table of course with Bob and Hilda and the 'management'. But this time we were not. We were on a table near the door. I was rather taken aback at that. And then I noticed on the menu that I was named to make the ladies' response when it came time for the speeches. Under the names there was a little witty line but under mine it said "she knows most who says the least", which I have always considered to have been a less than subtle remark aimed at me personally.

So, during the speeches they talked about the changes that had been made with Jimmy Adamson becoming manager and Harry becoming general manager and then it was my turn to respond. So I got up and thanked them for the flowers, fruit and cards I had been sent by the club and various individuals when I was in hospital. But, as for the latest news, I did not agree that it was in the best interests of Burnley Football Club. Harry, however, had accepted it so I would support him and stand by him. Then I sat down.

The silence was absolutely ominous. You could have heard a pin drop. I had no idea that I was going to say what I did; it just sort of came out spontaneously from the heart. I had seen how upset Harry had been on the day he had come home with the news. I had seen what it had done to him. He had given them so much, won them trophies, was so respected, worked for them nearly 24 hours a day and almost seven days a week. My mind went back to the incident on holiday years earlier when the German doctor had assumed that Jimmy Adamson was the manager.

My little speech was certainly unplanned. Harry had no idea what I was going to say. He didn't say anything immediately afterwards. After a few seconds' silence when nobody knew quite how to react, there was a round of polite applause. Then, well before the dinner finished, we left; quite early. A good while afterwards Harry did thank me for saying what I did and standing by him.

After the changes, his new place was sitting in the directors' box, not the dugout. That was an enormous change for him. It had only been a few weeks earlier when he had one of his outbursts and actually grabbed a linesman and made him look at one of his players who had been injured by a tackle. That was his passion showing through again. It was during a game against Wolves and it was quite a rough game.

After the changeover he lost all his close contact with the players both at Gawthorpe and in the changing rooms before and after a game. There were rumours in the local papers that Bob Lord would offer to make him a director but nothing happened about that.

And for me, there was the instance of being told not to wear trousers in the ladies' room. I had this nice navy and white trouser suit and with it being February and cold I wore it to sit in the stand because it was still winter. I still have a picture of me dressed in it with my hair done up in the beehive style that was fashionable at the time. Inside, in front of all the other ladies, I was told "trousers should not be worn in the ladies' room". So out I went into one of the other mixed hospitality rooms and did my usual cheerful socialising.

Harry and I still didn't sit together; I kept my usual seat with all the other ladies while Harry was in the directors' box. Quite soon he stopped sitting there because he'd be away at other games scouting, making reports and checking up on players. But it was obvious quite soon that he wasn't settling, the atmosphere wasn't right. He missed the day-to-day involvement. What he loved was the training; it was the side of football that he always enjoyed so much. He accepted the fact that he was still part of the club but I don't think he was given enough to do that was of interest to him or of a sort that he really wanted. You can only look and watch on the fringes for so long. All access to the players at Gawthorpe ceased.

Some time after the change was made, there was a presentation to him. Harry came home and showed me the cut glass decanters he received from the players. Neither Harry nor I are drinkers. I can still remember the comment I made to him.

"You'd have thought they'd known you long enough to know you don't drink, and long enough to know that a teapot would have been more you."

Years later, Jimmy Adamson's wife May made a point of telling me that Jimmy had chosen Harry's gift for the presentation.

There was one gift he received earlier, though, from Tom Thornber and the young lads. Maybe it was after a youth tour to Holland or Germany. It was a pair of silver serving tongs which I still use, on an almost daily basis. A genuine, little thought goes a long way.

One thing that irked me was an announcement by Jimmy Adamson that he planned to give Burnley some style. Style! How could anyone think that Harry's teams did not play with a great deal of style?

BURNLEY FOOTBALL Club made their official announcement on Monday February 23rd 1970. It was understood that both Adamson and Potts had signed new five-year contracts. The appointments had been a closely guarded secret and had come right out of the blue, reported Keith McNee. Players and staff assembled at Gawthorpe after a training session and Bob Lord made the announcement. The saddest thing

Arthur Bellamy remembered was Harry standing towards the back of the crowd. The players could tell he was unhappy when the announcement was given that Jimmy was the new manager and Harry would no longer be involved with the team in his role as general manager. Bellamy could see the unhappiness in his face.

Lord told them he had a very important announcement to make and that Harry was relinquishing the managership of the team and that he was sure that they would all want to thank him for what he had done over the years. The players were told that they should now take any problems to the new manager Jimmy Adamson. The ground was cut from under Harry Potts' feet. The team and all connected with it were now Jimmy Adamson's responsibility. Potts had a new contract, a good salary, but in effect, no further connection with the team.

As Lord continued his speech, Potts smiled but was seen to be clearly upset. He made a dignified response, expressing his gratitude for his twelve memorable seasons and all the support he had received. He went out of his way to thank Jimmy Adamson for his support as club captain while he was a player. "I could not hand over to a better fellow," he concluded, adding that he would continue to be at the club helping and looking.

Jimmy Adamson made his response, adding later that Harry would now be able to concentrate on matters away from the team. What those vague matters "away from the team" would be was never made clear. Harry Potts' days in the dugout were over. He was as good as banished. Ironically, in the few weeks prior to the announcement, Potts had overseen a run of five unbeaten games which had included four wins, the last of them being by 5-0 when Steve Kindon scored a hat-trick against Nottingham Forest. At any other club it might have earned the manager a reprieve. It seems reasonable to assume that Bob Lord had made his decision to replace Harry Potts long before the announcement.

The game before this run of five games began had been a home defeat to Wolves. It was a game that was rough, controversial and saw Harry Potts manhandling a linesman to make him look at Steve Kindon who had been laid out on the touchline, writhing in agony after a scything tackle had nearly crippled him. The referee, George Hartley of Wakefield, waved on play and as Potts was tackling the linesman, Wolves swept upfield. Derek Dougan was brought down well outside the penalty area but slid into it. The referee, yards behind the play, gave the penalty. Goalkeeper Peter Mellor saved it, was then injured in an ensuing challenge and Mike Bailey poked the ball home. Potts' fury increased, the fans raged and some invaded the pitch at the final whistle. Dougan, who once famously said that he would never allow a daughter of his to marry a referee, intervened and guided the referee off the pitch. "It was diabolical," said Potts after the game with a grim face. "Oh Harry, keep calm," his wife Margaret remembers saying to herself as she watched him grab the linesman.

Potts' programme notes for the Everton game on March 7th were, as ever, meticulous, measured and lucid. He was an articulate writer, extremely literate and fluent. In them he outlined the changes. There is not one single reference to how he must have been feeling.

"As I am certain you all know by now, last week was one of change for Burnley Football Club. Changes behind the scenes, which, I am sure are in the best interests of the club. Time will undoubtedly prove this, but the first thing I want to do at this juncture is to congratulate Jimmy Adamson on his richly deserved promotion to the position of club manager. At the same time let me emphasise that I am honoured to be appointed general manager and I can assure you that Jimmy and I will continue to work happily together in the future as we have done for so long in the past.

"We could not have a better man than Jimmy Adamson as our manager. He has proved time and time again that he is worthy of the sky-high reputation he enjoys within the football world. He was an outstanding player, a much-admired chief club coach and now he is destined to become one of the game's most prominent managers.

"I would like to take this opportunity of thanking all

those who have helped me during the twelve years as Burnley Football Club manager, between February 1958 and February 1970, including all the players it has been a privilege to work so closely with and all the supporters whose loyalty has been a priceless asset.

"I have been in an unusual position in that I have been one of the few managers who really has been allowed to manage and the same will of course apply to my able and greatly respected successor. I am very grateful to Mr R. W. Lord our chairman, who has always given me so much support, and to all the other members of the club's board of directors whose confidence in me has never faltered, which has been such a tremendous advantage".

These notes, so dignified and so eloquent, give no trace of the hurt and devastation he felt privately. The discussions between Lord and Adamson, regarding Adamson taking over, had taken place without Harry's knowledge. Even if Harry Potts had been fully aware of the manoeuvrings taking place and the decisions being made, it is arguable that he was too good a man, too trusting and far too honourable, to have known how to counter them. Potts, in the testimony of so many people who knew him well, was a man without one single trace of deviousness. It was, therefore, something he was unable to see in others. Harry's assurance in the programme notes that he and Adamson would continue to work happily together did not come true. It was a far from happy relationship.

Les Latcham, a key player at Burnley until his transfer to Plymouth, had a feeling change was imminent. "Towards the end of his time as manager you could sense that something was going on. Jimmy Adamson was slowly taking over all the team talks and the older players could see that he was going for the job. You couldn't put a finger on what the signs were but they were there, maybe a comment or a remark, a dig or a niggle, when Harry wasn't around."

A few weeks after the change there was a surprise meeting in the Turf Moor boardroom. Potts had no idea that every player at the club was assembled in there and wondered why he had been unexpectedly summoned. When he opened the door, having been guided there by one of the directors, he was astonished to find the entire playing staff. Captain Dave Merrington proceeded to give him a gift from the players, two Bohemia cut glass decanters. Then Mick Docherty stepped forward and presented him with two silver-plated candelabra. In an off the cuff thank you speech, Potts concluded by saying that football was like life, you got out of it what you put in. Nobody could ever say that Harry Potts did not put everything into it. And it was clear what his players thought of him.

Potts watched as new man Adamson's first two games in charge ended in defeats but then the 1969/70 season ended with just one defeat in eight games. If there was one bright spot it was the form of the mercurial Ralph Coates who was included in the Mexico World Cup squad, and who, against Chelsea in an FA Cup replay at Turf Moor, had given one of the finest exhibitions ever by any player in a Burnley shirt. He ran Chelsea ragged, yet the Londoners went on to win 3-1 in extra time. Sadly for Coates he was surplus to requirements and was sent home early from Mexico.

Just sometimes, however, an event takes place that reminds us that football is not the most important thing in our daily lives. In early July 1970 the crash of a Comet aeroplane in the mountains of Spain north of Barcelona was a tragic illustration of the smallness and closeness of Burnley and its surrounding areas. Just as the Hapton Colliery catastrophe had affected a whole town in the early 1960s, so did the holiday disaster in Spain when 112 passengers died. Forty of them were from the Burnley area. Among them were nearly half the members of a Padiham football team. Such a tragedy impinges on the lives of everyone in a town where so many families know each other, and so many lives are intertwined. Death came without warning to the people on board Flight DA 1903 from Ringway, Manchester, due to land at Barcelona. The newspaper report suggested that the only consolation was that the deaths would have been instantaneous. In truth there were no consolations and the town was devastated.

At the football club, for so long the town's pride and joy, the inevitable happened at the end of 1970/71. In Adamson's first full season as manager, Burnley were relegated. Fate, finances and injuries conspired to undermine another season's attempt to stay in the big time and Potts, from his position as general manager, without any influence on team affairs, could only watch helplessly. The football world was truly saddened as the last small-town team finally lost out in the endless battle to make ends meet and compete with the city clubs.

The statistics for that season are cruel. It began with the transfer of Brian O'Neil to Southampton for £75,000 in the summer. Goalkeeper Peter Mellor dislocated a shoulder before the season started and then Martin Dobson broke a leg. These injuries were to set the pattern for much of the season as other injuries occurred. There are many who think that the sale of O'Neil was the major factor and there was no one to replace him.

Adamson had declared: "Burnley will be the team of the '70s. We are building one of the finest stadiums in the country and we have a great young team to go with it. In the next few years we will win the championship not once but several times."

If ever a man's words would come back to haunt him time and time again, they were these.

Bob Lord announced that Burnley would buy, but that the asking prices for most players were beyond their budget. One player Harry Potts, in his new role, had his eye on was a young Paul Fletcher at Bolton Wanderers. He was one of several players Potts and Joe Brown watched as they took in games far and wide, including Scotland. Fletcher was, indeed, bought and though he had little impact in the relegation season, arriving only in March, he would become a key member of the later team that regained Burnley's place in the top flight. Potts always knew how to identify talent. Wherever he travelled, and at whatever game he attended, speculation followed as to who he was watching – even Derek Dougan was mentioned after Potts attended a game between Blackpool and Wolves.

190

Departure

After ten games and not one win, Burnley had accumulated just three points and scored five goals. There was general depression among supporters and continued criticism of the slow, slow, passing style and holding of the ball in midfield, so that any surprise or the use of Kindon's pace element was lost. Potts was powerless to intervene or comment. Ralph Coates was not having the best of seasons and injuries continued to play havoc with team selection. Even Malcolm Allison felt moved to analyse the Burnley problems in his *Sunday Express* column. He urged the Burnley board to find £100,000 to spend on new blood and he bemoaned the bad luck that Burnley were experiencing.

And then, at last, Burnley notched their first win of the season, beating Crystal Palace 2-1 at Turf Moor. The crowd of 13,000 sounded like 40,000, said Dave Thomas afterwards and Bob Lord was prompted to announce that the club would not be relegated. By Christmas, though, just two wins had been recorded and the third did not arrive until the end of February.

Hope returned at Easter when there were two consecutive victories and at one stage with five games to go and a game in hand Burnley could just have avoided the drop if other results had gone their way. Had they done so it would have been the greatest escape since Colditz. But four of those final five games were away from home and it was all too much. In farcical, rain-sodden conditions, the First Division curtain came down at home to Derby County and another defeat. A 1-0 away victory at Chelsea was meaningless and then the nightmare season ended at Wolves with the 22nd defeat.

There had been just seven wins and only 29 goals that season. In the third round of the FA Cup there was humiliation at Oxford United as they were booted out 3-0. Bob Lord accepted that it had been a disastrous season but added that no way could Burnley afford to go out and pay six-figure sums for players. In his drawer, he said, he had the names of 34 forwards whom Harry Potts had watched.

The general agreement within the club was that if there was a reason for this catastrophic relegation it was to do with the failure of the club in the years from around 1963 to 1966 to recruit enough young players of sufficient outstanding calibre, who would then have been mature first-team players by 1970/71. There were no more Irvines, Coates, Lochheads, O'Neils and Morgans. Instead there was a mixture of players bought at what one might call bargain prices, players from the youth team of 1968 and just a smattering of the older players who had come through the system, including John Angus who was well past his best and played just two games.

At the end of April 1971, Potts received a letter from Tom Whalley of the Ex-Clarets Association. He and all the members of the association wanted to record their thanks and appreciation for all that Harry had done in his time at Turf Moor. Tom Whalley had been one of those people who had seen the writing on the wall some time previously. He had privately predicted that relegation would happen and that not all was well between Potts and Adamson. His letter contained one sentence that related to relegation and "the tragic events of the 1970/71 season which had been a personal forecast of some long standing".

The season of humiliation, injuries and demotion ended with the sale of Ralph Coates to Tottenham. If supporters had been dejected, they now felt desolate at the departure of one of their favourite sons. With Coates coming from the same village as Potts, it added insult to injury. Harry Potts did not talk to his wife about how he felt. She knew, anyway, that he was desperately unhappy without him having to say a word. He had no meaningful role. His contributions were marginal. Manager Jimmy Adamson was not always cordial with him according to one player of the time; the partnership was no longer one between Potts and Lord, but Adamson and Lord. Potts would stay, kicking his heels, becoming more and more isolated (he used the word "lonely" to a trusted friend), for one more season.

During that season he did have one task to perform,

according to Les Latcham. "What Harry did as general manager I'm not really sure, except for having to rebuild the scouting network. When Jimmy Adamson took over he told the scouts, including Jack Hixon and all his north-east assistants, that they'd now be answerable to Dave Blakey. Jack Hixon thought that he might have been offered the chief scout post, but he wasn't, and he was not best pleased. So he left Burnley and took his network with him. Harry, who always maintained it took seven years to build a scouting system, had to start from scratch. Hixon continued to discover players like Alan Shearer but now they went to Southampton, not Burnley."

The loss of the disgruntled Hixon was a disaster. As the supply of great players from the north-east ended, Turf Moor endured its first season in Division Two and not until the final six games did any hopes appear that Burnley might just begin to find solutions to their problems. An outstanding goalkeeper was signed from Chesterfield – Alan Stevenson. A, by now rare, homegrown star, Leighton James, made the number eleven shirt his own. Colin Waldron and Martin Dobson grew in stature. Striker Frank Casper blossomed and struck eighteen goals. Paul Fletcher, not a prolific scorer, was nevertheless a great leader of the line and target man.

Prior to these final six games, it had been a season of inconsistency, of winning games and then losing, of being on the promotion fringes only for hopes to fade. There were more calls from the crowds for Adamson to resign. Potts might just have felt that Bob Lord would recall him. But then the final six games became six consecutive wins. Quietly and almost unnoticed a new optimism grew, criticisms of Adamson faded. The passing and possession style began to pay dividends and more than one manager described Burnley as the finest team of the second division.

The season thus ended on a high note, but not for Harry Potts. On June 30th 1972 he was dismissed. It is reasonable to assume he was astute enough to see that Adamson had fashioned a new and potentially successful team. Potts, by now a totally marginalised figure, realised that his position at the club was almost completely irrelevant. He could most certainly have sat tight and banked his generous salary if there had not been a reported fallout between him and Lord. The details of the argument are unclear. But it was obvious Harry Potts had become a reminder of a more golden age. He was no longer kicking a football on the training fields of Gawthorpe; he was simply kicking his heels in an office in which he served no purpose.

There were times when Potts felt a real sense of loneliness. No one knew that better than his great friend the Reverend Alan Reid who remembers the dull, drab, Friday morning when Harry phoned him from his office and asked him to come down for a chat and to provide some welcome company. Reid recalls how Potts confided in him that he was so fed up, and that he felt there was simply nobody in the club he could trust or talk to other than secretary Albert Maddox. Reid remembers how miserable and dejected he was.

People in this position know full well when it is best to leave with quiet dignity. Other people around them simply want rid of them. The dismissal of Potts was ratified at a board meeting on that Friday and the minutes are brief but illuminating. Under normal circumstances, both Potts in his role as general manager, and Adamson in his role as manager, attended board meetings. This was one meeting that Adamson did not attend.

The meeting proceeded, various matters were discussed, and then not until normal business had been concluded did Potts and his legal representative enter the room. The minutes report, "it was resolved that in the best interests of Burnley Football and Athletic Co. Ltd. that the services of Mr Harry Potts as general manager be dispensed with and that the termination of his services agreement with the Company dated 22nd April 1971, take effect as from today June 30th, 1972. It was further resolved that Mr Potts be offered the sum of £28,125 in full settlement and discharge of all claims of whatsoever nature or kind which he might bring against the Company..."

Departure

In blunt terms, Potts was sacked. There were no words such as reluctant, amicable or mutual. They were conspicuous by their absence. We can only guess what was meant by "in the best interests of Burnley Football and Athletic Co. Ltd." It was a bittersweet end to his time at Turf Moor.

At the same time the Potts/Adamson partnership was floundering there was just such a situation at Manchester City's Maine Road. The fatherly Joe Mercer, sometimes referred to as 'Uncle Joe', had been moved upstairs following Malcolm Allison's campaign to be made team manager. The word 'promotion' had been used to describe Mercer's move, but, as with Potts', it was anything but. Both men were moved out of the way. Allison and Adamson were two brilliant, innovative coaches, but their man-management and inter personal skills were less impressive. Relations between Allison and Mercer disintegrated to the point of them barely speaking to each other. The parallel between Turf Moor and Maine Road was striking.

There were several parallels, too, between Potts and Matt Busby; their man-management skills, their paternal approach and wisdom, their attitudes to the game and maybe above all their basic belief that you put out the best eleven players and let them get on with it, with just minimal instructions.

"Go out there, enjoy the game and just pass to a red shirt," was Busby's simple instruction. But if Busby scored over Potts it was perhaps in the area of mental toughness and coping with the politics of football. Martin Edwards, the former chief executive at Manchester United, made a telling comment about Busby. "All the great men have to be tough at some time otherwise they get washed away." While Busby was durable, hard-edged and political enough to be able to hold on to a position at Manchester United for many, many years, the nature of Harry Potts was such that he just did not know how to avoid being washed away at Burnley Football Club in June 1972.

'HARRY POTTS GOES' said the headline on Tuesday July 4th in the *Burnley Express*. Ironically, so too did hundreds and hundreds of Burnley people as they set off on their annual holidays. They left by road, rail, sea and air with great long lines and queues of people clutching bags and suitcases at railway stations and bus depots.

At Turf Moor, a joint statement was issued to say that satisfactory arrangements had been made under which Harry Potts would relinquish his duties as general manager as from June 30th 1972. Bob Lord added that the matter had been settled in the most amicable manner. He was unlikely to say anything else. Later in the year at the August AGM, he announced Mr Potts had received beneficial treatment, which few people in his position had enjoyed. He assured the assembled meeting that Harry had been handsomely treated. He further added that the arrangement that could have been successful had not worked out. There was no elaboration on that. One can surmise that it was a reference to the unhappy relationship between Adamson and Potts, and Potts' feeling that his role was a waste of his skills and energy. On paper it was the classic dream partnership of two gifted men with complementary talents. In reality it was anything but. As for the "handsome treatment", the sum of £28,000 appeared in some newspapers. Clearly this figure had been leaked to the Press.

The football world expressed its surprise. In the *Lancashire Evening Telegraph* Alf Thornton described Harry Potts as one of football's quiet men but with a flair for falling foul of authority. He was completely and utterly absorbed with his club, earning great respect for his unswerving loyalty. No manager was a shrewder judge of a good player and he had made a fortune for Burnley Football Club.

An era was over and Potts spoke at length to Joan Seddon of the *Evening Star*. He had no immediate plans, he said. His attitude was that the news would get round. He had been without a job before and you just wait for something to turn up. It was at this point he admitted to knowing for a little while that the departure had been coming but in no way would he deviate from the agreed statement. He felt fit; he was fifty-one but looked ten years younger. He had put out no feelers and was in no hurry.

196

"It's a great feeling when your body is toned up and feeling healthy. Never forget it's the game that counts. You get out of it what you put into it, put your whole heart and soul into it and the rewards will follow. I am the game's greatest enthusiast and I always will be."

He wrote to his daughter Linda on July 7th, just a few days after his departure. "I have enclosed some cuttings which tell of the events which came to light this week and I feel much better now that it is all over. It didn't come out as sensational news as far as the papers are concerned, but it is better for me that way..." Harry and Margaret slipped away for a few days' quiet holiday. If there was indeed anything sensational to reveal, the papers caught no hint of it.

In just a few weeks the players would be back for pre-season training. For the first time in many years Harry Potts would not be there with them. Neither would he be there at Turf Moor to see the Burnley team regain their place in Division One, with the players coming good, some of whom he had bought in earlier seasons. But if he was worried about what he would do without football he would not fret for long. His football career was far from over.

LOOKING BACK I think he must have known he was going to leave, but though he said nothing I suspect he was asked to go. Maybe his presence there was making certain people feel just a little uncomfortable and he couldn't have had any real job there once Jimmy Adamson became manager. I can't put my finger on anything specific but perhaps if I said there had been troubled waters, various incidents, and little tales would come to my ears that made me wonder if things were going on behind the scenes to push Harry out completely. It certainly seemed that he was kept away from the team. I think he was bored, he was missing the side of football that he always enjoyed so much and that's why I knew that if an offer came along he would take it and the fact that when it came, it was Blackpool, well it was just perfect.

We were hit quite hard. Yes, he had received a financial settlement but there was a mortgage to pay, a large tax demand and he was too young at 51 for any kind of pension. Linda was married but there was a young son in an apprenticeship to support. And there were his parents to support and help as well. So he went on the 'dole' and what a miserable experience for him that was. The unemployment centre took to seeing him in a private room to spare him the embarrassment. The man who had given Burnley Football Club all those wonderful years was now going down to Padiham to sign on. I had to sell my own little car, the Triumph Herald. There was a vacancy for a school nurse in Padiham but this meant I needed a car again. Life was difficult for a period. Thank goodness the Blackpool job came along.

CHAPTER ELEVEN

BESIDE THE SEASIDE

WHEN HE left Turf Moor, Harry had the job of telling his mother. "Better if we both went together," he said. I didn't see why, but I agreed to go with him. Mam Potts' first comment was, "What are dad and I going to do now on Saturdays?"

"Well, you're Bob Lord's friends," he told her. He contacted Bob Lord and arranged for them to retain their seats.

When Ken, then 11, found out that Harry was no longer at Turf Moor he took down all the Burnley posters that decorated his room and replaced them with stock car posters.

The first job Harry got following his departure was scouting for Blackpool. I'd often go with him to keep him company and I remember when he was doing it, he would never take any notes or write anything down at the time. Some people would sit there and scribble things down or draw diagrams but Harry used to say if they did that they must have been missing half of the game. During the drive home from wherever we had been he would barely speak but that was because I knew he was going over the game in his head and not until the Sunday morning would the paper come out, long sheets of foolscap, and the writing would begin. He would spend hours doing it all from memory including diagrams of free kicks and things that had happened. He had no problems writing and I know his notes for the programme at Burnley weren't just a few empty words; there'd be two pages of small print. It amazed me how his mind stored all the football and then out it came onto paper so many hours later.

Ron Suart, Blackpool's chief scout, would often phone and they would talk for hours. They were great friends. Harry had little notebooks as well and diaries going back to all the young lads who had come down to Burnley. I remember going to Crewe to watch one game. Harry told me to "watch their goalkeeper entertaining the crowd." Bruce Grobbelaar is the name that comes to mind although he wasn't the one that Harry had been sent to watch. But if he recommended him to Ron Suart, he didn't follow it up. He went to Liverpool.

And then the Blackpool manager's job came up. "Go for it," I said. "It's up to you, you are the one who is going to do the travelling." As we lived on the Simonstone side of Burnley we didn't need to move house so it was ideal. It wasn't a difficult journey and he was very happy that we could continue to live there. It meant there would be no great upheaval.

I got the impression that not all the Blackpool board were for him but the vice-chairman Cliff Sagar was there and we knew him. Some of his relatives lived in the village. Cliff had a business in Burnley and was often at Burnley games, though he lived in Blackpool. And so Harry got the Blackpool job and it turned out to be such a good arrangement because on Saturday mornings I would drive to Blackpool with him, have some lunch in the town, do a bit of shopping and then make my own way to the ground.

Doesn't life work in funny ways and coincidences? I was introduced to the directors and their wives and Frank Dickinson was the chairman. Of course he had been there when we first turned down the move to Blackpool when Harry was a player many years before. "It was through you we didn't get Harry all those years ago," he said. "Well," I said smiling, " I only said what I was told to say. It was to do with the house, wasn't it?" They were a lovely couple, Frank and Betty Dickinson.

Harry spotted one or two things straight away like there was nowhere for the players' wives to wait after a game. It struck me as odd that I never seemed to meet any of the wives after a game and it was because they waited outside the ground in all weathers or sat in their cars for their husbands. Then there were the queues of people waiting to play bingo in a club next door, the ground. Harry saw that they could have been buying lottery tickets or doing something to raise funds for the club. Harry suggested to the club that there was a market there and a chance to do some fundraising. Then he organised a Christmas party for the players and their children and they were really delighted with that. He just seemed to have this knack of thinking of the needs of others and then doing something about it. It was clear that the players and wives had enjoyed the party and as he came out afterwards young Alan Ainscow said to me with a cheeky grin, "Great party, can I call you Mrs Gaffer?"

There was one party where the players did comic turns and little 'acts'. Some of them came to me and said did I think Harry would mind if they did a sketch about him? I said he would love it because he always had a sense of humour and a schoolboy sense of fun. So one of the sketches was about them being out in all weathers training on the beach. It could have been blowing a gale some days but whatever the weather there was Harry saying with a smile, "It's a great day for football ,isn't it?" Another one was "It's a grand day for football, isn't it, let's go and see what's what?" Harry thought it was hilarious, and at his funeral when Paul Fletcher got up and told stories about him, it came across then that Harry was always up for a bit of boyish silly fun and he enjoyed that kind of thing with his players.

When Harry had been there just a little while he sorted out the problem of the wives having to wait outside even when it was raining. He found an empty room, took an old TV of ours, a table, a chair and other furniture and we managed to load it all into the car and the car boot. The wives and their children were so appreciative. That was typical Harry.

They started up what they called the Tangerine Club when Harry was there. It was in a building opposite the ground. They might as well be playing bingo in our Tangerine Club next door and raising money here for Blackpool Football Club, Harry said. I certainly saw a difference in the commercial ways in which the two clubs were run. The commercial side at Burnley was becoming really strong. At Blackpool, it was hardly started and, of course, on the playing side I could see that the way the clubs produced young players was so vastly different. It was the foundation at Burnley but at Blackpool nowhere near as advanced or successful.

I loved his time at Blackpool. On our way home from a match we would stop somewhere for a meal and have some special time together. There were lovely shops in the town and there was Lytham St Annes just a little way away. At Easter weekends, if there was more than one match or a Saturday followed by a Tuesday game, Harry would book us into a hotel and we could relax; enjoy the sea air; walk on the beach. What a change that made from the more intense time he had at Burnley. I'm not saying he put less effort into Blackpool but there did seem to be more time for us together. And of course there was the contrast between the two years he spent with so little to do at Burnley and then the fulfilment and satisfaction that came from having a proper job again at Blackpool. As far as I know, while he was at Blackpool there was no contact with Bob Lord.

But a strange thing happened and I think it must have been towards the end of our time at Blackpool. In the weekdays I would often walk round my favourite places at home and there was one walk I was doing around Whins Lane and the fields. Just as I was getting down from a gateway, a car came along. It stopped and Bob Lord was driving. Down went the window and he asked with some surprise, "What are you doing here?"

"Well Bob," I replied, "this has been my patch since I was nine years old." He looked tired and weary, he did not look a happy man and he just sat there in the car and then said slowly, "I made a mistake, I made a mistake."

"Well," I replied, "we all do sometime or another, you are not the first and you won't be the last." The conversation ended because someone I knew came out of her nearby bungalow to chat. To this day I've often wondered what else he might have said. I know it wasn't right at the very end of Harry's time at Blackpool but it was certainly at a time when Burnley again weren't doing very well. I sensed he would have liked someone to talk to that day but he drove off. Maybe he had realised that what I said at Mitton Hall might have had some value and had a grain of common sense and truth in it.

I said what I thought at that dinner and was true to myself. I never had any qualms about speaking my mind to people. I was confident and professional, well used to mixing with many of the people who came to the Burnley hospitality rooms. I had learned to speak up and to mix with people; at hospital with consultants, doctors and civic dignitaries. How well I remember that it didn't always go down too well in the Turf Moor hospitality rooms in a Burnley where there were strong distinctions between the men and women, and the latter were expected to know their place. It was perhaps fine to be seen but not heard. Maybe my free and easy attitudes were a result of my happy childhood and the easygoing nature of our household. I was happy to talk to anybody and everybody. Maybe that was why Harry's mother so often made hurtful, barbed comments about me and never thought I was good enough for him. Alice Paisley had said way back in 1949 that Mam thought "no one was good enough for our Harry".

I know other people who thought highly of her. With others she could be generous, warm, and giving. But now, looking back, was it a clash of personalities. It was as if we were destined not to get on, and yet ironically it would be me who would help her and tend to her right into her old age until the very end.

A lot happened during Harry's time at Blackpool. In 1974, I was ill with hepatitis. Our daughter Linda married Philip. Harry's father died in 1975. My mother had a stroke in 1976. Following his father's death they all wore black armbands at one of the games. I went back to doing a bit of clinic nursing and then towards the end of Harry's time there, it got a bit tense because there was a group of businessmen wanting to take control. We called them the Blackpool Mafia Group and it was not in their plans to keep Harry and he knew that. But that was towards the end and for four years he was his old self again and threw himself into the job of doing as much as he could for Blackpool Football Club. Football was all he knew; thank goodness he had Blackpool to go to.

WHEN BOB Stokoe left Blackpool to take over at Sunderland, the Blackpool directors said they were in no hurry to appoint his successor. Secretary Des McBain explained there was no pressure to act quickly and that they had the time to choose the right man. In the running were Jimmy Armfield, Lawrie McMenemy, Ian McFarlane and Gerry Summers, with McMenemy the favourite.

It was suggested there were three contenders, one of them being Ian St John, but that the two main contenders were Stan Anderson and Harry Potts, while Gerry Summers was the tip in the *Daily Mirror*. The *Sunday Mirror* reported that a two-hour board meeting following a home defeat against Sheffield Wednesday on December 16th ended with a 50–50 split between Potts and Anderson and that no decision had been reached.

At a later meeting a decision was made to appoint Potts, which caused more than a few raised eyebrows among fans who expected to see a younger man. But the board members who selected him had looked at his record at Burnley, his success with youth players and his vast experience of running a small-town club.

Des McBain remembers that McMenemy seemed to fill the room when he arrived for the interview and that the directors felt that with his huge personality and strong mind he would be too much to handle. He went to Southampton instead to weave his magic. Potts was interviewed in a hotel by the River Wyre and told the panel that he could still do a job and was in no way finished as a manager.

He took over at a time when Blackpool were reasonably successful and entertaining thoughts of a return to the top division. Since his departure from Burnley, Potts had in fact being doing some scouting for Blackpool. He arrived at a time when Blackpool were pressing hard at the top of the division. Stokoe was not the easiest act to follow but Potts announced that he was ready for the challenge as he got to know his new team as quickly as possible.

Margaret Potts announced, "It's no use denying that Harry has missed being involved with football. We've been hoping for something like this and now that it has happened we're thrilled. He has kept in touch by watching matches every Saturday. We'll move house if the club want us to, but it's a fairly easy journey from our home in Burnley."

Meanwhile, she had taken up part-time school nursing to help financially until the move was sorted.

"Football has always been my life," said Potts. "When I left Burnley I kept in touch with the game by scouting for a number of clubs. Then Blackpool asked me to be their scout and now they have given me a chance to prove myself again. I feel their proper place is in the First Division and I intend to see they get that place. I find the spirit amongst these lads tremendous. It is everything I would expect of a team second from the top of the Second Division. If we carry on the good work at Blackpool we will go into the First Division."

Chairman Frank Dickinson was in no doubt that the right choice had been made. "We have taken a long time to name the successor to Bob Stokoe but we feel we have the right man."

Dickinson was realistic enough to acknowledge, though, that it was not a universally popular decision. Fans were largely disappointed. They had been upset by the way Stokoe had left and fully expected the appointment of a young tracksuit manager. When the board came up with a man who was 52, thought to be past his best, and now out of the game, there were many disappointed faces.

Potts' main advocate was vice-chairman Sagar. He knew the secret of Potts' success at Burnley and went as far as saying that Burnley's success had been Potts' success. Sagar wanted to establish a youth system at Blackpool as successful as that at Turf Moor. Potts was the man to do it, he thought.

It was at the end a unanimous decision, explained Dickinson, even though they had indeed interviewed several of those tracksuit men. "We have no regrets," he announced emphatically, adding that they had chosen a man with an impeccable pedigree who knew how to get the best out of players, who knew how to put an emphasis on youth and who had superb experience of developing young players. At one of the earliest public meetings in his new job, Potts vowed that youth would be given its chance and that this was the way to the future. He had seen it work at Burnley; he was confident he could instigate something similar at Blackpool. Already on the coaching staff was his former player at Burnley, Ray Pointer.

It was generally acknowledged that Potts initially was on a hiding to nothing. It was a two-edged sword, suggested the *West Lancashire Evening Gazette*. The team were riding high; Stokoe had worked extremely hard, things were in good shape, the club was as strong as any in the Second Division, and success was deemed possible. If the team slumped, however, there would be criticism and inquests. They had just lost two consecutive games. They were about to lose a third.

If the gods of football have a sense of irony it was on full display in December 1972. Harry Potts' first game in charge on Tuesday December 26th was a home game against Burnley of all clubs. Adding to the irony was that Burnley were on their way back to the First Division in some style. At last, Jimmy Adamson had managed to fashion a team of class and skill, with a passing style that was almost textbook in its fluidity and precision. Blackpool were up there at the top as well and the stage was set for a classic game. Potts could not have failed to smile at the way things had worked out. Sadly, by the end of the game that smile had gone, although the part of him that was forever Burnley might not have been too unhappy.

As is often the way of things, a game that had promised so much was a fiasco as the second half turned into a battle with four bookings and two dismissals, both from Blackpool. This must have been the saddest thing for Potts to watch as the bad-tempered affair went from bad to worse. Burnley took the lead in the ninth minute through Frank Casper; Billy Rafferty headed the equaliser but Casper scored the winner, lobbing the ball into an empty net. It was a game and a result with lasting significance. Burnley added the points to their promotion total. For Blackpool it was two more points lost as promotion hopes faded.

Three consecutive wins in March brought hopes alive again but a very poor away record undermined everything. The local derby against Preston resulted in a home win for Blackpool, salvaging some pride. But even after just half a season in the job there were already calls for Potts' head from some supporters at the final home game in front of the season's lowest attendance. To make matters worse, former manager Stokoe took Sunderland to the most improbable of FA Cup final wins over Leeds United. With yet more irony Blackpool lost the very last game of the season 1-0 at Sunderland.

Blackpool had also competed in the infamous Anglo-Italian Cup. It was a tournament in which football became secondary in several games as the English and the Italian teams kicked lumps out of each other. But Blackpool did well and it gave Potts particular pleasure. They won their four games against Torino, Como, Bologna and Roma but although they achieved maximum points, Blackpool missed winning their group and playing in the final by goal difference. They were second to Newcastle.

Burnley and QPR took the promotion places with Blackpool seventh on 46 points, having been almost level pegging in December. A section of Blackpool supporters were far from happy.

A full season in charge, though, was seen as the test and Potts was ebullient at the beginning of season 1973/74.

"I have no illusions. I know that I am expected to take this famous club back where it belongs: the First Division. I don't need reminding that when I was at Burnley one of our biggest gates was when we were visited by Blackpool in the Matthews–Mortensen era. This has to be my target. Nor can I have any complaints about the team I inherited. When I took over last Christmas Blackpool were third in the table."

After Blackpool lost the Christmas game at home to Burnley they didn't lose another home game. Most of the players were still at Bloomfield Road. "But," added Potts, "while the foundation of a good defence is essential,

I believe in the old adage that goals win matches. The tremendous heading power up front provided by Wyn Davies is most welcome."

Another close season signing was Paul Hart, a tall centre half from Stockport County. Potts demonstrated again his eye for a class player as Hart went on to have a long and distinguished career.

"But I don't think I am satisfied or complacent. In soccer one is always on the lookout for good players. So far as Blackpool are concerned I shall be looking to skill to produce results. What spectators want is good entertaining football. This we are trying to give them, and the three up and three down ruling will help keep interest alive at top and bottom. We can't all win prizes but we can entertain."

Potts was a great admirer of Alan Suddick, a player who was doing banana-kicks long before David Beckham. He told Bill Elliott, of the *Daily Express*: "Alan did everything I asked of him last season. I don't think there is a finer sight in football than to see a player like Alan really on song. I shall again look to him for midfield generalship. We have Wyn Davies, Keith Dyson, Billy Rafferty and Mickey Burns. Alan Ainscow is developing into a very exciting player. I have bought with the future in mind. We have some excellent youth prospects already... The future of Blackpool is in safe hands.

"We plan to make the top three come May next year," said Harry with bravado.

Glyn James, in his fifteenth season as a Blackpool player, paid tribute to Potts, telling Elliott: "Harry Potts pushes people but he does it in a nice way, a way in which people respond. He is a gentleman and there are not many of those about in football. I like Harry a lot. The players respect him and he has this tremendous knack of bringing out the best in young players. I presume this is a talent he has kept from his days in charge at Burnley."

In the same article Potts responded: "Some managers want to be gods. They want to be dogmatic and they forget that it's the players who count. I try never to lose sight of that fact and that is why I like to think we are a happy family here."

In the town of Blackpool itself the old was being replaced by the new as demolition gangs got to work on the oldest parts of the amusement areas along the Golden Mile. There was great hope that the football club would be transformed as well.

"I feel excited for the future of this club. If we get promotion (touch wood) then I know there is a team here capable of making an impact on Division One."

Before the new season began, however, Potts gave the Blackpool crowd a good demonstration of his famous temper. In a pre-season friendly against Manchester City he went berserk with Rodney Marsh, twice rushing onto the pitch to berate both Marsh and referee Peter Porthouse after Marsh had scythed down Alan Ainscow during an anything but friendly 0-0 draw. City's Mike Summerbee and Blackpool's Bill Bentley acted as peacemakers and placated Potts. "Why does a great player like Rodney Marsh have to resort to this?" Potts demanded to know as he was pulled off the pitch red-faced with rage.

In spite of a defeat in the first game of the season at home to West Brom, Harry Potts very nearly did make the top three with Blackpool in his first full season in charge. Supporters in the early stages of the season were not pleased. After nine games Blackpool had accumulated just nine points and a section of the supporters were already baying for the manager's blood. The *West Lancashire Evening Gazette* was scathing about Blackpool's moaning supporters and pointed to injuries, missed chances galore, and the absence of key players in various games.

The slow start to the season was boosted by a run of five consecutive wins in October and November, taking them from fifth from the bottom to fifth from the top in the space of five weeks.

"I always say to the team before they go out – go out and enjoy yourselves," Harry told John Morrell of the *Lancashire Evening Post*.

Harry obviously enjoyed himself, too, and must have had a wry chuckle when he was named Bell's Manager Of The Month for November and received a gallon bottle of whisky. Harry was virtually teetotal. The whisky was shared with his back room staff.

But, "What have we got to do to win back the crowds?" asked a rueful director as only slightly more than 7,000 spectators watched the fifth consecutive win against Swindon. Fans had cried for goals and fifteen came in just six games. Fans had called for youth. Youth had been given its chance. But only 6,535 fans watched them hammer five goals past Portsmouth.

By March, with Blackpool in fourth place, the word 'promotion' was being spoken, albeit quietly. Almost unnoticed, Potts' team had gently eased themselves into this promising position. That it had done so, said John Morrell in the *Evening Post,* was due to the quiet influence of Harry Potts, who told Morrell that football was about players and what they do during a game. "My job as manager is to set up a framework for success but to leave room for players to express themselves freely when they are out on the field. We never deliberately adopt defensive attitudes. These are dictated by the way a game goes. If you've got a defensive attitude you rarely win things."

Sadly, promotion was not achieved in 1973/74. Blackpool finished fifth, just two points behind third-placed Carlisle. Twelve games were lost and thirteen were drawn. Those missed chances galore in the early games cost them dear. The last game of the season at Sunderland was lost 2-1. Had that been won, Blackpool would have been promoted as their goal difference was better than Carlisle's. It was a heartbreaking end to the season. With just six minutes to go, Blackpool were leading 1-0 and heading towards Division One.

"We had the game sewn up," Potts recollected. "Our lads had done everything right in preparation and training, getting into the necessary mood for the big day. In the first half Alan Suddick executed one of his most brilliant moves leading to John Evanson shooting just wide. Before Sunderland had recovered, John next rattled their crossbar with a free kick."

Mickey Burns gave Blackpool the lead in the 50th minute but out of the blue, Sunderland equalised through Billy Hughes and then one minute from time he scored again to break Potts' heart. Just six more minutes and Potts would have become a Blackpool legend. Margaret had accompanied the Dickinsons to Sunderland to watch the game. She, too, experienced the heartache of being so close to success. On the way back they met with the team coach and they stopped for a meal together with Harry putting on a brave face in spite of the deep disappointment he felt.

Football is cruel and fans are fickle. During the next season fans would again be calling for Harry Potts' resignation.

CHAPTER TWELVE

AN INCURABLE OPTIMIST

AT THE ABC Theatre there was Larry Grayson or Rolf Harris. We went to see Mike and Bernie Winters often. At the Opera House there was Val Doonican or Max Bygraves. We used to get Sunday afternoon invitations to go to the ABC. At the Tower Circus there was the wonderful Charlie Cairoli and at the North Pier there was Ken Goodwin. Blackpool was such an exciting place, full of people in the summer, full of light and fun at Christmas and, of course, there were the world famous Blackpool Illuminations. Harry loved the occasion that he came back into his office at the club and found Freddie Starr waiting for him and enjoying a pot of tea from his mug. Harry didn't miss the chance to have a few laughs with him and took him to the showers and changing room to entertain the lads.

Occasionally we stayed overnight although the travelling backwards and forwards was never a problem unless the weather was really bad.

What deeply upset Harry, though, in his time at Bloomfield Road was the murder of a fan at the ground during a game against Bolton Wanderers. He was stabbed and it was just so shocking. Violence between rival gangs of fans was commonplace at matches in the '70s. I was sitting in my usual seat with the Chief Constable, Mr Parr just behind me. He came to most matches. We'd actually noticed some kind of disturbance but then an official came round to Mr Parr to tell him he was needed urgently. Before the message was completed, he was out of his seat, leaving us all wondering what was happening.

Our contacts with Burnley Football Club people were minimal although living in a small village the whispers and conversations reached our doorstep that things were not all that well within the club between Bob Lord and Jimmy Adamson.

It was during this time that Harry's father died and, of course, Harry was deeply upset. The players wore black armbands in the game against Sunderland that was also on *Match of the Day*. It was one of those truly nail-biting, gripping, exciting games. I went to all the Blackpool home games. Alice Paisley came to stay with Mam Potts for a while afterwards.

Another game I remember well was the cup tie between Blackpool and Burnley. We couldn't have had a better draw and how pleased I was when Blackpool beat Burnley. After the game the chairman, Mr Frank Dickinson came to the Ladies' Room and asked us to stay where we were. He reported that there was noise and trouble in and outside the Burnley dressing room with Jimmy Adamson unable to get in. We could all hear the chants outside the ground as well of "Adamson out, Adamson out..." It was obvious that things were far from well at Burnley Football Club.

Harry was never a person to gloat at other people's misfortunes, it just wasn't in his nature, but I think he felt a quiet sense of satisfaction after that result.

THE NEXT season, 1974/75, began poorly for Blackpool. There were only two wins in the first nine games. One of the defeats was at Chester in the League Cup. To a club struggling financially, the early exit from this competition was disastrous.

Potts must have felt a sense of déjà vu before the season started when star player and leading scorer Mickey Burns was sold to Sunderland for a fee said to be £166,000 in one newspaper and £180,000 in another. Financial losses the previous season had been heavy and the minimal increase in gate receipts had been wiped out by increases in players' wages. The wage bill was said to be in excess of £100,000. Travelling and training costs were more than £40,000. By today's standards these are trifling sums, but then they were crippling to a club like Blackpool.

Chairman Dickinson announced that total losses had been £86,576 and average attendances were down to 8,500. At the annual general meeting, supporters grumbled that promotion would never be achieved if the best players were sold. Dickinson countered by saying that the club had to sell. Harry Potts must have thought he was back at Turf Moor; he was well used to this kind of thing.

Blackpool captain Glyn James' comparison of Bob Stokoe and Harry Potts was a revealing one. "I had a lot of respect for Bob Stokoe but he was too rigid in his coaching methods. He allowed no room for expression like Harry Potts. Coaching is too rigid generally speaking – although I would not include Blackpool in that."

But James' kind comments regarding Potts were not echoed at director level. The new Tangerine Club would hopefully soon be up and running and bringing in new revenue to compensate for the fact that there would be no revenue from the FA Cup. Plymouth Argyle had disposed of Blackpool in the first round, resulting in more grumbles directed towards Potts. Stanley Parr, a director who had resigned the previous season, aimed a verbal broadside at the Blackpool chairman regarding his hopes that the Tangerine Club would increase revenue considerably.

"I hope you are right about this new club, Mr Chairman, because by God if you are not, your head is for the chopping block."

If this was not a happy club off the field, on it Harry Potts, ever the optimist, put on his cheerful face and from Scotland, where the club were on a pre-season tour, said that the aim this season would be to win promotion.

Tony Quested in his *Seasiders' Scene* column in the local newspaper praised Potts:

An Incurable Optimist

Harry Potts gets a strange gleam in his eye when he talks about the future of Blackpool Football Club. He predicts that Blackpool are on the verge of a brave new world where penny pinching gives way to economic stability and joy on the field will be unconfined. He is able to say there are exciting times ahead. Only an hour-long session with Harry Potts could persuade doubters that his words are not so many more pies in the sky. Harry Potts is an incurable optimist in an age of incorrigible pessimists. He hopes when others despair, plans when others surrender. And it is not difficult to catch his infectious zeal.

I have disagreed with his selection of various players or formation this season, as many supporters have, but when it comes to ideas to restore Blackpool from financial embarrassment to financial stability, his schemes are hard to challenge. Potts advocates the use of Bloomfield Road for any event that brings in cash but does not interfere with the playing side. He wants to see Blackpool try every conceivable and harmless money making scheme. And he will not rest until the Blackpool board see things his way. His ideas are infinitely sound. The feeling is the majority of directors will listen. His statement that if you are not prepared to take a bit of a risk you are going to be left behind reeks of commonsense.

Des McBain remembers his tidiness and correctness, plus a hands-on approach that meant that nothing was beneath him. In the summer as the grass at the ground was being cut, Harry would appear with a pair of long-handled shears and trim the edges of the pitch.

Things had to be just right. Cutting the lawns and the edges was also a garden job he did at home. But whereas Margaret liked curves and bends, Harry liked things in straight lines. On the occasion Margaret had a circular lawn she had to insist to Harry that it was only in the shape of a football.

At 53, Potts could have been regarded as one of the elder

statesmen of football managers. But he was still a tracksuit man although he would chuckle at the expression 'tracksuit manager'.

"It is an essential and major part of my job to get out there with the players. Also I like to keep myself fit. Passing your experience on to the players is what it is all about and you have to get involved to do that, not just stand on the touchline all the time. I find training with the players one of the most enjoyable aspects of my job. I don't get out with them every time, that's where a club's coaches come in. I always liked training as a player."

In these words to Tony Quested of the *West Lancashire Evening Gazette* are the core reasons why he was so unhappy at Burnley in his general manager role when the hands-on involvement was denied to him.

His influence at Bloomfield Road became more evident with the development of better training areas at a new, improved Squires Gate. His money raising ideas (he was a great supporter of the much-criticised Tangerine Club), youth development, and now the start of the work on improved facilities, showed the depth of his influence and involvement. He did not see Blackpool remaining as a sort of poor man's Burnley; he wanted to make it into, and saw the potential it had to become, another Burnley.

It was hoped that the Squires Gate development would be ready for the next season. If the council had no objections to the plans then it certainly would be. Blackpool had bought land from the council and planned to add changing rooms, a gym room, a bootroom and showers. Players would report directly to the new training area instead of being bussed to the old facilities from the ground. That, in itself, would save money. Potts was delighted with the plans and felt that he was laying good foundations at the club.

He genuinely felt that the tide was turning. This was a club with an illustrious past that had been in the doldrums for too long. In the corridors and offices old, yellowing, discoloured pictures showed the late Harry Johnston with the FA Cup surrounded by heroes like Stanley Matthews and Stan Mortensen. Other pictures showed yet more of the faded glories. Harry Potts was happy to admit that he saw parallels between Blackpool and Burnley and that he was trying to develop things along the same lines. Out of 35 players in the squad, 25 of them were under 21 years old. A quarter of them were local boys. The reserves had been third in the Central League. The glass-half-full side of Harry saw the transfer of Mickey Burns not as an opportunity for him to bemoan his luck at losing such a first-rate player, but as an opportunity for a good youngster to step into the breach. If the club had the right foundations then those youngsters would always be available.

Of course, he rued the last cruel result of the previous season but he saw promotion as being possible again in a division that was so very tight.

Harry's incurable optimism was, however, tested to the limit in August. For football the 1970s were a time of vicious antagonism and gang confrontations. It was probably the worst decade that football has ever experienced in terms of blatant hostility. It was a decade when the face of soccer support changed into something often quite dreadful in its aggression, brutality, vicious altercations and frequent bloodshed. The terraces were no longer a safe place to be. Every club had its gangs, some had several. Most were there not for the football but for the adrenalin rush that serious fighting brings. On many occasions it was more than just fighting, it was warfare. Aggression was endemic. These gangs brought mayhem and fear; many clubs lost support and income because law-abiding fans feared for their safety on the open terraces of unsegregated and badly supervised grounds.

It was inevitable that someday, at some ground, there would be a fatality. It happened at Bloomfield Road on August 24th 1974 when a 17-year-old fan, Kevin Olsson, was stabbed to death at the Kop end of the ground. The club was stunned.

Only days before there had been 135 arrests at Bristol City. There had been trouble on the terraces even at the pre-season friendly between Blackpool and Manchester

City. But the first ever soccer fan to be killed at a match was at Blackpool. It was so predictable. It was noted that it mirrored the violence and dissent on the football pitches up and down the land. On the pitch, the 1970s were a time of football thuggery and savagery when players in many games did their level best to cripple each other, while referees waved play on. The players, according to Burnley centre forward Paul Fletcher, who eventually signed for Blackpool, had a simple philosophy. If the referee didn't see it, then it wasn't a foul. The 1970s, even though it was a time of wonderful individuals and flair players, were not a good time for the game.

Experts blamed this widespread football hooliganism on the breakdown of whole rafts of social mores, the erosion of discipline in schools, the decline of the family, lack of parental control, violent television programmes, the lack of punishments to fit the crime, the disregard for authority and the absence of National Service which had instilled obedience into its conscripts.

Whatever the reasons, football grounds were no longer safe places to be, although chairman Frank Dickinson was adamant that the stabbing of the Blackpool supporter was not the fault of the football club. It could have happened anywhere, he said and he was probably right. Football grounds were simply the meeting places of groups who were determined to attack each other.

Kevin Olsson's death, near the tea bar at the back of the Kop, at the hands of a Bolton supporter who was reported to be just fourteen years old, would maybe make the authorities rumble into action, wrote the local papers. The authorities would shake their heads, make their pronouncements and outline their policies but it was all too late. Efforts at many grounds to keep fans apart were at best poor, at worst non-existent.

Sports Minister Denis Howell made his obligatory visit to the scene and he was quoted in the *Evening Gazette* as saying, "In fairness to Blackpool this incident could have happened anywhere and not necessarily on a football ground." But he did point out that Blackpool, like many other clubs, had failed to carry out recommendations to segregate fans. Kevin Olsson's father asked for arrangements to be made for him to speak to Howell. Howell did not have time.

"The louts today have no discipline," Harry Potts told John Roberts of the *Daily Express*. "It is tragic that this could happen. Jimmy Armfield, the Bolton manager, is as grieved as I am about this."

Just three days later Blackpool went to Leyton Orient and drew 0-0. It was a game in which goalkeeper John Burridge, one of the great characters of football, excelled. "We can build a very good season on performances like this," said Potts.

But by December too many draws and defeats made it clear that promotion was a distant possibility. Christmas in Blackpool meant waves crashing against the promenade and trams nearly blown over by the gales but it also meant full hotels and big crowds at all the shows. At the football ground, however, attendances continued to dwindle other than when there was a visit from Manchester United, now in the Second Division. A bumper crowd saw United win 3-0. At the beginning of December two consecutive home games resulted in a pitiful 4,922 people going to watch Blackpool beat Notts County 3-1 and then there were fewer than 7,000 to see Norwich City beaten 2-1. The two wins revived promotion hopes and on Boxing Day there was another win at home, against Oldham.

But it was all uphill. Over the preceding few seasons a procession of good players had been sold – Alan Ball, Emlyn Hughes, Gordon West, Tony Green, Tommy Hutchison, John Craven and then Mickey Burns. Yet, even minus his best player, Harry Potts still did his best to produce a team that would entertain.

He told Richard Bott of the *Sunday Express*: "Football is an entertainment. When a man has been working all week, he wants to be entertained. We can only bring the crowds back by giving them a positive successful side. We will not be defensive whatever happens." Injuries continued to bedevil him but he refused to complain even though as luck would have it, it was always his forwards who were on the injury list. The gifted Alan Suddick, frequently sidelined, was yet again unavailable. "You can bet though a lot of folk will leave their firesides when he returns in the New Year."

In January, when Plymouth Argyle knocked Blackpool out of the FA Cup, it did not stop a suggestion by one supporter to one of the local papers that Harry Potts be given a ten-year contract. Opinion, though, was mixed on his effectiveness. Some supporters were coming round to the view that Potts was slowly but steadily putting the club back on an even keel, working quietly away, seeking no publicity and most importantly putting a decent team together. Others thought that he was not the man to lead the club and that younger blood was needed.

But simultaneously, a former chairman of the club, Bill Cartmell, announced to the *Evening Gazette* that he was heading a group of influential shareholders with a plan to call for an extraordinary shareholders' meeting with a view to axing the entire board and overturning their decision to give Potts a new two-year contract. Cartmell added that he would make £155,000 immediately available for the purchase of a goalscorer – with the barbed rider that "players were more important than social clubs". The Tangerine Club had been quite controversial, with Cartmell and others regarding it as a white elephant that would not recoup its outlay. Now that it was built, Cartmell announced that his consortium would put more money into it to expand and enlarge it, so it would be far more viable. Overall, Cartmell was scathing in his criticisms but felt himself too old to be a new chairman. What was needed was a much younger board and if nothing was done the club would be finished in a few years. The Cartmell storm died down but it would resurface a year later.

Relief and a measure of joy came for Potts in February when a marvellous game in front of a bumper 16,000 crowd was televised on *Match of The Day*. Although the 1970s continued to be a torrid time on the terraces, the tragedy of the August stabbing was largely forgotten, except for the family of the unfortunate victim. But at last along came one of those wonderful games that football is all about. The match with Sunderland demonstrated all that was best about football. It was an absolute humdinger, crowned by one of the best goals ever seen and captured perfectly by the BBC camera angle. Potts admitted that the visit of Sunderland made him think again of the final game of the previous season.

The Sunderland game had everything: goals, thrills, drama, excitement, controlled competitiveness and a big crowd to add the vital ingredients of passion and atmosphere. By half-time, Blackpool had brought a face as black as thunder to Bob Stokoe as they swept into a two-goal lead, one of them scored by Wyn Davies, who had been the subject of more Cartmell criticism. After a blasting from Stokoe at half-time, Sunderland came back to equalise. Then came what many thought to be the turning point of the game when John Burridge saved a Sunderland penalty. Millions of viewers saw a steward behind the goal doing his impersonation of a hyperactive ape to unsettle the Sunderland penalty taker.

Billy Hughes missed the kick. Potts thought justice was done and that it should never have been a penalty in the first place. The steward, Bert Taylor, now part of Bloomfield folklore, said, "I was just trying to tell the referee I thought he had made a poor decision."

And then in the dying seconds came one of the goals of the decade. Paul Hart found Mick Walsh with a fine clearance out of defence. Walsh chested it down and made ground down the right. He then cut inside two defenders before unleashing a shot from 30 yards that curled round Jim Montgomery's diving body, hit the inside of the post and then the back of the net. The ground erupted. Potts went wild. Stokoe was acid in his put-down: "They were never as lucky as that when I was here."

Blackpool were back in the promotion race and another letter to the local paper praised Potts for putting together a talented and youthful squad, of whom Mick Walsh, scorer of that extraordinary goal, was but one.

In late February, Bill Fryer, that eminent and perceptive *Daily Express* reporter, put his spotlight on Blackpool. In his interview with chairman Dickinson it was clear that Blackpool policy was to allow Potts to develop youth and large sums would not be spent on one player. Surely it was far better to invest the money in improving facilities so that men would bring their wives and swell attendances, said Dickinson. Surely it was far better to develop a social club that would tap in to the thousands of annual visitors to Blackpool every year. But the priority was the youth policy, especially as this had been a season bedevilled with injuries to key players. And the man for the youth policy was Harry Potts. Currently Potts was playing a team that contained more young players than at any other time in Blackpool's history. The future was bright.

A 3-0 victory over Southampton had their manager Lawrie McMenemy purring with praise for his opponents. After seeing Blackpool tear his side to pieces he told Tony Quested: "If Blackpool can play football as good as this despite all their injury problems and in front of so few people they deserve to go up."

Blackpool played some glorious stuff to record their seventh consecutive home win and a run of seven games undefeated. In sixth place, Potts admitted, when pressed, that promotion was still a possibility. They were still in touch with the leaders.

But that was as good as it got. From that particular game on March 1st until the end of the season there was just one more win. Four consecutive draws followed. The season ended with three consecutive defeats. Meanwhile, that bone of contention the 'Tangerine Club' was still not completed. August was the target to cash in on the influx of summer visitors. The club had borrowed money from the brewery to fund it but if the wining and dining and nightclub facilities were successful it would supposedly generate £20,000 a year.

Blackpool's final position was seventh, creditable; but eight points behind the third promotion place. Many fans wrote off the season as a failure. But, in truth, it had been a season when key players had been badly missed and the young reserves who had come in had done a great job keeping the club in contention. Tony Quested saw it as the season Harry Potts' reserves nearly won promotion to Division One. He was adamant that people could be proud of the club and its efforts. Bill Cartmell, however, was still hovering in the background. Potts had one season left as manager.

When Glyn James announced his retirement on July 15th 1975 he paid another tribute to Harry Potts. "I have played under seven managers and Harry Potts is, with Harry Johnston, the most genuine man I have ever met."

But for Potts the perennial problems remained – the acute shortage of cash and the acute shortage of spectators. Everyone at the club was anxious to chip away at the block of debts but with current income it was almost a hopeless scenario. Hopes were pinned once more on the social club but ex-director Stan Parr again pointed to it as a folly and said that chairman Dickinson's head would be for the chopping block if it did not make money. Far better to have spent the money it cost on a centre forward was his view. Behind the scenes all was far from well, with another director hitting out at the way some board members had bought shares in Blackpool Football Club. Accusations flew back and forth with demands for an investigation by the Inland Revenue.

The one ray of light, however, was that Alan Suddick was fit for the new campaign. But no new players had been signed and leading scorer Micky Walsh was placed on the transfer list at his own request while Wyn Davies had been freed in the summer. Walsh announced he had no grievances against Potts; he simply wanted a wage upon which he could live comfortably. The season began with Potts admitting there was no cash for players; all income had to help to offset the club's debts.

The gloom at Bloomfield Road was in sharp contrast to the glitz on offer in the resort elsewhere. Freddie Starr, The Bachelors, Rod Hull and Emu were at the Opera House, Mike and Bernie Winters at the ABC. Sid James was at The Winter Gardens. There were clubs, pubs and shows galore along at each of the piers, plus a dozen cinemas. The Tangerine Club at the football club had a lot to compete with. The attendance at the first home game of the season against Leyton Orient was less than 7,000. Letters flooded the local paper with the same question. Why hadn't the money for the Tangerine Club been spent on two decent players? But the club opened in September with Matt Busby as one of the guests.

The season limped along in fits and starts but came alive with the FA Cup draw when the fates decreed that Blackpool would be at home to Burnley of all clubs. All was not well at Turf Moor and there were rumours of difficulties and differences between Bob Lord and Jimmy Adamson. A full house was in prospect at Bloomfield Road and, except for a plum tie against a really big Division One club like Liverpool, Blackpool and Harry Potts could not have wished for better. The significance of the game was not lost on the national papers. It was Potts versus Adamson. It was a reunion with Bob Lord, it was a local derby, and it was anybody's game. It was even an opportunity for John Roberts in the *Daily Express* to dig out an old story about Harry Potts' marriage to Margaret. Alan Brown had not only carried their luggage to the train at Preston, he then disappeared into a compartment. "Next thing," recalled Harry, "a chap came out head first – and Alan beckoned us into our bridal carriage! Alan was a pretty formidable centre half in those days".

Burnley were followed by 9,000 in a total of 20,573 and Potts could not have wished for a better result with a 1-0 win. At Turf Moor, the game and its repercussions are still talked about thirty years later. The personal triumph for Potts was a disaster for Jimmy Adamson, who left Turf Moor just days later. Onlt twelve months earlier Burnley had exited the FA Cup in the third round at the hands of non-league Wimbledon. Now it was Second Division Blackpool who turfed them out. It was a game of argument and controversy as Blackpool scraped through on the strength of a Bill Bentley headed goal in the 56th minute.

Prior to this, Burnley striker Ray Hankin had been sent

off and it was just about the last straw for they were already missing four regular first-teamers. Yet again Suddick was missing for Blackpool and a game full of needle and blood-and-thunder tackles ended with Burnley accusations that Blackpool had constantly conned the referee. "They must be joking," Blackpool coach Len Graham told Tony Quested. "Look at the cuts and bruises on our players' legs."

Blackpool rode their luck and could easily have been beaten had Burnley, with players like Keith Newton, Willie Morgan, Mike Summerbee and Brian Flynn on show, taken their chances. Even at the end, Burnley looked to have earned the draw when Waldron headed what seemed to be a perfectly good equaliser. The referee saw an infringement that few others saw and the goal was disallowed.

Controversy continued after the game. Potts dismissed the claims that Blackpool had been over-physical. "It is not a game for namby-pambies. Fans enjoy the physical side of the game. The important thing was our great display. We had twelve heroes out there."

But in the Burnley dressing room there were reports of violent rows, scuffles, flailing arms, bitter arguments and one player being restrained by assistant manager Joe Brown. Manager Adamson was locked out while all this was going on, although it was unclear if this was accidental or deliberate.

Perhaps the happiest person of all, though, was secretary Des McBain who reported a clear £4,500 profit on the game and club record gate receipts. As a gloomy and dejected Burnley coach eventually pulled away from Bloomfield Road, the smiles of joy on Blackpool faces would have lit the Illuminations. As a person, Potts would never have been a man to gloat; in fact from the part of him that was still Burnley, he would have felt a tinge of sympathy.

McBain recalls that Harry always praised Bob Lord and never knocked Burnley Football Club. He never commented on whatever had happened at Turf Moor between him, Lord and Adamson. But McBain certainly remembers that this was a game he wanted to win and he wanted to beat

Jimmy Adamson. Here was a chance to show he was not finished as a manager, and could beat the club he still loved and admired.

Nobody could have blamed him if he had felt a sense of deep satisfaction. *Daily Express* reporter Bill Elliot described Potts after the game.

"Former Burnley boss Harry Potts had the air of a man who had just discovered the secret elixir of life after his Blackpool side had won 1-0. His beaming smile produced an unexpected Blackpool Illuminations but his repeated invitation to join him for a celebration drink had to be graciously declined because of events in and around the Burnley dressing room. But Potts' joy was understandable. In the match programme he welcomed 'with great pleasure' his old club to Bloomfield Road and though that greeting was clearly meant, nothing in life is sweeter than beating your best friend. The fact that the match did not live up to its initial promise was not going to stop Potts enjoying every moment of what for him at least was a memorable victory."

'Cup Of Joy Revives Blackpool' was Tony Quested's headline in the *Gazette*. He went on to report how the win had galvanised the club and changed the whole face of it. Never before had the club officials been so keyed up for a game and he described it as a personal triumph for Potts.

On the Monday, Adamson and Bob Lord parted company. The relationship between them had never been comfortable. On one occasion, Adamson had ordered Lord from the dressing room after a game at Liverpool and selling a player a year was something with which Adamson never really came to terms.

For Blackpool, however, the cup triumph was short-lived. Southampton knocked them out at The Dell in the next round. League form, in spite of a decent home record, was not good enough to bring the club anything better than tenth place with a very ordinary 14 wins, 14 draws and 14 defeats. Harry Potts' reasons, not to be confused with excuses, were the same as ever. This was yet another season ravaged by injuries. At the time of the Southampton game he was without six players, including the key figure of Alan Suddick.

"There's an outcry when a big-city club loses two or three players with injury," he said, "but we have had a completely fit squad for only two weeks this season."

In response to a fan's question at a club forum as to why there were so many cartilage injuries at the club, he blamed the modern football boot for the glut of injuries. He claimed that the one basic type of boot then being manufactured gave little support to joints. Players throughout the country were suffering more and more cartilage, Achilles tendon, ankle and muscle injuries. Modern boots favoured speed. "Players are faster now but they get less protection for the vital joints from the modern boots." In view of the problems encountered by David Beckham, Michael Owen and Wayne Rooney among others, Potts' words echo down the years.

February brought more problems and disquiet. "Now is the winter of our discontent", wrote Tony Quested and cited the famous phrase as a good summary of the grumbling. Shareholders were asking ominously for the date of the next AGM. A group of supporters started a "Potts Must Go" campaign. Car stickers with the slogan appeared around Blackpool. "It would take a cover-up the size of Watergate to disguise the fact that all is not well," wrote Quested.

In March, the writing was on the wall for Potts as chairman Frank Dickinson revealed, "If anyone can put money in they can have my chair anytime." Harry Potts sparked a mini-revival by signing Malcolm Smith on loan from Middlesbrough but he returned after scoring six times in eight matches because Blackpool could not raise enough money to buy him. In response, ex-chairman Cartmell announced he was ready to return as chairman for a maximum period of two years in which he would put £250,000 into the club to pay off all the debts and start buying players. His condition was simple. He wanted the mass resignation of the entire board. "I want Blackpool in

Division One in two years," he said, adding that he would pay off Harry Potts' contract.

By the end of the month, the directors had agreed to resign en masse as long as Cartmell came up with the money within a few days. Margaret Potts spoke for her husband to the local paper. "Harry knew this takeover was in the offing. He's very happy at Blackpool where he has a good job building up the club development and youth work."

Amazingly, there was talk in the *Daily Mirror* and *Daily Express* of Potts being succeeded by Jimmy Adamson. When Adamson cancelled a proposed trip to Rotterdam to continue his discussions with Sparta, speculation was fuelled further.

Blackpool vice-chairman Derek Lewin reiterated that the board would indeed resign if Cartmell's offer of an immediate £90,000 and the rest later materialised by the next week. He said, "Against the background of this cash injection, and Mr Cartmell's emphasis that the new board would have no necessity to sell players or other assets, the present board feel that is in the best interests of the club and the loyal supporters."

On May 5th, arrangements for the afternoon takeover were set. "The programme", said Bill Cartmell, "is for me to go into the Bloomfield Road boardroom with my five colleagues, pay out the retiring directors and then take command of the club from that moment onwards. There is a possibility a new manager will be appointed today but I am not saying anything until I have talked to Mr Potts regarding his contract with Blackpool. Allan Brown is the chap I would like the position to be offered to. He would certainly be my number one choice."

Des McBain explained that Potts arrived for work as usual and was summoned to see Cartmell. The then Blackpool secretary was present as Potts was dismissed.

"And leave the keys for the car," instructed Cartmell.

"But how will I get home?" asked Harry, not expecting that this would be the day for his dismissal.

"There are trains aren't there?" replied Cartmell curtly.

Such is football, and McBain does not remember how Harry got home.

On May 6th, cock-a-hoop with his takeover, Bill Cartmell was in official control of Blackpool Football Club. "This place is in a chaotic state," he immediately pronounced. "This club has been going downhill with no brakes," announced Stanley Parr, who was to be a director.

Now ex-manager, Potts went into his office to clear his desk. "He has been paid up for the unexpired period of his contract which runs until September 30th but he is sacked from today," added Parr.

Ever the gentleman, Potts replied, "I shall follow the players' careers with interest. I wish Allan Brown every success and I hope I might be able to offer some other club the benefit of my long football experience in some capacity."

In a final tribute to Harry Potts, Tony Quested described him as a man of dignity as Potts outlined his thoughts in Quested's column. Football remained the greatest game in the world, he said, and he would like to stay in the game in some capacity. He had a lot to offer and regarded his dismissal as just one of the misfortunes of the game. His parting message to the players was to be as dedicated as possible and to give 100%. Then he allowed himself a brief reference to the horrendous injuries the club had suffered. "These last two seasons have been the two most frustrating years of my life with injuries but my enthusiasm is the same as when I was a boy."

Potts departed, head held high and, above all, with his dignity and pride intact.

Cartmell had stated he would give himself two years to see Blackpool back in Division One. Unfortunately things went the other way and they would be in Division Three two seasons later. For Potts the next job would come quickly and from an unexpected if familiar source.

CHAPTER THIRTEEN
BACK HOME AGAIN

WHEN HARRY was dismissed at Blackpool, he certainly wasn't as upset as when he left Burnley in 1972, or when he was moved from manager to general manager two years prior to that. That change made in 1970 broke his heart. But, towards the end at Blackpool, he could see what was happening and even at the beginning of his time there he knew that not all the directors were in favour of his appointment. The worries when he left Blackpool were again financial with a concern that suddenly there was no regular income. How would we run a car, the house and a mortgage? And we still had a responsibility for our mothers. Harry was always a worrier and nothing ever changed that.

So I was so pleased for him when Joe Brown, the new Burnley manager, asked Harry to come back as Burnley's chief scout. Dave Blakey had left and Harry was asked to replace him. Joe was another good honest man, full of kindness and respect for other people. It was Harry who had first appointed Joe at the club all those years ago and he and his wife Connie were our good friends. Things were not going well, though, at the club and there were difficult times when Harry returned in his new job. Good players had been sold. Some of the others were unhappy. The atmosphere at the club, after Blackpool had knocked them out of the cup, was terrible. I saw the newspapers and heard things and the team weren't doing well.

Bob Lord was becoming increasingly unpopular; well, he'd never been popular, perhaps less respected would be a better way to put it, and people in the town were getting restless with him. There had been particular anger when Martin Dobson was sold at a time when they were doing well. But, as ever, money was the inevitable problem. Here we were in this small-town and fewer and fewer people were watching Burnley. The club seemed to have less and less money and I heard that Dave Blakey had left because his scouting system was one of the economy measures. And yet finding young players from school or at a young age up and down the country was the way in which Burnley survived, so it was just a vicious circle. The great days were really over and a thing of the past, but that was another problem: there were still so many people who remembered them and didn't like to see what was happening at the club now. They'd recently had a couple of good years with Jimmy Adamson but all that had ended badly.

So Harry just jumped at the chance to go back as chief scout. He was delighted and I was so pleased for him. It was Joe's idea to bring him back and clearly Bob Lord gave it the OK. But the only contact between Bob and Harry was at the club. The days of Harry going up to Bob's house for long talks, and dodging the dogs, were long gone.

Wherever we went to watch a game (I often went with him), he would ring up and let them know he was coming and inevitably we would be asked to sit in the directors' box. Wherever we went he was made so welcome, it was obvious he was so well respected. I thought it was so lovely the way he was treated. In this new scouting job there was never any atmosphere or tension, he just enjoyed the matches, watching players, spotting talent and I realised sitting by him just how involved he was and how good he was. As general manager he knew he hadn't really been wanted at the club, but this was different. He and Joe were good friends. He was so relaxed and on the way home we'd stop somewhere for a meal – this was in the days of Berni Inns – he loved his steak and chips.

At Manchester United, Matt Busby always greeted him like an old friend. Mrs Busby would take me to her table in the hospitality room while Harry chatted to the men. There was no segregation there. At Liverpool I was always able to chat to Jessie Paisley. I had always exchanged Christmas cards with her because her husband and Harry were childhood friends. Bob's Aunt Alice lived next door to Harry in Hetton.

They were known as 'The Likely Lads' after the TV series due to their connection with the north-east. But I'd never met Jessie. One year Harry had mixed up the Christmas cards; some got two, some got none. I wrote to Jessie to explain and found out that Bob had Alzheimer's. I was able to tell Jessie of some of the experiences she might have and we are still firm friends.

One place I particularly remember was Chester. The welcome we got was just so wonderful and I can remember Harry saying to them that for a small club their hospitality was marvellous. In we went and it was a case of "Hello Harry" as if he'd been a regular visitor all his life.

Another visit was to Huddersfield and that was a time when he had his licence endorsed and I was driving him. On the way home, the fog came down and I have never been so petrified driving in my life. But Harry kept so calm and just said, "Stick behind this lorry, keep your distance, and you can see all his lights and don't try to overtake him, just keep nice and slow." Harry had lost his licence; he was always speeding in the same place, a stretch of road in between Gawthorpe and the Bishop's Palace. He was caught there three times and it was always on a Friday when he was racing back from Gawthorpe to Turf Moor for a press meeting, or over to his mother's house.

I always loved these trips and visits with him when he was scouting and I know he did. There was never any worry or anxiety about the result of a game. It was good to have time together as well; for years I had seen so little of him and I can truly say I was never bored by any football match.

Later into the 1980s, he began to get apprehensive about driving and he used to ask either Alan Reid or John Cavanagh, the headmaster of the local school, to drive him and one funny thing at that time was a trip he made to Manchester City. It was a bit rough round there at that time and out came all these little boys hanging round who said, "We'll look after your car mister." So he got some coins out and handed them over with a smile, and told me if he didn't, he'd come back and find the windscreen wipers missing… or worse.

And then, after not very long in the job, with results going badly, Joe left and Harry was offered the manager's job again. My own reaction was quite restrained. I can't say I was excited, nor can I say I was opposed to it, but I could well remember how he had been treated before and how distressed he had been. My attitude was one of, well so be it; if it's what he wants and it's a second chance, then I'll support him. In hindsight, perhaps deep down, I might have felt I'd had enough of football and was ready for a life without it.

Harry was sorry for Joe of course and there was no animosity between them at all; they were close friends but it's always sad when something like this happens. This is football and the way it works, was the general feeling. Harry was surprised but pleased to be asked to take over again. He certainly didn't expect it. I imagine Bob Lord felt comfortable with him around again and felt he could trust him. I thought back again to the time along Whins Lane when I was out walking and Bob had pulled up and stopped his car and said he'd made a mistake. I can only assume he would have turned the clock back there and then and had Harry back. I think towards the end, the relationship between Bob Lord and Jimmy Adamson was not a good one. But anyway, Joe and Harry continued their friendship, and when Harry was ill, Joe and Connie visited him both at home and in the nursing home. They were such good people and still are.

So back he went and it was as if he had been given a new lease of life. It was the old story: some players were pleased and some weren't. You can't suit all the people all the time. One or two of them passed comments and said Harry helped them get their confidence back and that's half the secret of football, just being confident, because they'd had such a bad run of not winning and then lo and behold in Harry's first game they won. But it's not as if the new manager is a magician, it's just the way things work out, and that's how things happen in football, quite by chance.

The welcome I got when I went back was mixed. Several of the ladies were pleased to see me, but there was the odd exception. Even so, it was like being back home. When I went back there as the wife of the chief scout, I saw how things had changed with the new rooms in the new stand. Bob Lord had received a lot of criticism for building another new stand but really the old one was dangerously unsafe. And now there were proper kitchens and meals instead of just light refreshments. The catering and kitchens were quite amazing. It had all been made very modern but still even in 1977 the 'ladies only room' was there and it caused another funny thing to happen when I was in there one day.

I had arrived for the game in good time and a visiting couple came in. They were obviously from the away team, so I took the lady into the ladies' room and made her welcome and chatted away like I always used to do. After the game, the gentleman came in to find his wife; he was either the chairman or a director of the team we had played. Perhaps he didn't realise this was the ladies only room, but he walked over to the bar to order a drink and Hilda Lord turned to him and said "Trousers are not allowed in here." So he turned to Hilda and said very nicely, "Well, I'll come in my frock next time."

There was another story about the ladies' room. My daughter Linda and husband Philip had brought baby James down to the ground. He was only a few months old, and he was in his little claret and blue bootees. So Linda and Philip and baby James went just inside the ladies' room, to collect their daughter Deborah who was with me, and they also thought they'd let Hilda see baby James because Hilda was Linda's godmother. But Hilda saw Philip's trousers and they were ordered out. So since then we have always said that this was the first time James was thrown out of Burnley Football Club. The second was when he was trying to make the grade as a player and Adrian Heath finished him. Life is funny sometimes.

It was during this time he did something else which still makes me smile. Our son Ken, then in his teens, played for our local village team. True to form, Harry, looking after the younger players, brought a very small and very young Brian Flynn home one Sunday afternoon. At that time Brian would have been either on trial or just signed on as an apprentice. Harry brought him home so that he could have a game with Ken's team. The trouble was he had no boots and we couldn't find any small enough. I don't know how they solved it, but he played. Brian then went on to have a wonderful career playing for Burnley, Leeds and Wales.

IN 1976, with Adamson replaced by assistant Joe Brown, Bob Lord continued to stress that the future of Burnley FC would always depend on its youth policy. Lord emphasised yet again that the club could not afford to go out and buy players and that the scouting system was more important than it had ever been. Ironically, the scouting system was then reorganised and nine part-time scouts axed. Having seen the system he had built up decimated, chief scout Dave Blakey announced that he was no longer happy and left. As a player he was one of that rare breed who had played more than 600 games for just one club, Chesterfield. It was Blakey's network which had uncovered players like Ray Hankin, Brian Flynn and Leighton James. Though Burnley wanted him to stay, Blakey was understandably unhappy.

"The position of chief scout is an important one," said Bob Lord. "The new appointment will be given our utmost attention. It may happen that the right man will come along soon and we will replace Mr Blakey quickly."

Lord and Brown lost no time at all in replacing Blakey who had left only four days earlier. They turned to Harry Potts and Potts' role was specifically related to the search for new talent. At the same time as his friend Bill Nicholson rejoined Spurs as an 'adviser' a delighted Potts returned to Burnley. "My heart has always been at Burnley. This is a day of great nostalgia for me. In a way it's a new challenge because although I have been manager of Burnley and Blackpool in the past, this will mean specialising in the recruitment of young players."

In January 2006 an advert was placed in broadsheet newspapers advertising the post of chief scout at Bolton Wanderers FC. It makes interesting reading.

Comprehensive knowledge base of UEFA registered leagues and sufficient understanding of other

*established and developing leagues within FIFA:
Experience of working alongside a professional
coaching and management team in the identification
of elite players: Experience of working in an elite
scouting network within a professional football
club: Strong IT knowledge and an understanding of
databases.*

Harry took up his new post, the days of elite players at
Burnley long gone, without so much as a mobile phone
or a fax machine. He had a telephone list, his little black
notebooks and a pen. Mention of IT and databases would
have had him scratching his head.

At Gawthorpe, on his first visit after an absence of four
years, Potts was visibly beaming with delight as he stood
with Bob Lord for pictures. Joe Brown, too, was pleased.
Potts was a man he admired and respected enormously.

Harry Potts did not interfere in any way with the
management side at the club during his term as chief scout.
He did not give unwanted advice and nor was he asked.
Joe Brown wanted to be his own man and Potts, being the
man he was, would never have dreamed of giving advice
that was unasked for.

Sadly, through no fault of his own, results just did not
work out for Joe Brown. The rot and malaise was too
far entrenched. In the season he took over from Jimmy
Adamson, the slide continued and on April 24th Coventry
City applied the final relegation blow, beating Burnley 3-1
at Turf Moor. Burnley were duly relegated from Division
One, then the equivalent of the Premiership, in 21st
position.

One more small-town club had finally lost the battle to
remain competitive with the city clubs. They have never
regained that eminence. The reason lay quite simply in the
fact that recruits to the club's youth training schemes just
did not match the levels, in either numbers or quality, of
the young lads who came to Burnley in the late '50s and
then the '60s. Since then, the names of the players who
went through the Gawthorpe system, who just were not

good enough and never quite made it, can be sprinkled like confetti. In the 1970s, there was an occasional bright star like Flynn, James and Hankin. Then there was a brief, small, last harvest in the early 1980s – Laws, Overson, Phelan and Trevor Steven, but even they, except possibly Steven, were nothing like the truly outstanding players of the earlier decades.

Joe Brown had just another half-season in 1976/77 with Burnley in Division Two. But a run of fourteen games without a win, from November through until February, was too much for Bob Lord who decided a new face was necessary. Brown left in an amicable and gentlemanly manner, "relieved of his duties" being the explanation, because of the club's precarious position. Brown accepted his fate as being the inevitable consequence of the poor run and as part of the hazards of life as a football manager.

It wasn't so much a new face, however, to whom Lord turned; it was an old and trusted face, that of Harry Potts. The wheel had come full circle. As Brown left and the team was in crisis so was the Lucas Aerospace factory, a vital employer in the town, where 280 workers were declared surplus. Both club and town were at a low ebb.

Brown was asked if he wanted to stay on in another capacity. He replied that he would prefer to leave because he did not want to be an embarrassment to the new manager. Perhaps he was thinking back to the time when Harry Potts had stayed on in 1970 under Jimmy Adamson.

Harry Potts told Bill Elliott, of the *Daily Express*: "I see no problem in starting over again at Burnley even though I obviously had no idea I would end up here as boss again."

He told Keith McNee of the *Burnley Express*: "I don't think 56 is too old to be a manager. I feel fitter than ever" This club means more to me than Liverpool does to Bill Shankly."

For the *Burnley Express* it was an opportunity to remind the Burnley public how Harry Potts had been one of the first and best players to perfect the art of diving for penalties. On a return to Burnley when playing for

Everton, he had both amused and outraged the Burnley fans by winning one penalty when he dived at least three feet from the area.

Jimmy McIlroy still smiles at the memory of how Harry Potts could win free kicks and penalties. "He was able to fall over a player's leg and win the free kick and he was so good at rolling the last three feet into the penalty box. There was one occasion when I won a penalty against Sheffield Wednesday by 'diving' over a defender's leg. As I was on the ground I could see from the corner of my eye that Harry was dancing up and down on the touchline, smiling, arms outstretched, fully appreciating my 'dive'. Harry Catterick, however, was incensed."

"Our immediate aim is to keep Burnley in the Second Division," said Potts. (This was a far cry from the days when the immediate aim had been to keep Burnley in the First Division.) "Given maximum effort, then if we get a few breaks as well, we could be approaching a turning point in the club's fortunes." In the short term fortunes did turn. In the long term his optimism was misplaced.

It was clear that crisis time had finally caught up with Bob Lord's Burnley three months before Potts' return as manager. "You could say we are on the verge of bankruptcy," announced the grand old man of football. Things were so desperate at that point that a fan, Danny Carr, who had won £507,000 on the football pools, offered to pay the transfer fee of £20,000 to enable the club to buy the on-loan Malcolm Smith, a player Potts had also tried to sign for Blackpool. Bob Lord refused the offer, keeping to his policy of keeping fans at arm's length.

When Potts assumed control again in 1976/77, the club were in 21st place in Division Two, the lowest point ever in the club's history, and other clubs were circling the best player, Brian Flynn, like vultures. Harry Potts' programme notes announced he intended to take a positive approach. It was still a great club. "Who knows what we can achieve?" he asked. The Houdini act began immediately when a run of fourteen winless games ended with a 2-0 win at home to Carlisle, moving Burnley away from the bottom two places. Unfortunately a leaky defence let in nine goals in the next two games. Then came three wins from the next four games and then three draws.

In March in his programme notes for the Sheffield United game, a 1-0 win in front of just over 10,600 spectators, Potts did something extremely rare when he openly criticised another manager. Attempts had been made by Sunderland to unsettle inspirational captain Peter Noble and the dynamic Brian Flynn.

"What really does dismay me, however, is some of the off-the-field happenings in this game. I want to place on record the fact that I totally resent it when the manager of another Football League club makes 'transfer' references to two of our players, in a manner which creates an unfair situation. In my opinion this sort of thing is wrong. Therefore I am pleased to be able to officially inform the many very loyal supporters of this club that despite what has wrongly been said by one Football League club manager, Peter Noble and Brian Flynn will be remaining as Burnley players."

The Sunderland manager was Jimmy Adamson; it was a very specific attack on him.

The move to safety continued. Two of the last three games were wins. An away win at Cardiff brought them almost home and dry and it was an excellent performance that could have been far more than just 1-0. Tony Morley and Terry Cochrane, with superb wing play, tore apart Cardiff. Cochrane, another crowd favourite, would be sold later.

"It's not over yet," said Harry Potts in the *Burnley Express*. "If things go against us it could be that everything might still be decided on the last Saturday of the season." But he was delighted with the result. "I can't remember us playing better since I took over as manager."

Burnley could have signed Cochrane for £10,000 less than they paid. When Harry was chief scout, he had heard of Cochrane playing for Irish side Coleraine. Bob Lord suggested he should go and take a look at him and Potts reported back that the asking price was £30,000. Lord, in his usual apoplectic manner, coughed and spluttered his indignation and announced that no way was he paying that much for an Irishman since they were all a bunch of amateurs. A year later, with Burnley having a sticky patch, Lord told Potts to go and look at Cochrane again, which Potts duly did. This time the price was £70,000 and a percentage of any sell-on fee. Lord went through the roof but Potts explained that Cochrane was now twice as good. Burnley duly bought him for nearly £40,000.

Alan Reid, Potts' great friend, remembers telling Potts several times that Cochrane wasn't very good. "Just you wait and see," said Harry. Again Alan Reid told Potts that Cochrane was not very good. "Just you wait and see," said Potts. Poor Cochrane had been put in a council house somewhere near the ground and his furniture had been dumped outside the house one day and it was Harry who got the tarpaulin to cover it all up with.

Potts' faith was justified in the end when Cochrane, by now more settled, became a great crowd favourite and was eventually sold to Middlesbrough for something like £250,000, a huge profit.

Security was achieved on May 7th. A 3-1 home win over Notts County was achieved in some style which meant that Potts had managed the near impossible and saved the day. There would be no Division Three just yet. In the Notts County game, Tony Morley excelled, revealing the skill, pace and talent he would demonstrate at Aston Villa and England after, inevitably, he, too, was sold. Sometimes the football gods are with a club and so they were with Burnley on May 7th when Carlisle lost at home as they conceded three goals in the last six minutes to Bristol Rovers.

Carlisle's defeat ensured Burnley's safety. The scenes after the game were jubilant and just as joyous as when Burnley had beaten Sunderland four years earlier to clinch promotion to Division One. When fans stayed behind to call for manager Potts to come out onto the pitch he duly obliged. They called him 'the saviour'. They called him 'Houdini'. They called him 'Doctor Potts'. The Notts County manager Ronnie Fenton, a Burnley old-boy, said if he was going to give anyone two points – it would be Burnley.

The *Burnley Express* called it the 'Great Escape', as Potts announced that the future looked bright, taking into account the experience the club had in the first team and the young players coming through. The 'Great Escape' was what it was and Potts singled out Keith Newton, still playing his heart out, and Peter Noble as the inspiration for the rest of the team. "I feel just as elated as the night in 1960 when we won the league title."

Having taken over in February, under his leadership the team had lost just four out of fourteen games and he was still managing to hang on to Brian Flynn.

Harry Potts had brought with him no great tactical skills, just his humanity and cheerfulness, his ability to bring stability and restore confidence, and his basic philosophy of playing to people's strengths. At one point with results poor, he had even asked the players for ideas as to what to do next.

"This place is in my blood for life," Potts told *Weekly News* reporter Bob Gray. "To be given the chance to help this club is not a job. It's a hobby. It's a passion. A fulfilment you get from doing something you really care about. Whatever the problems, I find pleasure in coming to work here. If I did anything I put the smiles back on the lads' faces. The lads had been through a tough time. When I think of training, I think of laughter out on the pitch and in the dressing rooms. Confidence and good humour is half the battle in football. I had to take away the fear. You can insist they enjoy their work. When that happens the results usually follow."

A grateful and relieved Bob Lord said in the *Burnley Express* that the credit should go to Harry Potts and that he would be the Burnley manager for a long time to come. "We are optimistic of a much better season all round next year under his leadership."

He added that Burnley had just ended a traumatic season but finances were better because of mid-season pruning and better gates since mid-season.

NEXT CAME the season when Steve Kindon came back to Burnley. It would be 1977/78. I didn't get to know too many players very well but Steve was always one of my favourites. Bob liked him too, I could always tell that. There was just something loveable and likeable about Steve. He was such a huge man, like a big bear. What a wonderful sight it was seeing him at top speed going for goal. He was such a big man he must have terrified other players, especially goalkeepers.

Things weren't going too well on the field, in fact they were down near the bottom again even though Harry had done so well at the end of the previous season, and then Bob found some money from somewhere and he and Harry managed to persuade Steve to come back and he just sort of transformed the season. I know that one reason why Steve came back was that he remembered how Harry had put him up for the night all those years earlier. Steve has always said he has never forgotten that and has made a living telling the story in his after-dinner speeches.

WITHOUT THE return of Steve Kindon in November 1977 it is possible Burnley would have been relegated by the end of the season and the miracle escape of the previous year would have gone to waste. Quite simply, Kindon galvanised the season after a poor beginning and transformed the team. Potts quite deliberately played to the big man's strengths. That one man can alter, so dramatically, the direction a season is taking is uncommon, but Kindon did just that in season 1977/78. Lord found the money for Potts to buy two players and the other he bought was Plymouth Argyle's Brian Hall, the former Liverpool winger.

Kindon's arrival provoked general surprise. He had just won a Second Division championship medal with Wolves. The right and wrong of bringing back former players is always debatable, but in Kindon's case it was justified. Kindon recalls the pleas they both made to him, how

Potts softened him up and then Lord applied the *coup de grâce*.

Kindon recalls: "I had absolutely no intention of coming back to Burnley. They were facing relegation to the Third Division and that wasn't in my plans. Five or six First Division clubs had enquired but I felt honour bound to talk to Burnley. I asked my colleagues how I could show interest but turn them down at the same time. Ask for a ridiculous wage they can't afford was the answer. I visited the club on a wet, rainy, miserable Tuesday morning and knew exactly what I was going to say and that I would not be signing. Harry and I spent the first hour in his office asking about one another's family. Signing for Burnley was never mentioned. That was what it was like with Harry. So when Bob Lord comes in and asks bluntly and gruffly, 'Has he signed yet, Harry?', Harry was a bit flustered. He replied, 'We're just getting down to the details, Mr Chairman', which was rubbish. We were just having a damn good chinwag. 'Follow me, Stephen', said Bob Lord and we went into his office. 'And what do you want?' he asked. I gave him a ridiculous figure. He nodded and agreed. I was even more flabbergasted when he said, 'And what else?'

"So, I asked for this and that and then some more. He agreed to everything. Harry Potts was stood behind, taking notes all the time. The negotiations stopped and then Bob Lord pushed seven pages in front of me to sign. They were nearly all blank. 'Come back to Burnley where we love you, Stephen. Just sign and we'll fill these later', said Lord, handing me his pen. I knew he would keep his word. Imagine that, I just signed seven blank sheets of paper. 'You can even keep my pen', he added as the one last extra. It was a gold pen and his pride and joy. So I signed. 'Is he ours now Harry?' said Lord. 'Yes, Mr Chairman', replied Harry. I was just about to pocket the pen. 'Then in that case, Stephen, now I'll have my pen back', said Mr Lord, smiling at Harry."

Years later, Steve Kindon did receive the pen. Bob Lord had died, Harry Potts had left the club, and Kindon, though living in Burnley, had moved on to play for Huddersfield.

One foul, sodden night there was a knock at his door and when Kindon opened it, there was a wet and cold Hilda Lord. After being warmly invited in, she explained that following Bob's death she was sorting out some of his affairs. She put her hand into her handbag and fished out the gold pen. "This is yours," she told him. "On the Saturday after you signed, there was a party at our house and everybody laughed when Bob told them the story of how he had tricked you with the pen. But here it is; it's yours". A stunned and moved Steve Kindon still treasures that pen.

For all of the first 23 weeks of season 1977/78 Burnley were in the bottom three. Not a single supporter could have dared hope that they would not be relegated. And yet relegation was avoided. In the words of Peter Higgs in the *Burnley Express*: "Suffice it to say that what they did was flippin' marvellous." Lord described it as a miracle. Both he and Higgs were quick to praise Harry Potts, "who even in the darkest days refused to lose faith in his players or his belief that all would come right in the end."

Peter Noble was named "the most honest professional in the League" in the *Weekly News*. But it was Steve Kindon who was player of the season. Prior to Potts signing Kindon, the anti-Lord brigade and a group of rebel shareholders were loud and vociferous in their chants of "Lord out".

Yet another player, Brian Flynn, had to be sold but Potts had managed to persuade Lord to release some of the money for the signing of Kindon and Hall. Kindon brought more than just twelve goals for Potts, he brought power and presence, and he brought a huge personality that could lift a dressing room in minutes. He was allegedly described by radio reporter Stuart Hall as having the "speed of a racehorse, the strength of a carthorse and the brains of a rocking horse."

Time has proved the latter to be entirely without foundation. All this is not to say that there were no other good players. There was Paul Fletcher, Terry Cochrane, Tony Morley, Alan Stevenson, a rejuvenated Jim Thomson, and, of course, the old warhorse Peter Noble.

Back Home Again

In the first 14 games there was just one solitary win. Headlines such as 'Clarets Have Big Problems' and 'X Rating For Sad Burnley' were common. Simultaneously it was announced that the club were a staggering £347,000 in debt, a massive amount of money at the time. While transfers had brought in £223,000, the huge wage bill at the club had swallowed that money. "We're not in danger of folding," announced Bob Lord, adding that the situation would have been worse but for economies already made at the club. "I believe we could have been more than half a million in the red but for the steps we took last season. But with a little bit of help from our friends we will carry on. A recovery is possible." That Potts managed to persuade Bob Lord to release money for Kindon and Hall in spite of the club's desperate economic position was nothing short of miraculous. Perhaps he simply used the inescapable prospect that the club were heading towards oblivion in the Third Division.

The second win came against Notts County on November 12th. Kindon announced his presence with a goal and was subsequently interviewed. He expressed his amazement that Burnley had actually wanted him back and repeated his earlier statements that he never had any intention of signing. And then he added, "But that was before I met Burnley manager Harry Potts. I looked at their position at the foot of the Second Division and thought joining them would be a bad move. But Mr Potts is the best boss I have ever played for. We chatted about the situation and I was won over by his enthusiasm and his ambition. Only 50% of me signed for Burnley, the rest signed for Harry Potts and chairman Bob Lord. I've always held both of them in high regard."

By the time the season was over, it was difficult to imagine Burnley had ever been in trouble. By the end of the season they had recovered from their disastrous start and finished so creditably that it was assumed that in the next season they would just carry on where they left off.

According to Kindon, Potts never gave him any tactical talks when he returned but simply let him play to his strengths and normal game. "He just told me to run at defenders, create havoc and score goals." It was the old Potts philosophy of scoring more goals than the opposition and that good players didn't need complicated plans. You simply give them their head and take off the tactical shackles.

In a November 0-0 game against Leyton Orient at Turf Moor, Burnley created chance after chance and squandered them one after the other. Any other manager might have blown his top and hit the roof. Potts merely smiled cheerfully and commented that he had never seen such a one-sided game. "For a man whose team is surely destined for Division Three, Harry Potts deserves ten out of ten for cheerful unflappability," said reporter Howard Booth.

"He's such a great bloke," said centre forward Paul Fletcher, "that you feel ashamed if you let him down, and of course what some folk forget, perhaps because he doesn't go around shouting about it, is his great record.

"I can't recall any great impact he had when he returned to the club as manager but his arrival coincided with two things. Firstly, during a run of poor results he eventually asked, 'Has anyone got any idea what we should do, or how we should play?' We had got into a rut and he didn't seem to know how to get out of it. It was me who answered his question when I suggested the Fletcher Plan. It was simple. What Harry had inherited was a team of workers without any flair. The flair players had all gone and been sold. What remained were the bread and butter players.

"The Fletcher Plan was simply this: if we couldn't be the best team with the ball, we could certainly be the best without it. In other words we could stop the opposition playing; we could run, pressurise, intercept and force a team who were basically better than us to make mistakes. And it worked. In the very next game against Bolton Wanderers we ran round like headless chickens and won 2-1. There are two ways to look at this. You either discredit Harry because he didn't know what to do. Or you give him credit for being astute enough to give the problem to the players to solve.

The cover of the 1947 FA Cup final. It cost just 6d (2.5p).

Telephone:
04l-332 6372/3

Telegrams:
"EXECUTIVE, GLASGOW, C.3."

THE SCOTTISH FOOTBALL ASSOCIATION LTD.
PATRON: HER MAJESTY THE QUEEN

SECRETARY
W. P. ALLAN, J. P.

ADDRESS ALL CORRESPONDENCE
TO "THE SECRETARY."

Our Reference TD/JS

**6 PARK GARDENS
GLASGOW G3 7YE**

14th August, 1972

H. Potts, Esq.,
c/o Burnley F.C.,
Turf Moore,
Burnley.

Dear Harry,

I have been meaning to write to you for some time. I am very sorry to hear that you have parted from Burnley F.C. of which you have always seemed to be part and as you know, it goes without saying, that but for you being Manager our Michael would never have been a player with Burnley.

I take this opportunity of wishing you and your family good health. I am sure that you still have a tremendous amount to give to football.

Very best wishes for the future.

Yours sincerely,

Tommy Docherty

Team Manager.

Tommy Docherty, then manager of Scotland, sends his commiserations after Harry leaves Burnley.

Harry was not out of work for long. He joined Blackpool as manager and is greeted by Cliff Sagar and Frank Dickinson.

Harry's staff at Blackpool included Eddie Quigley and former Burnley centre forward Ray Pointer.

the seasiders

BLACKPOOL

versus

BURNLEY

TUESDAY, 26th Dec., 1972

KICK-OFF 3.00 p.m.

**FOOTBALL LEAGUE
DIVISION TWO**

Official Programme 7p
75th ANNIVERSARY

Ironically his first game as Blackpool manager was at home to Burnley.

His spell at Blackpool brought him a Bell's Manager of the Month Award.

The cover of the programme for the FA Cup game with Burnley which ended Jimmy Adamson's spell as manager and prompted Harry's eventual return to Turf Moor.

The Blackpool squad with which Harry worked.

Happy times at Blackpool. The Bell's representative with ball, England goalkeeper Gordon Banks, Harry and impressionist Mike Yarwood.

Back at Burnley for a second time as manager.

THE FOOTBALL ASSOCIATION

LIMITED

Patron: HER MAJESTY THE QUEEN
President: H.R.H. THE DUKE OF KENT
Chairman: SIR HAROLD THOMPSON, C.B.E., F.R.S.·

Secretary:
E. A. CROKER

Telegraphic Address:
FOOTBALL ASSOCIATION, LONDON, W2 3LW
Phone: 01-262 4542
Telex: 261110

16 LANCASTER GATE, LONDON, W2 3LW

Our Ref: FD/TC/416   *Your Ref:*

11th December, 1978.

Mr. H. Potts,
c/o Burnley F.C.,
Turf Moor,
Burnley,
Lancs.

Dear Sir,

> Burnley v Crystal Palace
> Football League
> <u>4.11.78.</u>

This is to confirm the decision of the Disciplinary Commission which was conveyed to you and to your Club representative at the meeting held in Manchester on Friday, 8th December, as follows:-

"From the evidence adduced the Commission is satisfied that H. Potts was guilty of obstructing a Linesman during the match and, therefore, it has been decided that you be fined the sum of £50, warned as to your future conduct and ordered to pay the adjusted costs of the Hearing."

The exact amount of the costs payable by you is £58.32, and this amount together with the amount of the fine must be remitted to the above address within the next 21 days.

Please acknowledge receipt of this letter.

Yours faithfully,

for Secretary.

c.c. Burnley F.C.

Registered Office: 16 Lancaster Gate, London, W2 3LW
Incorporated in London   Registration Number 77797

Despite his status as a senior manager, Harry could still get into trouble. Interestingly, he was only fined by the FA. There was no suspension for "obstructing" the linesman.

BURNLEY

FOOTBALL CLUB

20p   Official Match Programme   Volume 9 Match 5

Billy Ingham scores the winner against Bradford City
Due to heavy rain this picture is not up to our usual standard

ANGLO-SCOTTISH CUP Quarter-final, 1st Leg

Celtic

TUESDAY, 12th SEPTEMBER, 1978   Kick-off 7-30 p.m.

*The programme for the notorious Anglo-Scottish Cup quarter-final with Celtic
which restulted in a riot by some of the Scottish club's fans.*

Margaret and Harry at his 70th birthday party.

One last "managerial" role. Helping with the local cubs.

Harry and Margaret's grandson James Webster who was on Burnley's books.
"As James came out, the way he ran, the way he held his arms by his side, was just
the same as his grandfather," recalls Margaret.

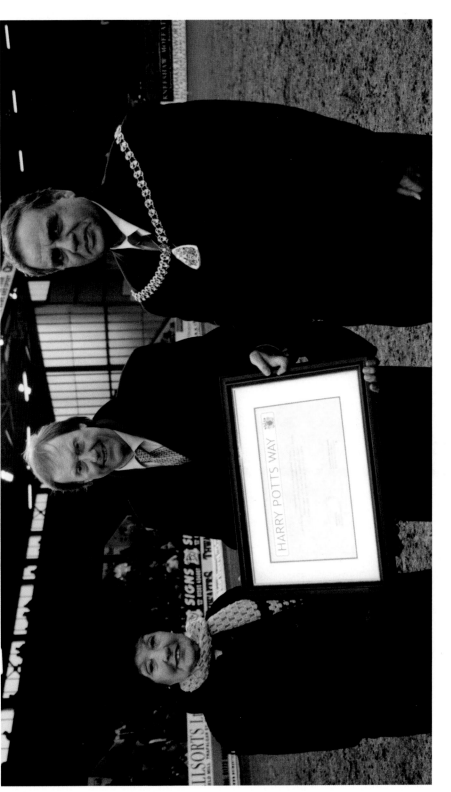

Margaret receiving the citation marking the change of name from "Brunshaw Road" to "Harry Potts Way." Pictured with Margaret are Barry Kilby the Burnley chairman, and mayor Rafique Malik.

The Potts family. (back row) James Webster, Alan Potts, Philip Webster and Lynn Potts. (middle row) Linda Webster, Ken Potts. Margaret (seated), Deborah Webster and Laura Potts (kneeling).

"Secondly, he signed Steve Kindon."

After Kindon's arrival, the points mounted up in ones and twos. After 24 games they were still bottom but a win at home to Stoke City lifted them from that position. The recovery was under way. After 30 games Burnley were still in the bottom two and Kindon had scored eight times in 14 games. But safety was still a distant target. At Christmas they had still been in the bottom group, but until the end of the season there were only three more defeats. In March there were five straight wins, the last of them being at bitter rivals Blackburn Rovers. It was a match marred by a sending off, eight bookings and violence on the terraces. It made the two points even sweeter. Potts was March Bell's Manager Of The Month. As usual the bottle's contents were divided into smaller bottles and shared. "In my opinion," said Southampton's Lawrie McMenemy, "Burnley are playing the best football in the division at the moment. Their revival has been amazing."

When league leaders Spurs, unbeaten in nineteen games, came to Burnley on April 1st, they might have been forgiven for thinking they would add another game to their run. A Burnley versus Spurs game: a reminder of the good old days. Potts rubbed his hands and no doubt thought back to all those wonderful cup games of the '60s. Prior to the game starting, Potts received a huge ovation from the crowd when he received his Bells' award. Spurs left, tails between their legs, having been beaten 2-1.

Towards the end of the season, when the press had noticed Burnley's staggering climb away from the foot of the table, they returned to Turf Moor and Gawthorpe to find the secret. "It's the boss," said Peter Noble. "He never flapped, never put the lads under any pressure, and of course has a great knowledge of the game. All the boss did was to tell us we were First Division players at a great club. We were to continue playing our usual style, give him 110% and go out and enjoy every game. If you had gone to our training sessions you would have thought that we were leading the First Division, not dropping perilously near the Third."

The papers lauded Gawthorpe again, the scouting system, the young lads coming through. They pointed to a youth team that had reached the semi-finals of the FA Youth Cup before being knocked out by Aston Villa. On the way they had beaten Liverpool and two other First Division sides who between them took the cream of the country's youngsters. Potts said the club still had 20 names a week sent to them by scouts.

A 4-2 victory over Cardiff took Burnley to the undreamed of heights of fourteenth place. Two home games rounded off the season and both were won. More than 11,000 spectators cheered and applauded the team and Harry Potts.

CHAPTER FOURTEEN
SWANSONG

IF THERE'S one season I do know a little about, or at least a game that was played in that season, it was 1978/79 when Burnley played Celtic in a cup game. Bob Lord and Harry yet again had something to celebrate when they won the Anglo-Scottish Cup.

It went so well until they had to play Celtic at Turf Moor and though Burnley won, the things that happened during the game were so dreadful that they came back to haunt Harry later when he was suffering so badly from Parkinson's Dementia. I don't know how many Celtic fans were there, but many of them behaved so badly that the game had to be stopped for quite a long time until the police had things under control. I have never seen Harry in such a state as he was after that game. People were genuinely frightened and terrified at the sight of great gangs of Celtic fans invading the pitch and trying to get at the Burnley supporters. It was so bad it was even headline news on the television that night and people who knew that members of their family were there were in fear for their safety. It was as if an earthquake hit not just the match but the town as well. Even today, more than twenty-five years later people still talk about it. You just don't expect things like that to happen at Burnley.

After the game we were kept back inside the hospitality areas until the streets had been cleared and the 'all-clear' given. We watched in astonishment from the windows above Brunshaw Road and if at that moment someone had told me that this same street would one day be renamed after Harry, I would have gasped in disbelief. It was mayhem.

It was the season after that when he finished. After they won that trophy I remember they had such a bad run of results. They just couldn't win and it went on and on and then on into the next season. That would be 1979/80. Harry would come home so tired. He had been managing almost without a break for more than twenty years and it was beginning to take its toll. For two seasons he had worked so hard to save Burnley from relegation. I could tell that there were some nights he came home just emotionally drained and worn out.

SEASON 1978/79 began well with a run of five undefeated games and the return of Leighton James. The Welsh international winger had been signed by Harry Potts as an apprentice in 1968, making his debut as a 17-year-old in November 1970. Burnley sold him to Derby County for a reported £310,000. From there he moved to QPR and now he was back at Turf Moor for a club record £165,000. This was eventually recouped when Terry Cochrane moved to Middlesbrough for £240,000. James' return to Turf Moor at the age of only 25, and already the owner of 37 Welsh caps, was welcomed by fans. The signing was seen as a huge tonic and an indication that ambition still burned brightly at the club. Events had moved so swiftly at the QPR end that James left without his boots and played his first game on his return in a borrowed pair. To have brought him back to Turf Moor was a huge coup for Potts. Although by James' own admission he was controversial and temperamental, Potts clearly felt he could handle him.

"How can a club fail when they have a manager as enthusiastic as he is?" said James. This was after his second talk with Potts who snatched him away from Sheffield Wednesday and Jack Charlton who was anxious to sign him. "To me this is home," he said to the local paper. "I like the club, the area and the people." Prior to signing he had watched one game at Turf Moor from the terraces, explaining that he could have gone into the Bob Lord Stand, but he didn't want any fuss.

James was back just in time for the Celtic game. "Come early" was the plea to fans by both club and police. Between 8,000 and 10,000 Celtic fans made the journey and the anticipation was intense. Burnley was literally invaded for the day. The green and white of Celtic totally filled the town and the approach roads to the ground.

If there are milestones in a club's history then Tuesday, September 12th 1978 was one of them for Burnley Football Club when scenes were witnessed and behaviour took place that had never been seen at Burnley before.

'Horrific' was the *Mirror Sport* headline. 'The Battle Of Burnley' said the *Daily Record*, Scotland's biggest selling newspaper at that time. "Scottish football disgraced again," said the latter. "Celtic fans charged the home fans, fought a pitched battle with police and eventually had the game stopped in an orgy of hate.

"Earlier in the day crowds of Celtic supporters had roamed the streets waving bottles and shouting abuse at shoppers," the newspaper went on.

"Some of the Scottish fans were so drunk they didn't know where they were or what they were doing," said Harry Potts. Celtic manager Billy McNeill was close to tears afterwards. A whey-faced Desmond White, the Celtic chairman, could only say, "It's a disgrace, a disaster. We at Celtic will have to discuss all the implications of this terrible night."

What happened was simple. Celtic fans were at one end of the huge Longside terraced area. Burnley fans were at the other. In between were the police and a fenced-off no-man's-land. To complicate things other Celtic fans had managed to get into the Bee Hole End behind the goals so that the Longside Burnley fans were sandwiched. After Burnley scored the winning goal in the 55th minute, a section of the Celtic support lost their self-control. A barrage of bottles, bricks and assorted missiles were thrown at Burnley supporters across the no-man's-land area.

Then a number of crazed Celtic fans tore down the fencing separating them from the Burnley fans and the barrage of missiles increased. When in the 80th minute fencing was uprooted and used as spears, many fans invaded the pitch to escape the mayhem. Unable to reach the Bee Hole End because yet more Celtic fans faced them there, there was only one way to go and that was onto the pitch. The alternative was to become involved in a mass fight on the terraces. The police, too, moved onto the pitch and were joined by some Celtic fans who were just as terrified as the Burnley supporters.

The players were taken from the field while order was restored. The game restarted because it was decided abandoning it would have provoked even more chaos.

When the inquests began, the following day, the comment was made that when Celtic fans came to Burnley some pubs were closed and there was nowhere to get anything to eat. But then alcohol was on sale inside the ground. Many of the Celtic fans who had managed to drink all day continued inside the ground. Those who had been unable to find a drink during the day made up for it inside the ground. The third group, who had simply gone to watch a football match, were caught up in the pandemonium.

The riot left two policemen in hospital, at least 60 people injured and eleven others with a date at Burnley Magistrates' Court in the following month.

As for the game itself, it was a cracker with big Steve Kindon and his surging runs providing an unanswerable problem for the Celtic defence. Steve tells a good story about the dressing room conversation while the teams were off the pitch. "There was a police request that some of us should go out and try to appeal to the Celtic supporters to calm down. Harry looked at me and suggested that I should go. 'Just one small problem, Harry', I said to him. 'It was me that scored the flippin' goal'."

That was a classic example of the counter-attack. Peter Noble won the ball in his own half and sent a great ball through the middle for Kindon to run onto. Kindon veered wide of the goalkeeper and put his shot into an empty net. This was simple football at its classic best. Every Burnley player was at his best except, ironically, the prodigal son Leighton James who had a quiet time in his first game. Perhaps in the circumstances it was quite understandable.

The return game later in the month in comparison was like a vicarage tea party, said one newspaper. There was not one bit of trouble in the ground and as a gesture the Burnley players kicked footballs into the crowd before the game. Potts was delighted and after they had won 2-1 described it as a terrific result. Not many teams do the double over Celtic, he added. Only a handful of Burnley fans were in the crowd to see another excellent Burnley display.

"A Kick In The Teeth For Soccer", wrote Keith McNee after Sunderland and Jimmy Adamson visited Turf Moor in September.

"Football reached a new low ebb in this nasty, niggling, grudge confrontation which gave the game a dreadful kick in the teeth," he wrote.

"Professional," responded Sunderland player and ex-Burnley man Mick Docherty.

"I am proud of my lads, I was sacked by Burnley so I get a special satisfaction from winning," added Jimmy Adamson, after what McNee described as one of the most disgraceful masquerades of a match ever at Turf Moor. Even with two players sent off and three booked, Sunderland hung on to their 2-1 win. Much of the aggravation resulted from the bad blood felt by Docherty and Adamson towards the Burnley they had left three years earlier against a background of great bitterness.

Potts was incensed by everything that he saw, although he didn't see the bitter confrontation between Adamson and Bob Lord in the stand. "No team of mine has ever, or will ever, play like that," said Potts. "I would rather pack in with the game completely than sink to Sunderland's level. Sunderland just went for the man. As a match it was a shambles and I was disgusted at the way Sunderland went about it." Potts claimed that one of the Sunderland players had even spat at a Burnley player.

They say that with age comes mellowness and wisdom. On a Saturday afternoon, however, Harry Potts continued to demonstrate that this is not a universal truth. If he remained calm and cheerful, sunny and amiable during the week, the demons still emerged on a matchday. In one game, in sheer frustration, he threw his cushion from the dugout at the referee. Fortunately it missed, and landed according to one spectator in the centre circle. Among his staff and some of the players he was affectionately called 'the Mad Hatter'. It was noticed one day that the top of his head was covered in bruises, abrasions and scratches. There was general puzzlement until it was realised that these were the result of him jumping up and down in the dugout and banging his head on the ceiling. His passion was undimmed.

When Burnley played Crystal Palace at Turf Moor on November 4th Potts was yet again involved in an incident with a linesman. As she watched from directly behind him, Margaret continued to wonder if he would ever learn. It was a game in which there were many mystifying refereeing decisions, a fact which was acknowledged by all the newspaper reports. Kindon was denied a perfectly legitimate goal when an infringement was spotted in the build-up that no one else saw. A clear penalty was denied when goalkeeper John Burridge hauled down Kindon. The referee then gave a penalty against Burnley for an identical incident when Vince Hilaire was felled.

With the crowd baying and the Burnley players incensed, it all became too much for Potts. When Kindon was impeded yet again right in front of him with no free kick awarded, an enraged Potts grabbed the linesman by the shirt and remonstrated with him. To compound matters, Potts refused to leave the dugout when ordered to by referee Ken Redfern, telling him he did not have the authority. Mercifully, Burnley won 2-1 but the hostile reception given to all the officials at the end of the game ranks as one of the most intense ever heard at Turf Moor. After the game Margaret was able to tell Harry that even the visiting Crystal Palace officials were baffled by the referee's decisions.

In his official report, Redfern wrote. "In the 75th minute of the above match my linesman Mr E McNamara drew my attention from his position on the touchline. Quote. 'The Burnley manager had just come to the touchline, grabbed me by the shirt and shook me vigorously.' I immediately produced my notebook and approached the home dugout and noted the manager's name. In the interest of both parties I then asked him to sit in the stand. Harry Potts refused this request and said: quote: 'There is no rule which says I have to do that.' I then informed him that all matters would be reported."

The linesman reported, "In the 75th minute I informed the referee of an incident which had occurred on the touchline outside the Burnley dugout. I was running along the touchline towards the halfway line when I saw the Burnley manager Mr H Potts standing on the line in front of me. I called him to move, as I couldn't pass. Mr Potts did not move and when I approached him he grabbed hold of the left side of my shirt below the collar and shook me vigorously three or four times, at the same time he was shouting at me in an incoherent fashion. I was badly shaken by this incident and immediately informed the referee. Mr Redfern took Mr Potts' name and asked him to leave the dugout for the stand. Mr Potts refused and he was informed by the referee that the matter would be reported."

Harry Potts' statement reported: "At no time did I shake the linesman vigorously and the reason he could not make out what I was saying to him was because of the uproar from hundreds of people in the stand who were incensed by the referee's attitude towards an incident which involved a Crystal Palace player practically pulling the shirt off the back of Burnley's player Steve Kindon to prevent him gaining a clear advantage. This was done not more than ten yards from the linesman."

There was widespread coverage in the papers and the feeling was that Potts would be banned again from the touchline. On December 11th he received news of the punishment imposed by the Disciplinary Commission.

"From the evidence adduced, the Commission is satisfied that H Potts was guilty of obstructing a linesman during the match and, therefore, it has been decided that you be fined the sum of £50, warned as to your future conduct and ordered to pay the adjudged costs of the hearing. The exact amount of the costs payable by you is £58.32, and this amount together with the amount of the fine must be remitted to the above address within the next 21 days."

It has to be said that Potts got away lightly. Most expected a lengthy touchline ban at least.

By the end of October, Burnley FC was in an upbeat mood. Money had come in from the sale of Terry Cochrane, the team was on the fringe of the promotion places; "Finances are on the mend" reported Bob Lord as the Development Association had pumped £107,000 into the club. Kindon was a match winner and the purchase of James had restored some faith in the club's hierarchy. Promotion was a serious topic of conversation. Potts explained the sale of the popular Cochrane by saying that he was unsettled, wanted an improved contract now that he was an international and that he had refused to come on as substitute in the late stages of one game.

Mansfield Town were the next club to be beaten in the Anglo-Scottish Cup as Burnley progressed to the two-legged final against Oldham Athletic. On December 5th at Boundary Park, a superb Burnley display swept them aside 4-1 on a skating rink of a pitch. Potts' tactics were spot on and his choice of trainers rather than studded boots for his players was ideal.

Right from the start, long passes were played through the middle, making it easy for attackers to run onto and impossible for defenders to turn and retrieve. Oldham had no answer to Steve Kindon who scored twice. Though Burnley lost the second game 1-0 at Turf Moor, the celebrations were long and loud as they were presented with the trophy. Big-city clubs might well have turned up their noses at such an insignificant event, but at Turf Moor it was valued highly after the last few years of struggle. They had beaten the mighty Celtic over two legs on the way. Who could say then that this trophy was not hard-earned?

In the FA Cup, First Division Birmingham were beaten 2-0 on their own ground to make things look even rosier. Their opponents in the fourth round were Sunderland, but by this time Jimmy Adamson had left. Things had not gone well for him there, which defused another potentially explosive confrontation. Severe winter gripped the country and played havoc with fixtures but after drawing the first game 1-1 at Turf Moor the replay at Roker Park was won 3-0 in some style.

These were heady days again with all-time record gate receipts of £36,000 for the Turf Moor game. There is no doubt Potts and his coaching staff had got the team and Burnley buzzing again. The win at Sunderland took them to Liverpool and a guaranteed near sell-out crowd and a further shared cash bonanza of at least £25,000. Not unexpectedly Liverpool beat Burnley but in the league things continued reasonably well with a 2-1 victory at Blackburn Rovers delighting everyone.

Captain Peter Noble wrote of Harry Potts: "After the traumatic events of last season a high final placing this time would be a considerable achievement and a further reflection of manager Harry Potts' qualities. At 58 he is one of the oldest managers in the League but he has the energy and enthusiasm of a much younger man and this, together with his great experience has undoubtedly rubbed off on the players."

But from that Blackburn game onwards, progress stopped. There were no more wins between then and the end of the season eight games later. A defeat at West Ham condemned them to another season in Division Two. Five of the last six matches were lost.

The finale was disappointing and from such a previously optimistic position not many weeks before Potts, Lord and Burnley were at a crossroads. "Just where do we go from here?" asked supporters after the tame, anti-climactic end to the season. Would the club remain ambitious or be content to drift along in the Second Division as gates dropped and interest dwindled? Even worse, if stagnation took place would there be yet another flirtation with the relegation positions in the coming season?

It had been a strange season, commented Potts. There had been some outstanding moments and aspirations had risen, only for it all to fade away in a season that seemed to have gone on and on because of the backlog of games to catch up on due to the bad winter. It had all become tedious and tiresome, commented the local papers. There had been a total of 58 competitive matches stretching back to the previous August. It was almost as if people had become tired of football by the season's end.

It was a widely held view that new players were needed and there was now a deliberate policy of bringing back former players. It was noted that Martin Dobson was unsettled at Everton. But this was in stark contrast to the days when Potts began his Burnley career as a player, and then when he went on to become its illustrious manager. Then all the talent was home-grown and a lot of it was outstanding. The wheels of this once dominant club were in reverse.

CHAPTER FIFTEEN

GOODBYE TURF MOOR

WHEN HE finished for the second time at Burnley in 1979, there was no real emotional upset like there had been in 1970 or '72. This was different. I could see he was so much more tired in the later years and he was feeling the strain and the pressure so much more. The demands were endless and he was not getting younger. It was probably no bad thing when he finished again.

They had such a bad start in August, September and October 1979 and that was when he and Burnley parted. The financial situation at the club was very bad when he went back in 1977, but they still had a couple of good players there, one of them being Brian Flynn, and you knew that they would eventually be sold. It was all so hopeless and thankless in many ways. There was no money, the crowds were getting smaller and smaller. As for younger players coming through, there weren't as many good ones as in the early years. And poor Bob Lord just hung on and hung on when really he should have retired as chairman. There was an atmosphere and so much dissatisfaction and Jack Butterfield, who had successfully raised so much money for the club commercially, left as well because he was so fed up with the way the club was run, or so the local newspaper said. Supporters and restless fans really were wondering just how bad things were.

So it was not surprising that Harry was replaced. I felt he was well out of it even though he had done remarkably well. To put it simply, I was ready for less football because of all the tensions. He was being pulled in all directions both in football and domestically. There were real stresses looking after my own mother who had suffered a stroke and stayed with us for a lengthy period. Harry was up during the night helping me with her. If she fell she needed lifting. He also went to see his mother every day although she was still physically well and able to look after herself and we continued to have her over every Sunday. We also took her meals and I did her garden. And all the time at the club there were the pressures from a situation where Harry, it seemed, had the job of trying to stop the tide coming in.

There were also the demands from Bob Lord. I vividly remember a telephone conversation I had with him one day. The phone rang at home. I picked it up.

"Is Harry there?" a voice gruffly asked.

"No," I answered politely.

"Well where is he then… he's not at Gawthorpe or the club," said a clearly exasperated Bob.

"Well, he's probably gone to his mother's," I replied.

"What's he doing at his mother's?"

"Probably helping her with the shopping."

There was a grunt and the line went dead without another word. I felt that all was not cordial between them and I've always wondered if the day had arrived when Harry would lose his temper with him and say something he would regret. It was time for him to hang up his boots. We had reached a time in our lives when we were due to have a life of our own together. Harry had missed his own two children growing up and I didn't want him to miss his grandchildren in the same way. It was time for Harry to give 'us' and our own life some time. Neither of us was getting any younger.

Brian Miller, a much younger man who had been at the club since he was a boy, took over. All I could think was "good luck Brian, you're going to need it".

It was from Bob Lord's daughter Margaret in 1981 that Harry learned that Bob was seriously ill. In between leaving the club in 1979 and Bob's illness in 1981 I am not aware of any further contact between them. But when he learned of Bob's illness he was terribly upset and asked me if I thought it would be a good idea to visit him. This was not the time to have regrets or differences, I told him. I encouraged him and so he went to see him. Harry didn't say much about it, but his sadness was clear. If their relationship had become estranged, they had nevertheless had so many years of friendship and success in earlier years. There had been a remarkable bond between them and the club's success was very much the result of that. Not many people knew how to handle Bob and tolerate him, but Harry was one. Theirs had been a real partnership and that was what we remembered. Of course we went to the funeral and we remembered him as the man who had built the club rather than the man who had nearly caused its downfall. When Harry visited him they put things right and their differences aside.

IT MIGHT well have been that Bob Lord had great faith in Harry Potts when, in May 1979, he gave him a new two-and-a-half-year contract at a salary of £17,500 a year. But, perhaps more importantly, Lord felt 'safe' with Harry, a man he clearly considered would not rock the boat and cause him aggravation as Jimmy Adamson had done. "I want to build a team, but the chairman wants to build a stadium and I think the chairman will win," Adamson once told Paul Fletcher. Despite producing a wonderfully entertaining and successful team between 1973 and 1975, the conflict between them had grown. A former player, who had returned to the town, met Lord in the Masonic Hall one night and asked him how things were. He had expected a positive answer. "Not good," said Lord and pointing to Adamson muttered, "and there's my mistake." He did not want a repeat of that and thus turned to Potts, with whom he once more felt secure and unthreatened.

In addition to his basic salary, Potts was also to receive bonuses of £50 per point, the same amount for drawn cup games plus £100 for any wins. If he were to be dismissed he would receive half of the value of the remaining months of the contract.

That most elegant and cultured player, Martin Dobson, returned from Everton in what was seen to be another inspired signing. At Everton, manager Gordon Lee had called him into the office and, though he had offered him a new two-year contract, he talked about eventually replacing him. The temptation, therefore, of a four-year contract at Burnley was a handsome one. He might well have rejoined Jimmy Adamson, now at Leeds United, but that would have meant moving house and his children's school. After an independent tribunal reduced the fee, Burnley snapped him up for £100,000. Potts phoned him and they met in a Southport hotel. "He was still the same guy that I had known when I last met him, the passion and enthusiasm was still there. He was the old Harry and Lord offered me a good contract."

But the season began as badly as the previous one had ended. There was simply no sign of a win and even the unflappable Potts was privately close to despair.

Dobson wondered what he had joined as game after game went by with only an occasional draw to lighten the gloom. "Within a short time of being there I wondered if I had done the right thing. I came back home after one of the pre-season training sessions and knew that they had problems there. It's difficult to be critical, I still have friends there, but the things that were there in the late '60s, when I first began, and then the '70s, had gone. I felt that the disciplined training that was once a feature had disappeared. It was too light-hearted, little things were allowed to happen that would once have resulted in the whistle being blown and the players being told 'Hey you don't do that'. There seemed to be a lack of focus and seriousness, it was not the Burnley that I knew in 1974. Then, every 'i' had been dotted and every 't' crossed, but not any more. Harry's old philosophy of 'go out and enjoy the game, control the ball – pass – and move – get it wide' still held good. But in the '70s the game had progressed and more was needed."

In August, Potts rubbished a new report by a sports scientist, Dr Vaughan Thomas of Liverpool Polytechnic. It claimed that football training was fairly undemanding and that footballers were nowhere near as fit as track athletes. "I would say the doctor who has made this report doesn't know what he is talking about," said Potts.

Then, just six months after signing the new contract, Potts left and his long, distinguished association with the club finally came to an end. Brian Miller, his assistant, replaced him. It would be the end of November before Burnley won their first game of the season. The situation was simple. Highly paid players, with wages among the highest in the division, had now gone six months and 24 games without a win. Potts had continued to shoulder responsibility and put on a brave face but as speculation and conjecture increased it became clear that his days were numbered. In one of his last statements he betrayed a rare moment of strain and dejection. "I think a great deal about this club but the results we have been getting recently are depressing."

The club statement as reproduced in the *Burnley Express* was short and simple. "An amicable arrangement has been reached between the club and Harry Potts that he should stand down as manager of the club. Both parties parted on friendly terms without any acrimony in any shape or form, all realising the serious situation in which the club is now placed."

Potts added nothing to this save to wish Brian Miller the best of luck.

Two years earlier the anti-Lord campaign had petered out because of the mini-revival Potts had inspired. "Providing I don't drop dead, I'll never give in, " retaliated Lord. But the inquests began again and the anti-Lord lobby resurfaced.

Fans had planned demonstrations and Jimmy Adamson stoked the fires. "The guilty man is Bob Lord," said Adamson. "In my opinion there's only one man to blame for the position Burnley are in. I said that Burnley would be the team of the '70s and to this day believe they would have been if someone else had not sold the best players." To this day, Adamson remains bitterly unhappy about the period.

The biggest accusations levelled against Bob Lord were that, since he had retired from business, he was clinging on to his position as chairman so that he could use the club to prop up his lifestyle with extravagant expense claims. He was accused of not running the club properly and he had become determined, come what may, to hang on. The local papers pleaded with him to step down but Lord countered with a tirade against them. He dismissed the anti-Lord supporters action group as four grown-ups and 20 schoolboys. He defended the high admission prices by saying they were a deterrent against hooligans, thugs and thieves. He had an answer for every criticism.

Burnley Football Club was close to bankruptcy but that was no fault of Potts. Within days of Brian Miller taking over, Burnley suffered one of the most infamous defeats in their history when they lost 7-0 away at QPR in a game televised on the BBC. Jimmy McIlroy, writing a column in the *Burnley Express,* expressed his feelings. Half of him felt a sadistic pleasure, he said, in seeing the club that had treated him so shabbily reduced to tatters. But when that feeling passed it was replaced with a deep sadness that this once great club had sunk so low and a sense of shame that supporters now had to endure the failings of the people at the top.

Bob Lord blamed his highly paid players for the disgrace. Supporters were shocked to discover the sums that Lord was still paying.

The club sank into the Third Division at the end of the season, with Miller powerless to stop the rot. It was so terribly sad to see a club that had once been a shining example of how a club could be run, producing its own talent, competing with the city clubs and being so successful, now in near ruins. The contrast between the club Potts took over as manager in 1958 and the near destitute one he left in 1979 was simply vast.

When Bob Lord eventually relinquished the chairmanship in 1981, only months before he died, the new administration found the club's affairs to be in disarray. It was described as a club where cheques sometimes bounced and bills went unpaid. One player was allegedly offered a £30,000 signing on fee which the club would not have been able to pay.

The position with the Inland Revenue on PAYE and National Insurance was chaotic. VAT matters were something to ignore and hope they would go away. On one occasion a creditor arrived at the club offices to demand payment of a sizeable unpaid bill. A voice could be heard from behind a door saying, "Tell him I'm not in". The great man who had built the club and the foundations of its greatness, and nobody can take that marvellous achievement away from him, was at the end helplessly and obstinately chairing its near demise. He was intractable in his determination to stay as chairman. The club was on the brink of closure.

Shortly after taking over from Potts, Miller declared that it would take a miracle to avoid relegation. There was none and relegation became a certainty with a home 1-1 draw against Bristol City. Their left back, Terry Cooper, cleared a certain goal from right under the crossbar. That would have given Burnley both points with just 20 seconds to go. Such is football. The once great club, the love of Harry Potts' life, was in Division Three.

Bob Lord passed away in December 1981. Harry and Margaret Potts were at his funeral. The partnership and bond between Lord and Potts, which had begun decades earlier, had been extraordinary. But in Potts' second term as manager, the relationship had deteriorated with little or no contact outside club matters. Their names are synonymous with not just the football club but also the town of Burnley itself.

Then, somehow, in the early '80s after Lord had gone, Brian Miller fashioned a dynamic and briefly successful team with one last harvest of good young players. Trevor Steven, Kevin Young, Michael Phelan, Vince Overson and Brian Laws, who had come together through the youth system repaired earlier by Potts, were mixed with an outstanding centre forward, Billy Hamilton, and the experienced elder statesmen, Martin Dobson and Alan Stevenson.

Miller and his exciting team took the club out of the Third Division and back into the Second. Potts, no longer involved at Turf Moor, was thrilled, but by the time of the promotion, sadly, he was in the early stages of the long slow journey into Parkinson's Dementia.

CHAPTER SIXTEEN

THE TWILIGHT YEARS

NATURALLY HARRY was unhappy to see them relegated at the end of the season he left. He didn't talk about it and he didn't talk about Bob Lord, but we couldn't escape knowing that things were bad at the club and that supporters were so very unhappy. Once again we had no income coming in so we started to worry again about where it would come from. Harry was still only 58, too young for either his state or football pension. Fortunately Harry had been advised to pay off the mortgage so that was one thing we didn't have to worry about.

Early in 1980, though, he was back in football when once again his friend Ron Suart, now at Chelsea, asked him to do some scouting. His job was to cover the Lancashire and Yorkshire area. Then in the mid-'80s, Martin Dobson, then the manager at Bury, used Harry as a sort of scout and consultant.

Three things stay in my mind. The first is how terrible things were at Burnley in 1987, when, if they had lost the last game of the season they would have disappeared altogether from the League. People asked how this could possibly have happened. This was a club that less than 30 years earlier had won the championship and there had been such a wonderful collection of players and now there it was on the edge of disappearing.

The second, and better, memory is the reunion and dinner of the championship team in 1985. Along with most of the team there was former Liverpool and England captain Emlyn Hughes, and Lancashire cricketers Clive Lloyd, the captain of the West Indies, and spin bowler Jack Simmons. They even had the trophy Burnley had won 25 years earlier on display. Just to see all those wonderful people together again brought back so many memories. There's a picture in my collection with them all arm in arm with Harry in the middle, Ray Pointer on one side, Brian Pilkington on the other and the trophy in front of them.

There was also a wonderful reunion at the Dunkenhalgh Hotel in April 1989 when dozens of former players and people associated with the club got together again. Of course, Harry and I were there and there was one lovely moment when we led the dancing. It was our 41st wedding anniversary as well. It was a wonderful night with so many faces from the past going right back to the 1930s and '40s. There was just an endless list and you looked around and you looked at them and you saw in that one room so much of the history of Burnley Football Club. Everyone talked about how great it had once been, and how proud they had been, and still were, to be linked with it. They talked of successes, of old glories, the good times and they talked of where the club was now and how wonderful it had been to see them back at Wembley again in 1988 for a cup competition which was specially for the lower clubs. It was the final and how ironic that it should be against Wolves, another great club fallen on hard times.

One of my newspaper cuttings says there were more than a hundred ex-Clarets at the reunion that night, some a bit grey round the temples, some a bit bigger round the middle, nobody quite as sprightly as they used to be. My clipping says, "It was an unforgettable night, a night for wallowing in nostalgia, a night for reminiscing, and for shaking the hands of old friends." It was all that and more. You looked at some of those faces and wondered if you would ever see them again.

The oldest player was the marvellous Ted Adams, 82 years old, and Burnley's goalkeeper from 1936 until the war. His pay was £7 if they won. Ted talked about a player called Billy Miller whose nickname was 'Golden' because he was so good. 'Golden Miller', of course, was the horse that won the

Cheltenhan Gold Cup five times in a row. Ted also remembered being the player who looked after a lad called Tommy Lawton when he came into the Burnley team.

What a night it was. Just about the complete championship team was there and for one night the clock was turned back as the conversations centred on those marvellous triumphs and Harry loved every minute of it.

We went home that night filled with nostalgia, particularly Harry. If one night could represent the wonderful life we had had, then that reunion was possibly it. Those people had come from the north and the south, from the east and the west, from Wales and Scotland and the length and breadth of England and that night it didn't matter if they'd played just once or one hundred times, they were all special. For many of them it was a first visit for twenty years or more. For some it would be the last time they saw each other. The stories they told each other lasted into the small hours, beginning with how they picked up their ragged training kit from the pile on the floor thrown there by Ray Bennion and Billy Dougal, and hoped it would fit. They talked about how they had to break in their iron-hard new boots and even left them soaking in water to get them softer. And then there were the old heavy lace-up footballs that got so wet and heavy that when they headed it they were nearly knocked out.

In his later years, Harry was a member of the Ex-Clarets Association, a group that worked to raise money for all kinds of charities and good causes. From the reunion dinner, for example, they were able to donate £750 to the Hospice Care for Burnley and Pendle Group. Burnley Boys Club received £250. But in 1991 the association was disbanded. "The End Of An Era", wrote Jimmy McIlroy in his newspaper column. It had been formed in the mid-'50s, had raised literally thousands of pounds and donated money to Burnley Football Club in the years when the club was so desperate. One of its biggest days was when it raised money for the Hapton Colliery disaster. The reason it disbanded was simple: the members were getting older and older and the request for younger people to step forward and take over went unanswered. Harry was still on the committee in 1991 when it finally ended. There's a picture of him I have with the committee at its final meeting and he looks so frail. His illness had taken a real hold by then. How good it is that the association was reborn some time later and today still works so hard under its new committee. The old association with its remaining funds provided Lifeline Alarms and sponsored a game at Turf Moor at which 50 or so former players made a nostalgic return to the ground. For some, it would be their last ever visit.

So Harry kept busy. Something else that he was involved with was a marvellous little club called Colne Dynamoes. There were several ex-Clarets either playing or on the staff. Colne is very near Burnley and Graham White, the founder and chairman, asked Harry if he would like to get involved. They really were a very famous little team and at one stage it looked like they would get all the way into the Football League, even though they started off as just a Sunday morning group of old school pals.

Harry wasn't yet 60 and having no pension to fall back on was a problem. But Harry did some Chelsea scouting work and the £50 a week expenses he usually got were very helpful. I remember the long phone calls he would have with Ron Suart. At this stage Harry could still write out the details of the games he watched, with diagrams of free kicks and all the details of the players. But his ability to do that slowly declined as his condition emerged and then worsened.

It's the story of football, isn't it, or any job for that matter. You enjoy the life, there is a salary coming in, and then the job goes and you wonder how you will manage.

AFTER LEAVING Burnley for the final time, Potts grabbed the chance to be involved again in football when Ron Suart, now at Chelsea, called him. "I've been involved in football all my life and I still think I've got something to offer the game." The opportunity came after the reorganisation at Chelsea with Geoff Hurst and Bobby Gould taking over as manager and assistant. "Ron Suart has been a life-long friend of mine."

Over the next six years, scouting for Chelsea and briefly for Bury, Potts watched from a distance as Burnley's fortunes eventually reached rock bottom on May 7th 1987. On that day, Burnley had to win the final game of the season in order to stay in the League. But even a win still meant that one of the other bottom teams had to lose to ensure safety. The football gods that day decreed that Burnley would survive and Lincoln City would be demoted.

More than 15,000 people saw the game. Many of them had seen the great years, the European games and the FA Cup final. Now they saw an impoverished club fighting for its very survival. On a November night in 1986 just 1,696 spectators had seen Burnley beat Colchester United 2-1. The empty seats, and vast spaces around the terraces and all around the ground, were a testimony to the years of decline. Harry Potts did not visit the club or see any of these bottom-of-the-table games.

For that game against Lincoln City, the media homed in on the town and the club, and Potts expressed his grief in the *Burnley Express* and said he never thought he would see the day it would happen. He pointed the finger at one fact that had affected small-town teams so much: the abolition of the maximum wage which made it it impossible for clubs such as Burnley to compete with the wealthy city clubs. Newspaper after newspaper featured the fact that two of the great clubs – Wolves were the other – were now in Division Four.

At Bury, Martin Dobson was player/manager and noticed that Potts was changing. "I brought Harry into Bury because I had total respect for the guy and invited him in on a sort of scouting/reporting basis. I knew he was missing the game so in '86 got in touch. I would choose a game for him to go to, and then he would come in on a Monday morning and we would talk through it. He would look at players for me; see the team we were due to play next. I'd hoped that he would give me some insights, spot the things that I missed. I wanted his advice on how to handle some of my own players and all their different needs and problems. I'd hoped to be able to tap into his vast experience as a manager. But sadly it didn't work out. I suspect that his illness was developing and his health was beginning to deteriorate. He found it difficult to remember things and focus. So we agreed to discontinue. It was very sad."

But in another footballing capacity, Harry Potts was still winning trophies. He helped with the football coaching at the local school in Read every Friday afternoon. This was a time when the Friday afternoon games session was commonplace in schools, and was then followed by inter-schools matches on a Saturday morning. Harry was there every Friday afternoon. Margaret later gave two shields to the school for presentation to pupils in memory of Harry. Then, with his friend Clive Bennett and Philip, his son-in-law, he helped with the local village cubs team in the late 1980s. For two consecutive years they won both the League and cup competitions.

Clive can still remember what a good team it was, and that Harry's grandson James was an integral part of it. James would go on to become a youth player at Turf Moor, play for a year as a professional and one day become player/chairman at Holt House, the home of Colne FC, where Colne Dynamoes had played when Harry had worked for them. By coincidence, Clive Bennett was a cousin of the Burnley winger Peter Kippax with whom Harry had played at Burnley in the great team of 1946/47. Clive had looked in awe in those years at Harry Potts. Now, here he was working with him in the village with their team of youngsters and Harry was as pleased to win trophies with them as he had been with his championship team of 1960. He was especially thrilled at one sportsman's dinner he attended with Harry. The great Denis Law came over to speak to Harry and Clive had long idolised him.

The financial plight of Burnley Football Club in the late 1980s was desperate and Potts was one of 25 former players and staff who wrote articles for a book compiled by Paul Fletcher in order to raise funds for the club. In his article he pointed to the club's best players being sold and the introduction of freedom of contract as being the biggest problems that the club had faced. It was also typical of Harry the man that in the same article he remembered a Burnley player, Steve Broome, killed in action during World War Two, more than 40 years earlier.

It was also in the 1980s that Graham White of Colne Dynamoes approached him with a view to him becoming scout/consultant. Harry accepted. In 1963 eleven schoolmates had turned up at Pendle Forest to play their first game as a team. By 1988 they had won the FA Vase at Wembley Stadium. It is not the purpose of this book to look in any detail at their remarkable story but as their successes increased and it looked likely that they would eventually join what was then the Vauxhall Conference, Potts joined the long list of ex-Clarets who aided Colne Dynamoes in one way or another. By the end of 1989/90 Colne Dynamoes had won the HFS Loans Division One by a record 26 points but admission to the Conference was denied. After the Conference it would have been the Football League itself. Shortly afterwards the club was disbanded. Jack Amos, of the *Northern Echo,* remembers meeting Harry at Colne Dynamoes.

"He was full-time scouting coordinator, even though he knew then he had Parkinson's Disease. 'I'm just proud and thrilled to be here,' said Potts. When the interview was over he offered to run us to the station but we needed first to see someone else at a pub somewhere in Colne. For Harry that was no problem; he took us to the pub first and insisted on buying the drinks when we got there. That's the kind of man he was; he'd just go out of his way for you."

The signs of Potts Parkinson's Dementia illness were clearly evident by the 1980s, but living in a small village community was a blessing. Suffering from Parkinson's and the emerging Dementia did not curb his boundless energy. He loved walking and walked miles round the country lanes, sometimes from Read to Sabden and back. Sometimes it was just a shorter walk, pushing his grandson James in the pram. But as the confusion grew and his condition worsened, neighbours kept an eye out for him on his walks. If he went too far they would telephone to ask Margaret if he would be all right and should they keep an eye on him? One neighbour, Cyril Law, the churchwarden, was a keen jogger and often met Harry along the lanes. There were other occasions when people who knew him would pass him in their cars and offer him a lift home. The trick, Cyril would say, was not to let Harry think that they were interfering or helping him. He would sometimes call in at Alan Reid's vicarage to stay and chat for an hour and then, as the smell of the dinner in the oven drifted by, it would remind him to get up and return home. But the signs of Dementia became more pronounced when he went on errands to the local shop and brought back the wrong items. Margaret would have to check with the shopkeeper that he had paid them the correct amount. She recalls, though, that even if he did give the wrong money the shopkeepers were too kind to say so.

SOMEHOW LIFE went on. He was admitted into hospital on cup final weekend in May 1985, for a small operation. He gave strict instructions he was not to be disturbed by anybody while the game was on. During all this time I was journeying backwards and forwards to his mother's house to do her washing and change the bedclothes. On this occasion she took hold of me and accused me of stopping her from visiting Harry. Usually when she said or did something like this I kept calm. They were not rows; you have to have two to have a row. But this time I just put down the washing, ignored the bedclothes and rushed from the house in tears. I don't know how I drove home. Linda found me terribly upset and I decided to tell her why. In some ways the weekend he had in hospital was a turning point. She went over to remonstrate with her, banging her fist on the table. Even that was my fault; I had brought up 'her' Linda badly!

I began to wonder if things could get any worse. Then the moment came when Harry returned from the hospital and, as he sat in his favourite rocking chair, we held each other. He looked so old and tired but I whispered to him that he would soon be out walking again and playing football with James. And then he looked at me. "It's me Mam, isn't it?" he said as if suddenly, after all this time, the penny had dropped. "Yes", I thought, "you've realised this years too late." I told him I would make no more visits to his mother on my own and that he must come with me. "I don't know what you said to Harry but he says I haven't to upset you again," she said. Yes, it was a turning point in Harry's understanding of his mother and me.

Even so, life with Mam Potts became even more difficult. One day a phone call came from her demanding that he should move across to her home, to live with her and look after her. As far as she was concerned, her house, not mine, was his home. He actually did go for a few days but he could hardly look after himself, let alone his mother, and he soon returned.

These were trying times. In addition, Mam's demands increased. She had a short stay in hospital. She had no real physical disabilities but when she was discharged we made her as comfortable as possible in the downstairs rooms of her home, making her a small patio outside the back door where she could sit in the sunshine. 'Home helps' took away some of the strain. Eventually, however, she became more and more reliant on neighbours for help, and upon me to drive over and look after her. It was Dr Iven who advised us that she must never come to live with us and that a 'home' would be the best thing. If it had been my suggestion she would have refused; as it was Dr Iven's, she accepted it. In 1988 she moved to the residential home Stella Maris.

Harry and I moved to Berkeley Drive in October 1989. It was a lovely, spacious bungalow, so much more convenient, light and airy, and from there he could set out on his walks that he loved so much. Once again, I worked hard in the garden and made it somewhere that he could sit on a warm afternoon and evening.

Somehow Harry and I managed to get a holiday in Majorca in 1989 but he would wander off on his own. A coach trip we took posed just the same problems. I could lose him in an instant. There were no more holidays. Just to think of that filled me with sorrow.

Then, after one particular nightmare motorway journey, the time came for him to stop driving. Giving up his driving licence was a sad moment. A car had been a part of his life for so many years; driving to games, visiting parents, scouting, he had covered the length and breadth of the country. One by one, the symbols of his independence were given up.

It became more and more heartbreaking as his condition worsened. Families with anyone who suffers from Parkinson's Dementia will understand. Alan drove us to Preston the first time we went to see a specialist in 1992 and I went in with Harry while Alan waited for us. The doctors and specialists gave Harry simple questions to answer and he couldn't answer them. They asked him to repeat three simple things they said to him, three objects maybe; a tree, a flower, a bird; and he couldn't repeat them in the right order.

I sat there and wanted to tell him the answers because I loved him so much but I had to stay silent. It was like wanting to help a child with difficult homework. We didn't want to hear the confirmation that he had this terrible illness even though we knew it was there. As long as it wasn't confirmed we could deny that he was ill and could pretend that he was well and that everything would be fine. But once the specialist confirmed what we already knew, all pretence disappeared and we knew it was real and inescapable. It was a matter then of dealing with it and adjusting to it.

Eventually, the most horrendous manifestation of his condition occurred. It was the time, in the early hours of the morning, he rushed out of the house into the street, knocking on doors and shouting about the Celtic game that had been so horrendous.

And so, remorselessly, cruelly, his capabilities diminished. Our lives became more and more restricted. By 1994 it was clear that I could no longer cope with looking after him and when the consultant asked me how I was coping the truth is that at that moment I was worn out and I burst into tears there and then in front of him. By now Harry was having intermittent respite care in various 'homes' but the consultant insisted this was the time for a proper break from him before I had a nervous breakdown. There was nothing like the range of drugs there is today, there was no stress counselling and there was minimal home support.

He moved into Dove Court nursing home in the summer of 1994 when Linda and Philip took me away for a badly needed holiday to Majorca with Deborah and James for company as well. How unkind life can be. Philip was hospitalised while we were over there. On top of that, while we were away the house was burgled. I was heartbroken, even though I was spared seeing the worst of the damage done because Ken had been allowed in to clear up the mess and make some repairs. It was while we journeyed home on the plane that Linda told me about Harry's permanent move to Dove Court. When we landed at Manchester she broke the news about the burglary.

After our return from the holiday, Linda took me to see Harry and I remember this first visit as if it was yesterday. We walked through the open plan lounge and dining room and went to the Sister's office. She was a little surprised when we asked where he was. "Harry's in the lounge, didn't you see him?" she asked. I had walked past him, not recognising the 'old man' asleep in the chair. I just burst into tears and couldn't face staying. The following day I made myself go, this time alone. The entrance doors were always kept locked in case patients wandered off. I rang the bell and in some trepidation was let in. And there was Harry. He was slowly walking down the corridor with a male nurse and as soon as he saw me, his eyes lit up and his face creased into a huge joyous smile of recognition.

"That's Margaret, that's my wife," he announced proudly to the nurse and in his joy gave me a hug and a kiss. We had what he always loved, 'a cuppa' and then, as he dozed off, I made my exit. And that was how it was on my almost daily visits: sometimes he knew me, and sometimes he didn't. Sometimes he thought he was in a hotel waiting for his players. On one occasion the Sister made a football out of a bundle of old newspapers and there he was, wanting the 'lads' to get out on the lawn training. I smile thinking about it. The staff members were wonderful and some of them would go out 'training' with him but how cross he got, bless him, when they didn't follow instructions. On one day he was indignant with me, telling me that they were playing at 'silly beggars' and not taking it seriously. Only someone who has lived through the experience of caring for someone with Parkinson's Dementia or Alzheimer's will understand the pain it causes to see loved ones behaving like this. Sometimes I saw the 'real' Harry and at others it was the Harry who didn't know where he was and couldn't recognise familiar faces. But the Sister and her staff were wonderful in their efforts to please and occupy him.

At Christmas 1995, Linda, Philip and James went to see him and found he was very ill. Ken went on Christmas Day and expected to see him in bed but he was in the lounge. They had taken plastic footballs with them and Harry was able to play with his grandson Alan. The footballer inside him never disappeared.

Later, the staff organised an outing to Towneley Park for Harry and some of the other patients. They were delighted that he knew where he was and they all had a grand game of football that day. When they got back to Dove Court, however, he insisted they take him back to Turf Moor, but the temptation of a good dinner back in Dove Court saved the day.

Stella Maris was only a few hundred yards away and I would visit Mam as well. It was all very tiring but I found peace and tranquillity in doing the flowers at Read Church, the place we were married. I was able to say prayers quietly by myself. I could visit at any time because in those days church doors were always open. Sadly that is not the case today.

The first thing his mother always asked was, "How's our Harry?" In the final months she became so frail and towards the end I would hold her hand, wipe her mouth, give her sips of water and talk quietly to her. And then at last, on one occasion very near the end she sat and repeated, "I'm sorry, I'm sorry... I'm sorry." It was as if in her last moments she knew and acknowledged how difficult she had been with me, and how unfair and selfish she had been towards our marriage. All I could say was, "It's all right Mam, it's over, and it's done with." I knew deep inside me that she was saying sorry for all those years of hurt. Now, none of that mattered. As I sat with her, as she faced her final days, those unkindnesses were no longer important. She passed away on October 23rd 1994, the day after Harry's birthday. She was 95. Alan Reid was a tower of strength and we both felt relief that Harry's mother had died first.

On medical advice, we did not take Harry to the funeral, or even tell him that she had died, and it was a strange sensation driving by Dove Court with Harry so close by, on the way to the interment. He was blissfully unaware.

We had our final Christmas dinner together in the 'home' in 1995. The staff laid me a place at his table but by now he looked so aged and fragile. We'd had so many wonderful Christmases together. It was a time he loved; the family get-togethers, the games, the fun, hats and crackers, presents and always a tree. Later that day there was another Christmas meal at Linda's house. I was surrounded by love, but there was no Harry.

There was a poignant moment a little later when I was given a photograph of him dancing with one of the staff. He always loved to dance and perhaps he thought it was me he was dancing with.

Visitors came and went; friends, ex-players and colleagues, family, his beloved grandchildren. Sometimes he knew them, sometimes he didn't.

Shortly after Christmas 1995 and the New Year celebrations I visited again. The decorations had been taken down and the piano, used for sing-songs and dances, had been moved into a corridor along with two armchairs. Nobody seemed to know where he was, but "he's in a quiet mood today," the staff told me. I found him sitting by the piano and there was the usual hug and kiss, and we shared some of his favourite sweets, 'pick and mix'. He had always loved choosing them in Woolworth's. Then after another minute or so he looked at me. "Did me Mam die?" he asked. I was quite taken aback. It was so unexpected. She had died many months earlier. I took his hand, apprehensive about telling him. "Yes Harry, you were very poorly at the time, perhaps you have forgotten," I told him gently.

Expecting a bad reaction, I waited, but to my amazement he replied, "Has she gone... up there...?" He pointed at the ceiling. Then even more surprisingly a huge grin filled his face and his eyes sparkled like I hadn't seen them in years. "Come here," he said, "give me a kiss."

We sat and held hands for a while until he drifted off to

sleep. Then the sound of the tea trolley rattling down the corridor woke him up. To the very end he loved his cup of tea.

"Peace at last," I thought. She had made demands on him all his life. He wanted so much to be a good husband but she could never leave him alone, and he was, I think, always afraid that he was not the son she wanted him to be. His loyalties were always torn. In that moment after I told him, he appeared content and at peace. It was as if knowing that she had died, he had found his release from a lifetime of obligation.

In the following two weeks he deteriorated. Whenever I had been to visit he had always been up, at the very least sitting in a chair. This time he was in bed and I knew the end might be close. He was still and silent. I felt for his pulse. The Sister called for the doctor who said he would send Harry to hospital if that was what we wanted; but if he was to pass away, this was where we wanted him to end his days; where he was loved, in a homely atmosphere.

And so it came to January 16th, all of us there, watching and waiting, looking at this brittle shell of a man who had once been so strong, muscular and beautiful; his schoolboy grin, the blonde hair, the tanned body. The first ever meeting we had on the coach back to Burnley, walking with him in the park while he signed autographs. The man who had achieved so much: the man I had come to love dearly, but nearly left twice, when his mother was so impossible. The final few days had passed by in a sort of blur, all of us sitting by his bedside; so much love, so much the sense of impending loss. The staff were so sensitive and knew that each remaining moment was precious. I stayed each day and had my meals there but came home in the evenings. The final hours were simply a matter of waiting for the inevitable. It was a matter of time.

CHAPTER SEVENTEEN

JOURNEY'S END

HARRY'S SON-IN-LAW, Philip, was one of the visitors to Dove Court. He and Linda had known each other since their schooldays and Philip would often catch glimpses of 'the great man', as he called him. And then came an invite to tea. Philip was nervous; he was just a local lad whose father worked in the cotton industry. Harry arrived back at home, weathered from all of his many hours outdoors but immaculately dressed. Within minutes, though, Harry had put him at his ease and Philip came to learn that Harry, the 'superhero,' was in fact 'just Harry', a kind, generous, warm-hearted family man totally absorbed in his football and Burnley Football Club. Philip remembers the occasion he talked to Harry about marrying Linda.

"I remember his grin and a little tear in his eye, and he said he'd better think about a new suit. On the day itself he was so generous and there was no expense spared. In his speech he trembled with emotion. Deborah and James could never have wished for a better granddad, with trips and presents and holidays. On holiday, it was always my job to go with him to the beach café for the drinks and ice creams. In later years, after he had left management, he would take me with him to places like Liverpool and Manchester United. Everybody knew and greeted him. At Old Trafford, when Manchester United played Chelsea, and Harry was then doing some scouting for them, Ken Bates met us in the car park. Seats were provided in the directors' box. This was the day it was absolutely clear that so many people in football had such respect for him as a procession of football greats came to talk to him – Dave Sexton, Tommy Docherty, Denis Law, Bobby Charlton, Jimmy Armfield and others who all made their way over. Then a ripple of applause began around us and a frail, elderly, well-dressed man came over to talk to Harry. It was Sir Matt Busby.

"Harry's world was football; everything else could wait. Cars were just things you sometimes put petrol in, if you remembered. He was constantly running out; red warning lights for oil and petrol were nothing too important. He would get in the car and if the petrol light came on, he would tap it, and if it didn't start to flash he would pronounce that all was well and there would be enough petrol to get back. My memory is of him constantly wiping the misted-up windscreen so that he could see while he was driving. The demister was something he never discovered on any car.

"What a good, kind man he was though, always smart; white shirt, tie, shoes you could see your face in. Had time for everybody but certainly didn't suffer fools gladly. When he flipped, he flipped, and maybe this was the 'Mad Hatter' side of him. How he loved Christmas and birthdays. He was a kid at heart and yet I never thought he was quite the same after he left Burnley in 1972."

It saddened Philip enormously to see the health and strength of 'the great man' deteriorate so cruelly. If, however, there was sadness that Harry never saw his grandson James play in the Burnley colours, there was tremendous pride some years later when the road outside the ground was renamed the 'Harry Potts Way'. It was a fitting tribute to Mr Burnley.

AT THE very end, Linda, Ken, Philip, Lynn and myself were at his bedside. It was obvious his time was over and we wanted to telephone the Reverend Alan Reid to ask him to be with us. God works in mysterious ways for at that very minute Alan walked into the room. Alan still remembers the moment because even after all his years as a vicar it was the first time he had ever been at someone's bedside when they had passed away. I remember his words too: "Go forward out of this world… in the name of the father who made you… in the name of the son… and in the name of the Holy Spirit… may your days be filled with peace."

And we wept. Of course we did.

The rest of the day was a blur, a seemingly endless round of cups of tea, telephone calls, decisions to make and talks about arrangements. There were just so many people to tell, so many things to do. Everybody who has suffered the bereavement of a loved one will know what it entails. You cope because you have to and because there is the love of the remaining family around you. How awful it must be to have to deal with all of this alone. By the time we got home, the news had been on the television and local radio. The football club issued a statement in the local newspaper. The following day it was in the national press.

The letters flooded in. I still have them: letters from supporters, from players, from dignitaries, The PFA, the Football League, the Football Association, the Lancashire FA, from nearly every League club, even some non-League clubs, and from family and friends. Few people come into this world and leave it having left a mark like Harry did. The people who didn't take to him, you could count on one hand. A letter came from his grandchildren Laura and Alan; it expressed what we all felt… "Words could not tell you what I'm feeling today, I lost someone who means so much to me, in every possible way…"

None of us expected the huge turnout at the church on a dry, but bitterly cold day. The cortège drove from Read, through Simonstone and Padiham, along all the streets we knew so well. Streets that Harry had driven along, countless times. On the journey to the crematorium we went past his beloved Gawthorpe, and then a heart-wrenching stop outside Turf Moor. Goodness knows how long those supporters had been standing waiting in the cold but there they were with distraught faces and bared heads. And then my emotions and tears came to the surface when I saw a banner that said "Farewell Harry".

A funeral is a mixture of things. It is a day of sadness and loss but it is also a day of happiness and memories. It is a final celebration of a life lived. Strange as it may sound, I kept thinking how Harry would have enjoyed it, but how he would also have been so surprised at all the fuss. And then when the day is over, and the following day, and the days after that, this is when you realise the enormity of it all. Your loved one is gone and the house is now finally strangely empty other than yourself. For a while, there are so many things to do, affairs to sort out, and letters to write but there was my family to help.

Even when he was in Dove Court, there was still somehow a part of him in the house and there was a purpose to my being there, getting ready to go and see him, wondering how he was getting on, wondering if he would recognise me or not each time I went. So many people will say that it always takes several days, if not longer, before the realisation sinks in that it has happened and that a loved one has left us forever.

But life goes on and the adjustments are made. Slowly, over time, the smiles and laughter return and I was honoured some months later in June when I was asked, as a tribute to Harry, to present the sports prizes at our local village Gala Day. I took my place behind the table of trophies and heard a little boy's voice from the front row.

"What have they got an old woman like her for – what does she know about football?" he said to whoever was next to him. Poor lad, so disappointed he was. I wonder who he was expecting; he would much rather have seen a footballer and collected an autograph. But afterwards I was amused. Perhaps now that he is grown up and maybe if he reads this book he will smile himself. If only he had known of all the football I had seen, all the things I had done, places I had been, famous people I had met, and the wonderful occasions I had been a part of.

THE FUNERAL took place on Monday January 22nd 1996. Cyril Law was one of the many people who filled the church and was also one of the churchwardens who led

Journey's End

the cortège into the church bearing their staffs. He had first met Harry in the 1950s, when Harry would contact him because Law was the Lucas Training Centre manager and also ran the football team. Harry would ask him about any prospects worth watching. It was Law who would meet Harry in later years during his illness, walking around the local area, and would make sure he knew where he was if he was walking up on the hilltops. "He won't get lost," Margaret would tell him, "he always knows where his cup of tea is."

Football people and family friends filled the Church of St John's, Read, for the funeral organised by Harry's great friend, the Reverend Alan Reid. From his family came claret and blue floral tributes in the shapes of a football, a shirt and a football boot. It summed up not just their love, but the love of everyone in Burnley, for this was a man who loved his family, the club and the town. There was a wreath from the Professional Footballers' Association. John Connelly and Alex Elder led the pallbearers organised by Brian Miller. There was Jimmy McIlroy, Arthur Bellamy, Brian Miller himself, Jimmy Robson, Peter Noble and Harry's grandson James Webster who at that time played for the Burnley youth team.

James was overcome as thoughts of his grandfather drifted through his mind. In the garden Harry would coach him, making him use both feet, telling him that there weren't many players who could use both. He would have him using his left foot to pass the ball against the garage and the garden wall and James remembered how at Dove Court right at the very end Harry could kick and control a ball down the corridors effortlessly and with such natural skill. It was Harry who set James on the sporting path and played golf with him on the pitch and putt course at Towneley Park. James would sometimes go along with Harry on football trips. He has never forgotten one to Anfield for a Liverpool versus Chelsea game and how they ended up in the away end with the Chelsea fans and he had to hide his scarf at the end of the game and having to sing with the Chelsea supporters. Or, when on another visit to Anfield, Bob Paisley took him into the dressing room and he sat next to Bruce Grobbelaar and Kenny Dalglish signed a poster. Today it is one of James' greatest regrets that Harry never saw him play as a youth or as a first-year professional for Burnley until manager Adrian Heath released him. Margaret, too, knows of the time he spent with James. "Before he went into Dove Court I would hear him muttering and mumbling as he watched *Match Of The Day* on television on a Saturday night. 'What's the matter, Harry?' I would ask him. 'Ee, there's none of them with a left foot as good as James,' he would grumble."

Following the service, the cortège drove to Turf Moor where a two-minute silence was observed by a mass of people who arrived outside the ground to pay their last respects, despite the bitterly cold weather. The first team and youth squad lined the pavement in an emotional tribute while the club flag flew at half-mast. Ordinary supporters mixed with the club's players in an extraordinary show of appreciation. One such supporter was Tony Scholes, who had left work early in Manchester to make sure he could pay his respects. He remembers the road being closed to traffic and the poignant sight of one former player, Billy Ingham, standing downcast and alone on the other side of the road. Tony Scholes was not the only person that day who shed tears.

Paul Fletcher, today better known perhaps for his stadium design work, and now managing director of Coventry City, was the Burnley number nine for nearly all of the '70s. He had always kept in touch with the Potts family after football and it was to him, on Alan Reid's suggestion, that Margaret Potts turned with a request that he deliver the eulogy at the funeral. Fletcher agreed with the proviso that it should not be overly serious and that it should highlight Harry's sense of fun and humour. He remembers him with great fondness.

"As a person he was such a nice guy and I think there was a part of him that was still a schoolboy. He had such a great sense of fun and humour and he loved footballers' pranks. Once on a coach returning from an away game we were in such high spirits because we had won. Jimmy Holland, the physiotherapist, would always fall asleep if he'd had a couple of pints and as he slept his mouth would drop wider and wider open. It was Harry who actively encouraged me to custard pie Jimmy with a paper plate and shaving cream while he slept there with his mouth wide open. Harry's sense of humour always managed to come out. There was an occasion at Gawthorpe when he was watching several of us practising shooting.

"Nearby, behind the goal, was a plantation of trees and if we booted the ball into the trees it was Harry who went in to fetch it. So when the ball went into the trees, back it came with Harry still somewhere deep inside the plantation. From then on we chipped every ball at Alan Stevenson in goal who then lobbed them back into the plantation. Thirty times this must have happened with Harry deep inside the wood kicking them back out, until at last he emerged covered in leaves and twigs and branches, red-faced, spluttering, forehead throbbing, veins bulging, absolutely furious. It was the only time I ever heard him swear. Harry never swore, but this time he did and yells out 'Can't you ******* ever hit the ******* target?' Then, of course, he saw us laughing, realised the joke, and started laughing at himself. That's the kind of man he was; there we were taking the mickey out of him and there he was able to see the funny side of it. That's why you were able to like him.

"When Margaret Potts asked me to give the eulogy at the funeral, I agreed as long as I could bring out this side of Harry. It's the Harry I remember. I can't remember exactly what I said but maybe I told the story of Harry and the bath towel. If we ever did a tour it was always tradition that on the second night Alan Stevenson and myself would host a cocktail party in our bedroom. So this particular time we told everyone that it was a fancy dress party and they must come dressed in something from their bedroom. Halfway through and everyone is there and then suddenly the door bursts open and in the doorway there's Harry, by now on the portly side, with just his bathroom towel round his middle...

nothing else… and in he comes and somehow contrives to fall over and lands flat on his back in the middle of the floor. All of us collapsed laughing. But that was typical of the man. He'd rather be doing something like that with the players than sitting down below with the directors."

Paul says today that there must have been such a thing as the 'Harry Potts Way'. "There must have been something; his record speaks for itself. You can't achieve what he did without having 'something' and he achieved things for Burnley Football Club that nobody else will ever do. Maybe he worked in an era when nice guys could manage and just send out their best eleven players to play. But times have changed and it's doubtful if that would work today. Maybe football had passed him by, by the time he finished his second spell. Sometimes it seemed like we were almost organising ourselves in training, and there was more to football than saying things on a hot day like, 'go out and enjoy yourselves, play like the Brazilians'. But you couldn't have done what he did without a basic 'Harry Potts Way' be it to do with behaviour, expectations, attitudes, looking after yourself, or maximum effort. But certainly, inside Harry there was always a little bit of the schoolboy and I rarely saw him when he wasn't smiling."

Fletcher went on to tell the congregation that a generation of footballers had, indeed, had their lives changed by Harry Potts and ended his address with Harry's own words as he recalled a typical pre-match team talk. "Go out with a smile on your face and a chuckle in your boots, and if you come back with a smile on your face you'll have won the game. I think it was Harry who won the game," said Fletcher finally.

When Joe Brown spoke at the funeral, it was to say that, "In all my years in football everyone asked about Harry and no one said a wrong word about him. And Harry never said a wrong word against anyone else. He never held any grudges although he may have had cause. He just thought the best of everyone. He was a really good man."

Later the Reverend Alan Reid recalled: "He was a friend to those players as well as a father figure. In 1994 Harry's health began to deteriorate so that Margaret could no longer give him the care and attention that she had given him in the past and so Harry went into the nursing home where he could receive 24-hours-a-day nursing and attention. In January 1996 it was obvious that Harry's life was coming to an end. As his trusted friend and vicar for 40 years something one day told me I must go and see him. The family, who had just telephoned the vicarage as I was driving over, were amazed to see me walk into the room almost before they had put the telephone down. Together with Margaret and the family, prayers were said for Harry's safe departure from this earth and as we all repeated a final 'amen' we realised that the final whistle had been blown on his life. The day of the funeral was a cold, blustery day, but Read Parish Church was filled to capacity with many famous names in the congregation. The coffin was carried in as we sang 'O love that will not go away' and the tears ran freely. The curtain came down on a true soccer giant, a devoted husband and father and a true Christian gentleman. In the Church he had been a sidesman and never missed his duty on the rota or at a meeting. He never once let us down."

While many people in the church that day remembered Harry as the football man, some remembered him as simply their grandfather. Deborah describes him as a wonderful grandfather; always telling them HP brown sauce was named after him, chasing away the swans that were frightening them as they fed the ducks one day or rescuing them from a field of bulls through which they had inadvertently walked. "He loved his Cadbury's Fruit and Nut and I bought him a huge block for his 70th birthday. There'd be tubs of ice cream at the cinema; playing crazy golf. He would throw us in the water at the swimming pool, play with us in the back garden, we would be together on family holidays and the special treat was letting us go into his office to help ourselves to the ginger beer he kept in a cupboard."

The Brunshaw Road which ran alongside Turf Moor was renamed the 'Harry Potts Way' in 2001. It was a fitting tribute to Harry the man, and Harry the manager of Burnley Football Club. The idea came from the London Clarets Supporters' Club, which approached the then Burnley MP Peter Pike, who then made the formal request to the town council. It was a suggestion endorsed by all the supporters' clubs and the Burnley directors. More than two hundred people stood alongside Margaret Potts and her family, representatives of the club and local dignitaries, who, as the rain fell, watched the nameplate unveiled in his honour. "He would have thought what a fuss this is," said Margaret. "He was such a modest man and would have loved his team to have been honoured in such a way, rather than just himself. All this is rather strange to his grandchildren. To them he was simply granddad."

Harry's daughter Linda watched the ceremony with the family. What she recalls is Harry on holiday, the fun and games that he would take part in. On a beach, somehow his fun and laughter always managed to draw a crowd of children who would join in with the games they played. "He was like a Pied Piper figure. One Christmas he bought us a puppy; Sandy. He actually had that pup in his bedroom with him on Christmas Eve and half the night in the bed so that he could stop it from crying and keep it a surprise until the morning."

On a Christmas Day years later he spent the whole day inside the Wendy House that had been a present for his granddaughter Deborah. "He loved dancing and things like the Gay Gordons and the Dashing White Sergeant. Typical. These were old-fashioned dances where you had fun and could really let go. Before that there were functions in the village he always supported, particularly one where funds were raised for the victims of the Hillsborough disaster at Sheffield."

Laughingly, Linda remembered the endless telephone calls when he had been in his prime as Burnley manager. "We had this kind of cubbyhole under the stairs in the '60s with a door that could be closed, and dad would sit in there for hours and hours on the telephone." And then as Linda's eyes misted over, she talked of how at her wedding, he had been so nervous, and had gripped her hand so tightly, you could actually see the veins in his hand bulging. She talked of her huge regret that he had never seen his grandson James play in the claret and blue strip of the Burnley youth team or known that he had been a professional for a year.

Harry's son Ken was there as well. The memories came flooding back: playing football with his father on the back lawn by the light of the car headlamps in the evenings. No matter what mood Harry was in when he came home, he always had time to kick a ball with his son. It wasn't until the 1962 cup final weekend that Ken realised just how important his father was. Later he took him to some of the 1966 World Cup games at Goodison Park and remembers the words, "This might never happen again in this country."

They went to several cup finals and many League games and Ken remembers how Harry knew every route and road to every ground and all the quick short cuts. He knew every train timetable, bus route, tube station in London, and the best parking spaces for every ground. But remembering to fill the car with petrol was another matter. "He never seemed to fill it up; just a few gallons would do." It was as if he hadn't time to fill it, such was his desperation to get to the football.

"On holidays, which he loved, there was always more football, more often than not with the waiters from the hotel, either on the beach or in the car park. At home there was always a football in the back of the car so that if we went out for a drive we could always find somewhere for a quick kickabout. Dad loved his steak and chips; it was about the only meal he could cook when Mum was in hospital. He loved sledging in the snow and bonfire night.

"The weather never seemed to bother him when he was outdoors but at home he loved nothing more than his coal fire, with his armchair pulled up close so that he could toast his feet. Then there was the time that he brought home a very young Brian Flynn one weekend. He was up for a trial but Dad roped him in to play for our seven-a-side team in a village game behind the houses. Brian demonstrated his talent by chipping the ball over the 6ft 4ins goalkeeper."

It was not surprising that Ken, too, wanted to be a professional footballer and he was not without talent. Harry fixed him up with a trial at Hull City but it was unsuccessful. In retrospect, Ken thinks this was Harry's way of letting him know that he wouldn't make the grade rather than just telling him himself. "Dad had told me it wouldn't be easy but probably knew I wouldn't accept it from him that I wasn't good enough. When Terry Neill told me, then I accepted it.

"Dad was a smart man, traditional and conventional. He always combed my hair, made sure it was cut once a fortnight, made me clean and polish my shoes. His values were time-honoured and old-fashioned."

Ken's son Alan also played football with Harry, but this was in the corridors of Dove Court. "Even then he had such skill with that ball, in spite of the Parkinson's. For a few minutes it was as if the years rolled back, he was so light on his feet." Shortly after Harry's death Alan played in a weekend match and had a particularly good game. "That's for granddad," he said as he came off.

Recognition for what Harry had done for Burnley Football Club was still not over. In 2003 fans voted for him as one of the club's top all-time legends. His name is on a plaque by one of the main entrances. On the day of the unveiling many of those honoured took part in the matchday ceremony and then paraded around the perimeter of the pitch before the game. When Margaret Potts appeared and made her way round the ground, representing her beloved husband, the waves of applause were an expression of love, affection and gratitude for what Harry Potts had done for the club and town just over 40 years earlier.

So many people have such good things to say about Harry Potts. Les Latcham, who played 178 games under him, is possibly best remembered because of the photograph of him with bloodied and bandaged head in the game at Naples. It is an image that has become an iconic representation of the way some players will give their absolute all for their club. Les, too, speaks readily of the 'Harry Potts Way'.

"Fitness was the thing with Harry. He was fit himself. And then he was always telling us that we represented the club. Give a hundred percent, he said. You would have the biggest stinker in the world but he wouldn't criticise you. Then he would do everything he could for all his players. To Harry, people had to take responsibility for their own actions, but he would have no truck with people who broke club rules. One such unwritten rule was no drinking after Wednesday, although a couple of half shandies were allowed if you took your wife out for a meal.

"Willie Morgan and another young player were told by Harry to moderate their drinking habits if they wished to make a career at Burnley Football Club. Willie heeded the advice and what he achieved in football speaks for itself. The other player left the club at the end of the season. Harry didn't just preach about giving one hundred percent; he always gave a hundred percent himself. And honest. He was such an honest man and always had his own high standards. He told you the truth and what you saw was what you got."

Brian Miller, who was a player for Harry and was then his assistant before taking over as manager, today is only too ready to speak warmly of him. "In the dressing room he didn't rant or rave, bully or shout. His philosophy was simple, and that was to go out and play, move forward, get onto the attack, and if the others scored we just had to score more than them. Worry about you, not the opposition, is what he said. As a man manager he was so good, you could relate to him, trust him, you knew it hurt him so much to drop a player.

"He was never a man to walk past you without a greeting, a word, or a conversation. He cared about the private and personal lives of his players and you knew he was genuine and honest. I wanted to play for him so much that once with a broken toe I cut a small hole in my boot to take off the pressure and out I went. He couldn't abide cheats, which is why he ran on to the pitch in the European game in Reims. One manager he didn't like was Alan Ball senior. I can still picture him and Harry on the touchline in their respective dugouts throwing stones at each other that they picked up from the shale track round the edge of the pitch. It was hilarious.

"He had such a great influence on me personally. When I became a manager myself I'd find myself asking what would Harry have done in this situation or that. He taught me that players respond to a manager who makes them feel that they are looked after and protected. At our peak he just had this knack of making us feel that we just had to go out and win."

The mention of Harry Potts' name brings an instant smile to Andy Lochhead's face. "Some of the things Harry did and said still make me chuckle. He loved to join in with the training. He was a very fit man, always led by example and if we did circuit training he always led the way. There'd be press-ups, sprinting, forward rolls and Harry always demonstrated. Well, one time he did them far too vigorously, got up too quickly, went terribly dizzy and started running backwards; he'd no idea where he was or what day it was. 'Course we all collapsed laughing.

"In London we always used to stay in the good hotels down there. One of them had these big revolving doors and it was a place we used a lot. It was always Harry and me who came out last. We had this little routine. I'd tell Harry not to forget to give the doorman a tip. So Harry always gave him the same tip. 'Here,' Harry used to say chuckling, 'I'll give you a tip; back Burnley for promotion this season.' He said it, without fail, every time we came out of that hotel and I laughed every time he said it.

"We had some real comical moments with him. We did a trip to Folkestone once to play a friendly, and the big invention back then was the Hovercraft. After breakfast Harry calls us round, tells us to get ready and says he has a real treat organised for us – he's taking us all for a trip on the new Hoovercraft.

"You could laugh with him, yes, but he was no pushover, you knew the limits. He fined and dropped me for a game for some boisterous behaviour in Blackpool and then we had a young reserve in the early '60s called Peter Simpson; he didn't play too many games for Burnley. One day he came in and he had dyed his hair blonde. Harry took one look and sent him away to wash it out. You couldn't do that to a player today."

What everybody remembers is Harry Potts' utter devotion to Burnley Football Club and the passion he showed towards it. Woe betide anyone who had a bad word to say about his club. There is a story, possibly apocryphal, that on one occasion after a game he returned to his office to find a radio reporter using his telephone to broadcast his report. It was none too kind, and hearing it a furious Potts grabbed the telephone from the reporter's hands and shouted down the telephone and across the nation's radios that he had been talking a load of rubbish!

And for Margaret...

HIS MEMORY is everywhere and I never feel he is far away. I wear his old anorak when I'm working in the garden. His old rocking chair that he spent so much time in during his last months in the house is still here. I can hold the watch, now faded and broken, that he was given to mark the winning of the Championship. The clock he was given at Shrewsbury still ticks away in the lounge. The cabinet has mementoes, trophies and pictures. Each of them reminds me of a special occasion or something different. There's even an old biro inscribed "stolen from Clement Freud" that he gave me when he interviewed Harry long, long ago. There are photographs and pictures on the walls and I have a score of photograph albums and boxes of letters from all manner of people. One letter from my granddaughter Laura is very special. She wrote it when she was at university and had been to Wembley as part of a Coca Cola competition with a medal presentation by Ray Clemence.

"When we stepped out onto the hallowed turf," she wrote, "it really was a moving moment as I only wished Granddad was there to share the moment. I played well and I did this for him. It was a real honour to have changed in the same place as him, touched the bath and walked through the tunnel just like Granddad did fifty years ago. My only wish is that he could have been there to see me follow in his footsteps."

In another box there is a gold compact from Everton after they won promotion, a Blackpool scarf, and some black and gold ribbons from Wolverhampton Wanderers. I still have a presentation rose and wheatsheaf arrangement decorated with black and gold ribbons from the banquet for the cup final between Wolverhampton and Blackburn Rovers. I remember that game well. Hilda and Bob Lord had been invited to the Blackburn Rovers banquet while Harry wouldn't tell me where we were going that night. It turned out to be the Wolves' banquet. They'd won and of course Harry had been their coach. When we got back to the hotel, Hilda Lord saw me with all my presents and said, in her Hylda Baker manner (for those who don't know Hylda Baker, she was a comedy actress famous for the catchphrase "she knows, you know"): "Not a patch on Burnley's dos. Anyway, where've you been?"

"To the Wolves' banquet," I replied.

"How did you get there?" she asked. She looked very envious.

These things would not be valuable to everybody, but they are to me. Burnley FC have most of Harry's memorabelia at Turf Moor.

The Reverend Alan Reid still wears his lovely Crombie overcoat; Harry was always known for his coats and raincoats and Stuart Hall made good-natured fun of that. The Reverend Reid drove a lot with Harry in the later days and they'd visit clubs and grounds everywhere scouting, and Harry loved to have Alan for company. It was such a lovely coat and I gave it to Alan who then enjoyed surprising people when he was wearing it. Alan always says, "It knows its way round all the boardrooms." He was at Burnley one day and bumped into Andy Lochhead in the stand somewhere and he complimented him on the coat. "Yes," said Alan, "it's at home here, it's been here many times before." Then Alan told him it was Harry's coat and Lochhead grinned, "Yes, I thought I recognised it." That coat became quite a talking point as Alan later had the same conversation with other players like John Angus and Alex Elder when they were at the club as guests one day.

Just so many memories; sitting by the fireside in our home when we were first married, all those years ago, making rugs from the kits that you could buy; the way he would come home after a game and say, "Oh Margaret, I'm in trouble again," when he'd had a row with a referee. Then there was Sandy, the spaniel puppy Harry bought for Linda and Ken; sometimes even now I can still hear in my mind the sound of its scampering feet, slipping and sliding on the linoleum we used to have. We had no fitted carpets in those days and had a carpet square or a rug and you'd turn them round every so often so they wouldn't get worn out in the same place. There were the lovely times we had with our good friends Connie and Cliff Roberts; I can still picture Harry playing the game at the age of 56 when they opened the new pitch at Read. In the cine films now made into videos I have a treasure trove of precious moments I can see again: Harry on the beach, playing cricket, surrounded by children, always surrounded by children. And now at last there is the book I have always dreamed of seeing written.

CHAPTER EIGHTEEN
ROOTS AND WINGS

AT QUIET moments, as I look back at my life, and the experiences I have had, I am forever convinced that there are two lasting bequests we can leave our children. We can give them roots and we can give them their wings. When I read this some time ago I thought how true it was. It is such a simple truth, but it has never left me.

How lucky I was in my own childhood; how fortunate I was that my own wonderful parents gave me the love and room to grow and blossom. For that is what our childhood is: it is the willingness of parents to let us flourish; it is the encouragement they give us; it is the room they give us to develop and mature, in the warm, secure, love-filled environment of the home. And then, it is their courage and unselfishness in letting us go when the time has come and they can do no more. Just as a fledgling bird takes its first hesitant flight from the nest, so do our own children need to take their first early steps. They become, and will be, what we provide for them, not in material ways, but simply in the richness of the nourishment we give them, and the independence we bestow.

They are what we allow them to be, and what we give them from inside of ourselves. Roots and wings. The two things they need above all else. The two most important things we can give.

It is what Harry and I always tried to provide for our own children. It is what my parents did with me, it is perhaps what Harry's mother was unable to do with him; she gave him roots but she was unable to release him and let him go. The roots she gave were strong, secure and loving; but she could never find it within herself to give him his wings. She clung to him for all of her life and most of his.

As the years go by, we let our children test those wings. They make their first faltering journeys in life. If they are fragile and insecure then they might fail. But if we give them wings that are strong and secure, they will find their own way, but will always know where to come back whenever they wish for support if they need it. And then, when our own parents pass away – my own father one Christmas in 1961, my mother more than twenty years later – we have the strength, the character and the ability to cope and carry on with our own lives.

I can look back over the years and think of so many things, some of them painful, but so many others that fill me with pride and pleasure. One thing that happened so early in our married life, nearly fifty years ago, when the children were still so very young, and Linda was just eight years old, is still imprinted in my mind.

It was the time when we lived in Wolverhampton, perhaps it was 1957; she would be eight years old, and I was in the kitchen baking. Little Linda, in her gentle, caring way was looking after, and playing with her younger brother Ken. Breathlessly, they ran in to tell me that there had been an accident and a cyclist had crashed into a tree as he swerved to avoid a cat.

The cyclist was badly hurt. In and out of the house Linda ran to fetch cloths, water and towels. It seemed like an age before help came. While we waited we tended to the dreadful injuries to his face, removing broken teeth to keep his airways clear. At last the ambulance arrived, but in those days they only had very basic equipment, little more than a stretcher and blankets. The driver and his assistant had only the most rudimentary, basic first-aid knowledge, unlike today's paramedics with all their high-tech equipment.

And so we looked after him until that help arrived, and in those moments, I saw and knew then that Linda would grow to take life in her stride. She, like me, became a nurse and perhaps the seeds were sown, and the roots took hold, on the day we helped that stricken cyclist.

Some weeks later we had a visit from him, to thank us. The surgeons had told him that whoever had aided him with their vital help had saved his life.

How fortunate I am to be still so active and busy. Yes, age has slowed me down but my garden remains my pride and place of relaxation. It is still where I work, so often, and in most weathers. And then at the day's end I can sit and reflect on a job well done. At other times, images from years ago and the pleasure they bring fill my mind.

Ken: racing across the tarmac at the airport to help us catch the plane to Portugal in the summer of 1966. Harry had to stand in for Bob Lord at the Inter-Cities Fairs Cup meetings. Our holiday was booked for Corfu but we agreed to go to Portugal on condition that Ken could come with us. Linda had just started work and stayed with Philip's family.

The last-minute changes resulted in a mad dash when we got to London. The flight, we discovered, was ready for take-off and we were sent onto the tarmac at the very last minute as the plane waited. "Run for it," yelled Harry and the three of us ran as fast as we could with me trying to be elegant in my cream Chanel suit and high-heeled shoes. Can you imagine doing that today? I can still picture the sight of Ken running ahead with Harry and me struggling behind them. I can sit by my fireside as the day comes to its close and relive so many things that we did. These are the simple memories that I cherish. The mad dash with Ken across the tarmac at the airport is one of them.

We didn't see much of Harry because he was on Inter-Cities Fairs Cup business and Ken and I befriended a family from Sheffield, or I should say they took us under their wings. They clearly thought Ken and I were on our own. Feeling sorry for us, they insisted that the children played together and the mother regaled us with stories of all the football VIPs in the hotel and how she would do her best to get their autographs for Ken, especially Matt Busby's. On and on she went. We kept quiet; it was always our agreement that we should never say who we were. Oh dear, how boring this lady was, trying to be kind and helpful, thinking that we needed looking after.

This went on for quite a few days, until one afternoon on

the way back to our rooms we stood by the lifts on the ground floor. There we were in our towels and costumes, and there, too, was the mother and her two children fussing round us, still promising us that she would get us the autographs. The lift doors opened and from one of them out stepped half a dozen of the pressmen, including Bill Fryer of the *Daily Express*. "Ah hello, Margaret," he beamed, surprised that I was there in a swimming costume with a towel over my shoulders. The Sheffield mother looked askance. Almost simultaneously, the adjoining lift door opened and who should step out but Harry and Matt Busby. Matt greeted us warmly. They grinned at us. Ken ran over to greet his dad and the secret was out. I don't think we saw the Sheffield family again.

I remember, too, another holiday in Crete when Harry was recognised by a head waiter. Previously the best tables were booked; but once he saw Harry we were out on the terrace where we wanted to be.

Then there was the time in Majorca, not long after the match with Hamburg where we met a German journalist who recognised Harry after watching him play football on the beach.

The wings to fly: the time comes when your children meet their future, the person with whom we hope they will spend the rest of their lives. You want so much that their happiness will be long and lasting. Of course Harry and I had our difficult times; of course his mother caused us tensions and heartache. How often have I sat and vowed that I would never cling to my children like Harry's mother clung to him. You let them go; you free them so that you can't hold on to them with endless jealousy and possessiveness. Linda and Philip had been at school together. We knew their friendship was deepening and just before Christmas in '67 Linda approached me to say that they wanted to become engaged. It was one of those special mother–daughter moments. But they were hesitant and apprehensive about approaching Harry; he was old-fashioned in so many ways. They had no need to worry. When I told Harry he was delighted and Philip still remembers how Harry nearly crushed his fingers when they shook hands. That was a wonderful Christmas.

Harry Potts – Margaret's Story

Now, years later, I know that our instincts to encourage them gave them the wings to fly and the ability to set up their own home which was strong and secure.

"Do you wonder where I go every Wednesday when I borrow your car, mum?" asked Ken one evening and smiled. In 1977 Ken married Lynn, a lovely, homely girl from Euxton, near Chorley. As a boy he'd had a pony, later it was a Land Rover and he loved to go stock car racing which is where he had met Lynn. Of course, a mother likes to know everything her son does, where he goes, who he sees, just like Harry's mother had done with him. But I had always left it to Ken to tell me in his own good time, however much I would like to have known. I sensed this time that it was news about himself and Lynn that he wanted to share. I was on pins with excitement and I can still hear the reply I gave him. "If you want me to know, you'll tell me, in your own good time – if I ask, you probably won't." Just before his wedding, he held me and hugged me tight. Then, gently, he kissed me and I could feel the love and emotion. "I'll always love you, mum," he said. "We'll come and visit, but you won't be like Nanna Potts will you?"

The pathos in his voice was clear, for sadly he had sensed some of the tensions we'd had. As a tiny, young boy when he had just started at infants school, I had been to collect him and then called to see Nanna and Granddad. On this occasion she was on her own. She grabbed me by the collar, and held me against the closed door. How she called me and shouted at me for not letting her help to decorate "our" Linda's bedroom. As she harangued and berated me, Ken ran to hide behind the sofa. She eventually released her hold, the scene ended and we left. As we did so, when we got outside, Ken slipped his hand into mine and spoke in that innocent, childlike way in which small children express their thoughts. "Never mind mummy, never mind… she's very old, isn't she? She'll soon be died…"

Just before Linda and Philip got married she said: "Please Mum, Philip and I don't want any habit-forming visits."

Yes, there were some terrible times with Mam Potts and sometimes the children saw them. I vowed that day I would never be the same with any of my family.

302

Roots and Wings

I haven't met anyone whose grandchildren are not their pride and joy. I love mine so much, and so did Harry. It was December 1975 when Linda's Deborah was born and yet it was like a lovely spring day. What pleasure I felt, knitting and crocheting for our first lovely grandchild. James was the next to arrive and many years later, when he was a youth team player at Burnley Football Club, there was a game I saw him play. It was in Manchester, the final of the Lancashire Youth Cup. Burnley won and my heart almost stopped when I saw the resemblance between him and Harry. As James came out, the way he ran, the way he held his arms by his side, was just the same as his grandfather with whom he kicked a ball and practised so often. Through half-closed eyes it could have been Harry. Sadly, Harry never saw James play for Burnley.

It was Ken who called us to say that Lynn was expecting their first child. It was Harry who was the first to see Laura in 1979 when he called at the hospital on the way to a meeting. And then you sometimes wonder at life's coincidences. As our fourth grandchild, Alan, was due to be born on January 1st 1982, my dear mother died. I remember it so well. In awful weather and on wintry roads we drove to Ken's at Leyland to help, my bags packed, ready to give support. But Alan wasn't for coming, false alarm, so somehow on roads that were hazardous and dangerous, we got back to our own home, slithering and sliding in all directions. By now it was almost two in the morning. Within minutes, the phone rang again but this time it was the rest home in Padiham, and the doctor to say that my mother was very ill and was now sedated. By this time the roads were so treacherous and icy there would have been so much risk of an accident to Harry and myself if we attempted the journey.

I so desperately wanted to be with her; she had given me so much love, so much support, the roots to grow and then the wings to fly, and yet here in her hour of need, as the life was slowly draining away, we had to make this choice. We decided we could not risk the roads. The next call was the one I didn't want. Peacefully, but without me by her side, she had passed away. I owe her and my father so much.

If I am what I am, it is because of them and the times we had together at Trapp Cottage. What they did for me, I have never forgotten, and it has formed the basis of all that I have tried to do for my own children, and then with my grandchildren. At such times Harry was always my support with his physical presence. My dear Harry, who was so generous and trusting with money, helpless with cooking, and uninterested in anything domestic but had so much patience with children.

What is life but an endless procession of births, christenings, weddings, birthdays, family celebrations, silver, ruby, golden weddings, anniversaries of this and that, and then at the end, the passing away of loved ones? A parent dies, and a grandchild is born. The wheel goes round: regeneration, life's endless replenishment. On Linda's birthday in April 1986 we took Deborah to Rosegrove Station to see Charles and Diana arrive in Burnley. Charles had moved on to somewhere else in Burnley but I 'willed' Diana to come and speak to us – and she did – so slight, pale, coy and shy. "We are three generations," I told her, as Deborah gave her the flowers she had brought. Three generations, renewal, the cycle of life. I felt so proud.

Harry's grandchildren are his legacy: Laura, now a sports teacher; Alan a policeman, athletic, and still with a love of football; Deborah, a primary schoolteacher who teaches all the sport in her school. And James, the footballer and golfer, who so nearly achieved the football dream.

I sit quietly, thinking, sometimes in the sunshine while the shadows lengthen and the sun lowers in a cloudless sky, or sometimes sitting in my favourite chair in the conservatory when the rain falls down on the roof from a grey, damp sky. The wheel has turned full circle and I am back so close to where I grew and spent my childhood. Back to Simonstone and Read; Whins Lane, Huntroyde and Higher Trapp so very close by; our old cottage but a short walk away, a place that was filled with so much love, warmth and friendship. Back to the lanes and pathways, the woods and bluebells, the hilltop walks, the spring lambs and farmers' fields. The irony does not escape me: I can close my eyes content; I am close to the church where Harry's and Bob's headstones stand almost side by side. I am back home; back to my roots, loved by my children and grandchildren, never to be totally dependent on them I hope, the only grandparent remaining, so proud of all my family. I cannot ask for more.

EVERYONE WHO walks by Turf Moor can see the sign that says 'Harry Potts Way'. Nobody will forget his name. As Alan Reid so often says, "Harry lives on".

On one wall of the lounge of Margaret's home hangs a picture of their wedding. Behind the picture in the frame is the card that she attached to her floral tribute at his funeral. The message is simple.

"In loving memory of a dear husband xx. We didn't quite make the 50. But you left some golden memories. Love you. Margaret."

Index

As Harry and Margaret Potts are mentioned on practically every page there was little point in putting them into the index. Below are the major players and places in their lives.

Index

Index

Index